Mass Customization

Mass Customization

The New Frontier in Business Competition

B. Joseph Pine II
IBM Advanced Business Institute

Foreword by Stan Davis

Harvard Business School Press
Boston, Massachusetts

LIBRARY OF CONGRESS CATALOGING-IN-PUBLICATION DATA
Pine II, B. Joseph.
    Mass customization : the new frontier in business competition / B. Joseph Pine II ;
foreword by Stan Davis.
        p.   cm.
    Includes bibliographical references and index.
    ISBN 0-87584-372-7
    1. Technological innovations—Management.   2. Manufactures—Technological
innovations—Management.   3. Service industries—Technological innovations—
Management.   4. New products—Management.   5. Competition.   6. Mass
production.   I. Title.
HD45.P537   1993
658.5'75—dc20   92-17506
                                                                        CIP

To the women in my life:
Julie, Rebecca, and Elizabeth

Mass Customization

Contents

Foreword

MASS customizing is an oxymoron, which is the putting together of seemingly contradictory notions, like jumbo shrimp and artificial intelligence. Or, as my then teenage son told me a few years ago, "Oh, like a parent's joke."

Until recently, things were either custom made or mass produced. It is only in the past decade or so that these opposite types of manufacture have been blended together, and the blending is not limited to the production of goods. We are experiencing the mass production, distribution, and delivery of customized goods and services. And, as methods of organizing adapt to business changes, mass customizing is finding its way into this arena as well.

If you want to understand and be able to use the power of mass customizing, then it is most helpful to appreciate the logic behind the concept. This logic is not limited to business, nor did it originate here. The religious notion of the trinity, the governmental notion of balance of power, and the psychological notion of ambivalence are variations on this same logic: to allow for the co-existence of opposites, to embrace contradiction as an indication of a larger truth. The key is to embrace and transcend the paradox, rather than be limited by it. Mass customizing is an exemplar of a profound shift occurring in many aspects of life, and I welcome the opportunity to explain how I first saw this trend and crafted the term that is the subject of this penetrating book.

Unlike examples from other domains, the applications of the

paradox to economic life require technologies that can handle contradictions. Pre-industrial technologies were not suited for this task because they were premised on small volumes with high unit costs. Industrial technologies, as Joe Pine amply shows, were premised on the opposite approach: high volumes and low unit costs. Business had to wait for today's technologies to merge the two into mass customization, the production and distribution of *customized* goods and services on a *mass* basis.

A decade ago, I came to appreciate a progression in which dimensions of the universe are understood by science, art, and religion as different expressions of universal truths. People build institutions, such as businesses, governments, churches, and schools to realize the practical applications of these truths. The institutions are only as powerful as the truths upon which they are built. Our interest here is business, and the progression that I put forth in *Future Perfect* was that "fundamental properties of the *universe* are transformed into *scientific* understanding, then developed into new *technologies*, which are applied to create products and services for *business*, which then ultimately define our models of *organization*."

Using this progression, I examined two interrelated conceptions of the universe and then applied them to business. One was about "parts/wholes" and the other was about "either/or" constructions. The results of these experiments led, among other insights, to the notion of mass customization.

The parts/whole notion began for me with what is known as a mechanistic interpretation of the universe: the whole equals the sum of the parts. Newton's world was built upon this approach, and it found technological and commercial application in what became the industrial economy. If an enterprise was very efficient, then the whole might be worth more than the sum of its parts; if it was very inefficient, then corporate raiders told us the breakup value of the whole was worth less than the sum of the parts. But, more or less, the whole was the sum of its parts.

An alternative notion holds that the whole exists simultaneously in every one of its parts. A simple example of this startling conception is that the genetic code for our entire body is in each of our cells. It is only the limits of our engineering skills, then, that prevent us from recreating whole people from individual cells. It happens in nature all the time, and genetic engineering is trying to build this process into a commercial capability.

The same holistic potential exists in business and in organization.

The whole business exists in every product, service, and customer. The whole organization exists in every employee. And so on. When an airline loses a customer's reservation, for example, the customer does not respond mechanistically and say, "It is only this one small part [a single reservation] of the whole that is not good." The customer, in fact, responds holistically, saying that "you don't know how to run an airline." The entire airline is on the line in that one moment. And those moments happen all the time in every business.

Customers respond holistically, and it is only the limits of our conceptual skills and social engineering that keep us from actually creating these new, holistic forms in business. Why not, then, consider that "mass" is to "whole" what "customization" is to "parts"? The whole and its parts go together.

The other conception was the either/or way that we tend to view things. I was struck by the parallels between business and science. About a century ago, a major debate in physics was about the nature of light. One experiment had "proved" that light was composed of particles and another "proved" that light was made up of waves. Each was true, and contradicted yet could not disprove the other. The physical models of reality were either/or constructions, unable to represent opposites simultaneously.

Today management has much the same problem. We still build most of our models around false dichotomies. To name but a few, we speak of strategy *versus* operations, cost *versus* quality, and centralized *versus* decentralized. The way out of the dilemma for scientists, finally, was to abandon the perspective of irreconcilable opposites, and to embrace interpretations that accept contradictions without trying to resolve them. Quantum mechanics does that in physics, mass customizing does that in business.

Pine has taken this development and used it effectively as an emblem for many of the transformations occurring in the way we conduct business. He shows its emergence in industry after industry, how it creates a firmer basis for competition, and why those who still adhere to the earlier, industrial model falter in the face of this paradoxical blend.

Mass customization does not occur in isolation, with other elements holding firm. It is, as he demonstrates through a monumental array of examples, intimately linked with time-based competition, manufacture at the point of delivery, customer self-design and direct access, modularization, zero inventories, shrinking overheads, declining need for working capital, enhanced logistics, infomediation, and electronic value chains. None of these are free-standing elements. They all require and reinforce one another to greater or lesser degrees.

Very mature businesses either try to prop up their declining life-cycle curve with marginal improvements, or they evolve fundamentally different ways of conducting business. Using some of the approaches named above will allow them to grow in multiples, rather than just marginally. The irony, however, is that in the process they will redefine the very enterprise itself.

In Pine's capable hands, mass customization is not merely a buzz word or a tool, it is an expression of the future. As an umbrella concept for a host of techniques, it is not something that one can simply tack onto an otherwise steady state of business conduct. It has such an extraordinary dynamic of its own, that while you may be seduced or compelled to adopt it, beware that its successful employ will likely take you to ways and worlds far beyond your original intentions.

Boston, Massachusetts   Stan Davis, author of
June 1992   the award-winning
                                         Future Perfect and *2020 Vision*.

Preface

AMERICA gained its world economic dominance through the system of Mass Production, the frontier in business competition for most of the twentieth century. America is losing that dominance in large measure because Mass Production could not handle the increasingly turbulent market environment of the past twenty or thirty years. Companies in other countries have been quicker to shift to a new system of management, Mass Customization, which both causes and thrives on turbulence.

Mass Customization is the new frontier in business competition for both manufacturing and service industries. At its core is a tremendous increase in variety and customization without a corresponding increase in costs. At its limit, it is the *mass* production of individually *customized* goods and services. At its best, it provides strategic advantage and economic value.

As a technological capability, Mass Customization was anticipated in 1970 by Alvin Toffler in *Future Shock* and delineated (as well as named) in 1987 by Stan Davis in *Future Perfect*. What has emerged is even more than Toffler envisioned twenty-two years ago and Davis described five years ago. Mass Customization is a new way of viewing business competition, one that makes the identification and fulfillment of the wants and needs of individual customers paramount without sacrificing efficiency, effectiveness, and low costs. It is a new mental model of how business success can be achieved, one that subsumes many of the "silver bullets" of prevailing management advice such as time-based competition, lean production, and micromarketing. Further, the development of Mass Customization as a paradigm of management explains why product (and service) life cycles are decreasing, why development and production cycle times must follow, why businesses are re-engineering their processes, and why hierarchies are flattening and transforming into networked organizations. Mass Customization integrates all of these into one cogent system of management that describes what is going on today in industries whose markets—small or large, local or global—are characterized more by turbulence than by stability. This book shows you how to grasp, implement, and benefit by this competitive reality.

My exploration of this new frontier in business competition is the result of five interlocking experiences. First, in 1986, the IBM business unit in Rochester, Minnesota, embarked on a "bet your business" project that resulted in the Application System/400™ midrange computer. I led an effort to involve customers and business partners in the development process of the new system, an activity that broke down the walls separating development programmers and engineers from our customers. It allowed me to understand that customers were not members of an amorphous, homogeneous market but real people with real problems to be solved—and each one was different. Therefore, each solution had to be different as well.

Then, after the AS/400™ was announced in 1988, I joined a startup strategic planning group formed to make IBM Rochester a truly market-driven organization. We segmented our customers into various markets, targeted select markets, ascertained their wants and needs, positioned the system into those markets, and provided requirements to development. While learning more about markets and customers in this position, I was fortunate to participate in a task force charged with developing a vision for the direction of the AS/400 in the 1990s. During this activity I read Stan Davis's profound book *Future Perfect*, and quickly became convinced that for continued success we would need to develop the capability to customize the AS/400 not only for the various target markets, but for the individual uses of the system by each distinct customer. Mass customization became one of the pillars of the system vision.

The third experience was the opportunity to spend 1990–1991 at MIT in the Management of Technology Program. I quickly settled on Mass Customization as the subject of my thesis and spent a year researching and writing it and the papers that formed the beginnings of this book.

After graduation, I joined IBM Worldwide Headquarters to work on re-engineering our requirements process. I learned the enormity of such a task in a company as large as IBM, and many of the dos and don'ts it takes to be successful. Finally, at the end of 1991, I joined the management research function of IBM's Advanced Business Institute (ABI). This group researches new and emerging management ideas for use in the customer executive education courses conducted by the ABI and for IBM's management consulting practices. Here, I was able to learn from the ongoing research we conducted and supported as well as complete my own research and writing.

This book, then, is the result of both business and academic experiences. It is aimed at both business and academic audiences, although the needs of executives, managers, and professionals always took precedence when I was deciding what to include and how to say it.

Outline of the Book

Part I, "The Shift from Mass Production to Mass Customization," provides the *what* and the *why* of this new frontier. Chapter 1 begins with a story that will seem familiar to all—but with a twist—and introduces the concept. Chapter 2 briefly discusses the history of production to explain how we arrived at where we are today, and shows that Mass Production is a system with inherent limits. Reaching these limits over the past twenty or thirty years led to declining competitiveness for many companies and for America as a whole.

Chapter 3 begins with a discussion of a number of industries to see how companies have responded to these limits and shows how these responses have coalesced into the new system of management, Mass Customization. Chapter 4 explains why increased turbulence in an industry indicates that it should shift from Mass Production to Mass Customization and provides a tool with which you can determine if your company needs to make this shift.

Chapter 5 discusses how the practitioners of Mass Production focused on common themes that naturally resulted in a number of detrimental effects that left them open to new forms of competition. Chapter 6 describes these new forms and shows how companies discovered Mass Customization by focusing on different themes with corresponding positive effects.

Part II, "Exploring the New Frontier in Business Competition," provides the *how* of Mass Customization. Chapter 7 offers a number of case histories of businesses that are shifting to this new system of management to show you how your company—depending on its circumstances—can also make this shift. Chapter 8 describes the five basic methods of mass-producing individually customized goods and services, with many examples and guidelines for how to use each method. Chapter 9 explains how companies are focusing on re-engineering their processes to achieve high variety and customization and provides a progression of structural innovations that can be used to transform the organization for a more turbulent world. Finally, Chapter 10 provides the limits to the system of Mass Customization to make you aware of the dangers that may exist, and speculates on what the landscape of business competition will look like in the future as more companies enter the new frontier.

Customizing This Book

Unfortunately, it is not yet possible to understand the individual desires of readers and customize trade books to fulfill those desires. So, let me provide some information that might allow you to customize this book to fit your needs:

- *If you have time to read only two chapters*, read Chapter 3 on what Mass Customization is and Chapter 8 on how to do it. Of course, if you only have time to read two chapters, chances are you did not begin by reading this preface. . . .
- *If you are familiar with the history of production* and the effects of Mass Production, just browse through the tables and figures in Chapters 2 and 5 and read only when something sparks your interest.
- Many industries and companies are discussed throughout the book. *If you are interested only in your own industry*, skip the discussion of others at the beginning of Chapter 3 and use the index to find references to your industry and companies in it. You may even find your own company listed.
- *If you are already convinced that Mass Customization is the way to go* and just want to know how to go about doing it, you may want to skip or browse through most of Part I and get to the meat in Part II. *If, however, you need to convince others of the merits of Mass Customization*, you will want to read most of Part I, particularly Chapter 4.

- Endnotes are used extensively for three reasons: to provide inter-esting, useful, but more detailed information without inter-rupting the flow of the passage; to cite supporting research and materials for the point at hand; and to provide additional sources that can be used to explore facets of the discussion. *You can easily read the entire book without referring to an endnote*, but you may want to look up notes pertaining to a topic or discussion you find particularly interesting.
- *Read the Appendix only if* research methodologies and statistics make you giddy with excitement, or if, after reading Chapter 4, you remain unconvinced that market turbulence can indicate the shift to Mass Customization.

Last, and most important, providing the *what* and the *why* of this new system of management in Part I is crucial to establishing the intellec-tual foundation for the competitive and economic shift from Mass Production to Mass Customization. Do not let its detail or length deter you from getting to the *how* of Mass Customization provided in Part II.

A Final Note

It took academics thirty or forty years to figure out the process and organizational innovations that companies like Ford, Gen-eral Motors, and Du Pont were making early in the twentieth century, and the complete story behind the success of post–World War II Japan is subject to continuing debate. The system of Mass Customiza-tion is still emerging. So even if academic research cycles are declining in step with development and production cycles, there is still much to learn. I encourage you to participate in this learning process through research if you are in academia and through implementation and shar-ing your experiences if you are in business. If you would like to discuss, debate, or query any aspect of Mass Customization with me directly, please contact me at the address below. I look forward to hearing from you and learning more about how companies are shifting to Mass Customization, the new frontier in business competition.

May 1992   Joe Pine
                                IBM Advanced Business Institute
                                Route 9W
                                Palisades, New York 10964
                                U.S.A.

Acknowledgments

MOST authors are supported in their endeavors by a number of people without whose contributions the work would not have been possible. I have been supported by more people with greater contributions than usual.

I am first of all indebted to those managers in IBM who have given me opportunities to work in a diverse number of areas, constantly driving me to learn, improve, apply, and broaden. They include Satish Gupta, Dean Tulledge, Pete Skiko, Gary Okimoto (now with Stratus), John Woods (now retired), Judy Kinsey, Dave Schleicher, Don Van Ryn, Tom Furey, Roy Bauer, Vic Tang, Bob Chappuis, Jim Kelly, Larry Osterwise, Steve Schwartz, Dick Sulack, and Al Barnes. Others at IBM who have greatly influenced my experiences and thoughts include Laurie Baker, Don Kerlin, Steve Heuer, Kent Holcomb, Sue Aldrich, Julie Ransom, Bob Haines, Margaret Hainsworth, Jim Rogers, Mike Beasley, Gerry Jacobs, and Steve Haeckel. For sparking my interest in Mass Customization and helping flesh out its implications for the AS/400, a special note of thanks to IBM Rochester's system vision task force, particularly Mark McNeilly and Bruce Jawer, who reviewed drafts of the book as well. I am also enormously grateful for all the assistance I received while researching and writing this book, including secretarial support from Kim Kaster, Barbara Cicchetti, Marie Rex, and Jennifer Gagliardi, graphics support from John Mullaly and Jeanine Sacheli (now with CBS), and information support from the staff of IBM's Technical

Information Retrieval Center, most notably Ottie Moody and Ed Wickersham.

This book began taking shape while I was at MIT (in 1990–1991) in the form of various papers and, most notably, my thesis. For their contributions to the development of the resulting ideas and concepts, I am particularly grateful to professors Mike Piore (my thesis adviser), Jim Utterback, Rick Locke, Arnoldo Hax, Shlomo Maital, Karl Ulrich, and Mike Cusumano. My fellow participants in the Management of Technology Program that year deserve special mention for sharing their own knowledge and experiences in class and at parties, and for putting up with my talking about Mass Customization all the time. My car pool members—Mark Emery and Paul Hunter of Bell Atlantic and Dave Wright of General Motors—were especially tolerant on that last point, and especially helpful in discussing ideas and reviewing work-in-process. Dave, who has read and reviewed virtually everything I have written on this subject, has had a most positive effect on the quality of the final manuscript, not to mention my basketball skills.

The contents of this book are in large measure a synthesis of my own ideas and research with those of others who have been examining the end of Mass Production and studying the terrain of the new frontier. In addition to Mike Piore and Stan Davis, I owe an intellectual debt in this regard to Andy Boynton of the University of Virginia (my thesis reader) and Bart Victor of the University of North Carolina—my friends and research partners—as well as to Charles Sabel of MIT, Michael Best of the University of Massachusetts, Bill Davidson of the University of Southern California, James Brian Quinn of Dartmouth, B. Charles Ames of Clayton & Dubilier, George Stalk of The Boston Consulting Group, Nathan Rosenberg of the University of California at Berkeley, Tom Peters of The Tom Peters Group, Peter Drucker of Claremont Graduate School, Gary Hamel of the University of London, and Phil Kotler of Northwestern University.

The examples and prescriptions contained in this book flow from the many companies that are leading the way into the new frontier. While too numerous to mention, many people in these companies deserve accolades not only for their achievements, but for spending the time with me to describe what they have done and how they have accomplished it. I discovered many of these companies through reading various business publications, most notably *The Wall Street Journal, Fortune, Harvard Business Review*, and *The Planning Review*. I owe each of the more than 250 people who personally took the time to respond to my overly long research survey my gratitude.

The Harvard Business School Press staff have done a wonderful job in marshaling my work from the first (also overly long) draft to final publication. Dick Luecke deserves special mention for recognizing the promise in my initial work and hastily completed outline and for a great editing job. Thanks also to the press's anonymous reviewers who recommended many excellent changes to the draft. In addition to these reviews and those of many others previously mentioned, the book is also much better because of my extensive discussions with and the recommendations of Paul Ruscher of Viking Press, my father, Bud Pine, and my wife, Julie.

Julie, successful at IBM in her own right, endured the uprooting of her family to the East Coast, the many long evening and weekend hours it took to complete first my degree at MIT and then the book, and, perhaps most of all, being the first reader of much of what I wrote. Thank you, Julie, for your love and patience.

Last (and first) of all, I owe the greatest debt to the Lord Jesus Christ, with whom anything is possible, without whom nothing is worthwhile.

PART I

The Shift from Mass Production to Mass Customization

CHAPTER 1

Once Upon a Time

THERE once was an economic power that dominated the world's industrial production. This country was the world's leading manufacturer and its predominant exporter of goods. Much of its success was based on its basic research, its ability to invent, and its unparalleled technological leadership. A time came, however, when it began to decline relative to its international competitors and was challenged by another country whose ships, filled with new products, arrived with increasing frequency.

Several decades earlier, the two nations had been engaged in a bitter war, but they had become allies. Some time after the war, the upstart country focused on its manufacturing prowess, eventually gaining renown for its new and unique production processes that turned out goods of high quality.

At first the dominant country had no fear of its lowly ally, which focused only on low-end products with small profit margins. It was not known for its quality, and all of its products were basically imitations; inventiveness or creativity was not its strong suit. But the upstart country kept plugging away, improving its manufacturing processes, quality, exports, and market share in a number of industries.

As the number of industries in which the upstart country challenged the dominant one grew, people began to examine how and why this was happening. Articles were written, reports were commissioned, and books were published to explain the new and powerful manufacturing processes of the upstart country and to recommend how it could best be emulated. Many factors were identified to explain its success, including:

- A focused, orderly, and systematic manufacturing process that depended on the combination of highly skilled workers, automated machinery, and a new way of moving materials and goods through the factory.
- Strong and continual gains in productivity and quality, thanks to the involvement of workers in improving the process.
- Highly skilled and well-educated workers who maintained clean work environments and had high marks for attendance.
- Continual, incremental technological innovations.
- A high level of cooperation among national competitors, which helped the rapid diffusion of process innovations.
- A high degree of reliance on subcontractors for innovations and production skills.
- A strong education system.
- A culture that was unique and relatively homogeneous.

Thoughtful individuals in the dominant country warned of dire consequences if the nation as a whole did not change its ways and rise to the challenge. But the nation's business leaders did not know quite how to respond. As the upstart country continued its march toward larger and larger market share, fears arose that it would eventually overwhelm its bigger ally and the rest of the world with its exports, putting domestic firms and even entire industries out of business. The dominant country was faced with the prospect of losing the economic superiority it had held for so long. Time appeared to be running out.

A Parable for Modern Times

In this story, the country that feared losing its dominance of world manufacturing is not America, but England in the latter half of the nineteenth century.[1] The country whose manufacturing prowess it feared was not Japan, but the United States. The way of manufacturing developed in this upstart country was not known as "just-in-time" or "lean production" but as the American System of Manufactures.[2]

Despite the efforts of many industrialists, the English never quite caught on to this new way of manufacturing, and England eventually lost its dominance over world production and exports. It did not happen overnight, but took many decades. While American pioneers were exploring and mastering the western frontier, industrial pioneers concentrated in New England were exploring and mastering a new frontier of business competition by focusing on the process of production, developing interchangeable parts, and utilizing the flexibility and ingenuity of American workers. By the 1880s, thanks to the American System of Manufactures, the United States had overtaken England as the world's leading manufacturer. By the turn of the century, the United States had one and a half times the industrial production of its rival.[3] The America of the nineteenth century became the world's premier manufacturer thanks to its highly skilled and educated workers, quality goods, low costs, rapid innovations, and technological leadership.

In the twentieth century, the American System was itself transformed by Henry Ford and others into the system of Mass Production.[4] This became the next frontier for American companies to master. This new way of producing goods—with its emphasis on the smooth-running flow and operational efficiency of the assembly line, specialized machinery and worker tasks, and great economies of scale through standardized products—not only solidified America's leadership position but propelled the country to become the world's dominant manufacturer and exporter. Through its system of Mass Production, America won the economic battle with England.

In hindsight, it seems to have been an inevitable victory. World dominance seemed to be America's birthright, as it had once seemed to be England's.

Need history repeat itself in the current battle between America and Japan? Must Japan become the world's leading manufacturer and exporter by the turn of this century? And if so, will it seem to have been just as inevitable to people a hundred years from now?

No, the battle has not yet been won; the outcome is not inevitable. England lost its leadership not through economic predestination, but through the daily decisions of the thousands of managers in English businesses, as well as those of their counterparts in America. And the daily decisions of American managers and executives today will determine whether this country retains its leadership position.

As in the English experience of a century ago, there is no shortage of explanations for what is happening. Numerous books and studies have investigated America's difficulties, and nearly all argue that they are not the result of purely short-term forces: something fundamental is happening. As an example, the MIT Commission on Industrial Productivity concluded:

Relative to other nations and relative to its own history, America does indeed have a serious productivity problem. This problem in productive performance, as we call it, is the result of major changes within and outside the United States in the past four decades. It is manifested by sluggish productivity growth and by shortcomings in the quality and innovativeness of the nation's products. Left unattended, the problem will impoverish America relative to other nations that have adapted more quickly and effectively to pervasive changes in technology and markets.[5]

Similarly, there are no shortages of recommendations as to what America, and individual companies, can and should do to regain lost competitiveness. The list of "silver bullets" to which managers are supposed to subscribe grows every year. Too often, however, there is no recognition that the fundamental changes are not hitting all industries equally, and therefore there is little recognition that not all companies are facing the same circumstances and should not implement the same solutions in the same way.

What is really necessary is an understanding of the fundamental changes that are occurring in both market environments and business competition, and why they are happening now; where these changes apply and to what extent; and how executives, managers, and employees in individual companies can recognize these changes and transform their businesses to succeed in an increasingly turbulent world.

The New Frontier in Business Competition

The companies that responded properly to these changes are now exploring and beginning to master yet another frontier in business competition, one whose terrain is decidedly different from that of Mass Production. These companies have discovered that the silver bullets management gurus have been promoting can be integrated into a powerful new system of management. They understand that not only can higher quality yield lower costs, but so can greater variety. They have found that customers can no longer be lumped together in a huge homogeneous market, but are individuals whose individual wants and needs can be ascertained and fulfilled. They have determined that reducing product life cycles and fragmenting demand can yield powerful advantages for those causing these changes relative to those forced to react to them. Leading companies have created processes for low-cost, volume production of great variety, and even for individually customized goods and services. They have discovered the new frontier in business competition: Mass Customization.

In this new frontier, a wealth of variety and customization is available to consumers and businesses through the flexibility and responsiveness of companies practicing this new system of management. In the past twenty years, the number of different items on supermarket and pharmacy shelves has exploded, allowing manufacturers and retailers to reach ever-finer granularities of consumer desires. You used to go to a fast-food restaurant for a mass-produced cheeseburger, french fries, and a shake; now the same restaurant provides a half dozen varieties of burgers along with chicken sandwiches, salads, pizza, fajitas, burritos, submarine sandwiches, spaghetti, carrot and celery sticks, bottled mineral water—you name it and it is standard fare today, being test-marketed, or under development.

The most prototypical mature mass production industry, automobiles, is a hotbed of innovation and variety. As innovation advances, market segments fragment and models proliferate. The same is true in service industries such as telecommunications and financial services, which have long held to the same basic tenets of Mass Production as manufacturers. Henry Ford's dictum, "You can have any color car you want as long as it's black," is long gone from the automobile industry.

However, just ten years ago, you could have any level of phone service you wanted as long as it was pulse or Touch-Tone. Today you can have Call Forwarding, Call Waiting, and Voice Mail, while message forwarding, caller ID and caller ID blocking, and literally hundreds more services are on the drawing boards. By connecting a PC to your phone line, you can access numerous personal services, including travel agencies, catalogue stores, news providers, and message services.

In financial services, you can bank at automatic teller machines (ATMs) whenever and wherever convenient, and choose from among thousands of financial and insurance products those few that match your needs. You can do all your banking through your PC or Touch-Tone telephone.

The leading pioneers of Mass Customization[6] are providing tremendous variety, and individual customization, at prices comparable to standard goods and services—and often better. Want to tour Europe? Call a local travel agency to choose one of a half dozen or so standard tours; or call the country's leading provider of tours to choose the individual elements of your vacation—when to leave, where to stay, what to see—for the same price. Want to purchase a high-quality book for a young granddaughter or niece? Find the right source and you can obtain a customized book with a story about her, her family, and her own friends. You may already be receiving a newspaper, magazine, or catalogue with text and advertisements different from the same issues other subscribers receive, precisely because your personal interests and desires differ from theirs.

In industry after industry undergoing turbulent change, the companies that have come out on top—domestic or foreign competitors—are those which have discovered the power of Mass Customization. In automobiles, apparel, lighting controls, power tools, refrigerated warehouses, travel services, midrange computers, watches, power supplies, pagers—the list could go on—the leading companies use flexible information, telecommunications, and manufacturing technologies, but more important, flexible, knowledgeable workers and new management methods to shorten their cycle times, lower their costs, enhance their flexibility and responsiveness, and increase their variety and customization—all to satisfy more closely the individual wants and needs of their customers. Not only are these companies the pioneers of the new frontier in business competition, they are at or near the top in market share in their industries.

Of course, not all companies in all industries need to achieve both low costs and high levels of variety and customization, for not all industries are undergoing the same changes at the same rates. But to choose to remain mired in the old ways of Mass Production when fundamental changes are altering the competitive landscape of a particular industry—demanding new management responses, new technologies, and new ways of doing business—is to court disaster. It can be equally disastrous to be unaware of the new possibilities for competitive advantage inherent in Mass Customization.

It is time to understand what fundamental changes are occurring, and what exactly are the possibilities opening up within this new frontier in business competition. But to understand where we must go, we must better understand where we have been.

CHAPTER 2

The System of Mass Production

IN THE history of economic affairs, the system of Mass Production prevalent in America today is relatively new. For centuries, economic production was based on the notion of *craftsmen*. Everything was crafted by the hands of someone who had the requisite materials, tools, and most important, skills. Craftsmen were also called *artisans* and their skill (or know-how) in turning raw materials into finished goods was not only an art but a source of pride.

The Industrial Revolution brought a general replacement of hand tools with machinery and mechanization as the primary instruments of production. As Michael Piore and Charles Sabel of MIT relate in *The Second Industrial Divide*, over time the use of machinery led down two distinct paths. The first was a continuation of the basic idea of Craft Production:

Its foundation was the idea that machines and processes could augment the craftsman's skill, allowing the worker to embody his or her knowledge in ever more varied products: the more flexible the machine, the more widely applicable the process, the more it expanded the craftsman's capacity for productive expression.[1]

The second, Mass Production, involved a different idea: "Its guiding principle was that the cost of making any particular good could be

9

dramatically reduced if only machinery could be substituted for the human skill needed to produce it."[2] These two paths can be seen today in the different management systems that produce a Rolls-Royce and a Chevrolet; a Tiffany lamp and a Wickes lamp; a Paris designer original and an off-the-rack dress from T. J. Maxx; and a five-course meal at a five-star restaurant and a cheeseburger and fries at McDonald's. For a time these two paths were less distinct, blurred by the simultaneous use of highly skilled workers *and* mechanization. This was the time America began its surge into economic prominence.

The American System of Manufactures

From the Industrial Revolution came a mechanistic "factory system" common to the United States, Great Britain, and the other newly industrialized countries of Europe in the nineteenth century. In the middle of that century, however, the factory system in the United States took on a nature so distinctive that it became known as the American System of Manufactures, or simply the American System.[3] It was indeed this system of production that fueled the growth of the United States as an economic power. Between 1875 and 1899, just as the American System began to dominate the American economy, commodity output per capita grew at an annual rate of 2 percent versus just 0.3 percent for the first three quarters of the century.[4] As Table 2-1 shows, the manufacturing share of commodity output grew from 17 to 53 percent between 1839 and the end of the century. This growth was at the expense of agriculture, which was itself undergoing tremendous increases in productivity at the same

Table 2-1 Sector Shares in Commodity Output, 1839–1899 (percentage of total output)

Year	Agriculture	Mining	Construction	Manufacturing
1839	72	1	10	17
1849	60	1	10	30
1859	56	1	11	32
1869	53	2	12	33
1879	49	3	11	37
1889	37	4	11	48
1899	33	5	9	53

Source: Adapted from Robert E. Gallman, "Commodity Output, 1839–1899," in William Parker, ed., *Trends in the American Economy in the Nineteenth Century* (Princeton: Princeton University Press, 1960), p. 26.

Table 2-2   Characteristics of the American System of
Manufactures

• Interchangeable parts
• Specialized machines
• Reliance on suppliers
• Focus on the process of production
• Division of labor
• Skills of American workers
• Flexibility
• Continuous technological improvement

---

time,[5] demonstrating the truly explosive nature of the change caused by the American System.

What was at the heart of the American System of Manufactures that caused it to be the driver of the U.S. economy? Table 2-2 lists the key characteristics of the American System that differentiated it from both craft production methods and the factory systems of Europe, which had become increasingly mechanized in the seventeenth and eighteenth centuries. The first characteristic was the defining principle upon which the system rested: *interchangeable parts*. Prior to the development of the American System, each part of a product had to be individually fitted to each of the other parts in the manufacture of that product. This involved time-consuming effort throughout the entire production system: filing down edges, testing, and filing again until sufficient fit was achieved. Interchangeable parts greatly simplified the production process and saved enormous amounts of labor. Perhaps even more important, interchangeable parts facilitated the effective repair and maintenance of products, which even for the relatively simple ones of the time required more skill than did their original manufacture. The American System, first developed in the firearms industry, was heavily supported by the U.S. government because the ability to repair firearms in the field was so important.[6]

Along with interchangeable parts came the *specialized machines* necessary to produce the parts to the tight tolerances required to eliminate hand fitting. Formerly general-purpose machines were adapted to all sorts of specialized functions with successive innovations throughout the production process, as economic historian Nathan Rosenberg tells us:

Americans had developed and applied the milling machine, a device of extraordinary versatility, to a wide range of purposes in shaping the metal parts of the musket. In so doing the machine had, in the United States, progressively displaced the highly expensive operations of hand filing and chiseling of parts. In fact, the development of specialized forms of the milling machine may be considered one of the really distinctive contributions of America to the system of interchangeable manufacture. For it was through the use of these machines that a high degree of uniformity of metal parts was achieved, far beyond what was possible by hand filing.[7]

To ensure exact interchangeability, systems of gauges and fixtures were developed as key components of the new machinery. The gauges allowed both operators and supervisors to monitor machines so that any discrepancies could be immediately detected. To prevent small differences in how parts were fixed to the machines from multiplying across each operation, a reference point was designed into each part and the fixtures specially designed for the reference point. Together, the innovations underlying these first two characteristics of the American System greatly increased quality, uniformity, and productivity.

The third characteristic, flowing from the second, was the *reliance on suppliers* that the use of specialized machinery entailed. The entire machine tool industry, beginning in about 1820, was created in response to the needs of practitioners of the American System.[8] Although the first practitioners built their machines in-house, they soon relinquished this function to the burgeoning machine tool industry because it enabled them to focus more fully on their own production problems, avoid the costs of machine development, and share the technological advancements made by machine tool suppliers. These same advantages accrued to suppliers of raw materials and noncritical components. As Rosenberg states, "American firms showed a much greater talent than British firms for coordinating successfully their relationships with other firms upon whom they were dependent for the supply of essential inputs."[9]

The fourth characteristic of the American System was a *focus on the process of production* that previous advancements afforded company owners. Rather than simply providing isolated craftsmen with all the materials they needed to manufacture a product one at a time, resulting in differences in quality and workmanship depending on who made it, company owners focused on the entire organization and how the production process could be managed to greater effect.[10] They developed a functional organization of the factory, where materials and semifinished products were moved from one station to another in batches. Along with this transformation came increased supervision and worker accountability for schedules, quality, and material usage.

A further result of process focus was the *division of labor*. As the production process was standardized and routinized, it was argued that focusing workers on only a piece of it would quite naturally lead to greater efficiency. While craftsmen were not pleased with the loss of responsibility and eventual loss of skill, the division of labor did indeed increase efficiency and productivity.

Despite the loss of some abilities, the American System was still fundamentally based on the *skills of American workers*. This was attested to by a British parliamentary report of 1868 that examined American industry and reported that the American worker

understands everything you say to him as well as a man from a college in England would; he helps the employer by his own acuteness and intelligence; and, in consequence, he readily attains to any new knowledge, greatly assisting his employer by thoroughly understanding what is the change that is needed, and helping him on the road towards it.[11]

Even as machines were being made to automate work, companies found them most productive when used by craftsmen to enhance their skills instead of replacing them.[12] And there were many skilled hands around. As gains in agriculture productivity accelerated in the mid- to late 1800s, many of the new industrial workers came off the farm, where they were accustomed to working with tools and devising ways of making their tasks easier and quicker to perform.

English observers were "struck by the absence in American factories of the organizational rigidities so familiar in the European [factories], by the concern of workers for personal advancement and material welfare, and by the belief of workers and managers alike in the boundless adaptability of American labor."[13] The American System thus retained a high degree of *flexibility* from its roots in Craft Production and its focus on the process of production rather than on individual products. Such flexibility was not found in European factories, nor would it continue in American factories in the years ahead. The dependence of the American System on worker skill, know-how, and flexibility extended to industrial suppliers, particularly to the machine tool industry, which, as Rosenberg notes, was important to the American System because

it came to constitute a pool or reservoir of the skills and technical knowledge which were essential to the generation of technical change throughout the machine-using sectors of the economy. Precisely because it came to deal with processes and problems which were common to an increasing number of industries, it played the role of a transmission center in the diffusion of the new technology. The pool of skill and technical knowledge was added to as a result of problems which arose in particular industries. Once the particular problem was solved and added to the pool, the solution became available, with perhaps minor modifications and redesigning, for employment in the growing number of technologically related industries.[14]

Thus, not only were the successes of individual companies due in large measure to the skills of workers trained in the craft tradition, but the diffusion of the American System throughout large sectors of the economy was itself due to their skills, flexibility, and ability to apply what they learned to a far-ranging set of problems.

American entrepreneurs of the nineteenth century were great imitators, innovators, and inventors. Armsmaker Colonel Samuel Colt and hundreds of his contemporaries introduced product development and improvement initiatives that demonstrated the final defining characteristic of the American System: *continuous technological improvement* in both product and process. As an anonymous American said to Alexis de Tocqueville in 1832,

There is a feeling among us about everything which prevents us aiming at permanence; there reigns in America a popular and universal belief in the progress of the human spirit. We are always expecting an improvement to be found in everything.[15]

The American System, an extremely successful method of production by the middle to late nineteenth century, was an object of envy among European rivals. While no single company was a perfect model for all of its characteristics, these eight—interchangeable parts, specialized machines, reliance on suppliers, focus on the production process, the division of labor, the skills of its workers, flexibility, and continuous technological improvement—accurately describe the American System of Manufactures and were responsible for its success.

Mass Production

As the American System moved into the twentieth century, these factors were not enough to support the growth of many large enterprises as they sought to meet the demands of an increasingly geographically dispersed economy. Beginning in the late 1800s but not reaching full development until the 1910s and 1920s, a related but distinct system of manufacturing formed that, while it owed much to

Table 2-3 Principles of Mass Production

From the American System

- Interchangeable parts
- Specialized machines
- Focus on the process of production
- Division of labor

Additional Principles

- Flow
- Focus on low costs and low prices
- Economies of scale
- Product standardization
- Degree of specialization
- Focus on operational efficiency
- Hierarchical organization with professional managers
- Vertical integration

its direct ancestor and in fact overlapped it in time, went far beyond it in organizing production for efficiency and low costs. This system became known as Mass Production, or *Fordism*, after Henry Ford, under whose leadership the system was most purely implemented.[16]

Mass Production was the direct descendant of the American System. Interchangeable parts, specialized machines, process focus, and the division of labor were particularly important to Mass Production and were taken to new heights in the system, so much so that rather than mere characteristics of the system they could be called principles of Mass Production. The additional principles of Mass Production that differentiated it from its predecessor are listed in Table 2-3.

Just as the defining principle of the American System was interchangeable parts, the principle of *flow* defined Mass Production. This principle, which involved the automatic movement of work to the worker, was first used in continuous process industries such as the refining of petroleum and distilling of alcohol, but could also be seen in cigarette manufacturing, flour milling, and the "disassembly" lines of slaughterhouses.[17]

It was Henry Ford and his cadre of production engineers, notably Charles Sorensen, who put the principle of flow to full use in the Model T assembly line, rearranging the functional organization of their factory into a moving line where each worker assembled a piece of a car, which moved on to the next worker for the next assembly step, and so on. This innovation became synonymous with Mass Production. As business historian David Hounshell describes it:

In "moving the work to the men," the fundamental tenet of the assembly line, the Ford engineers found a method to speed up the slow men and slow down the fast men. The assembly line would bring regularity to the Ford factory, a regularity almost as dependable as the rising of the sun. With the installation of the assembly line and the extension of its dynamism to all phases of factory operations, the Ford production engineers wrought true mass production.[18]

When Ford's engineers introduced the assembly line to Model T production in October 1913, the amount of labor time spent making a single car dropped from 12 hours and 8 minutes to 2 hours and 35 minutes. Six months later, Model T's could roll off the assembly line at the rate of 1,000 a day, with the average labor time dropping to just over an hour and a half.[19]

One of the reasons that the principle of flow was never fully developed in the American System was that its practitioners did not focus on lowering costs; their aims were primarily better quality and higher output, and in fact they typically charged more for their products.[20] But the second principle of Mass Production, also put into effect by Ford, was to *focus on low costs and low prices*, in order to create products for the "masses." It was this cost focus that created the need for assembly-line flow. Out of these two concepts came the third principle of Mass Production, *economies of scale:* the larger the enterprise and the greater its output, the lower its costs. In the American System, companies increased output by adding more machines and more workers in the same ratio that already existed in the factory, which did little to lower costs. In Mass Production, companies increased output not only by adding inputs but by increasing the throughput of the machines and the productivity of the workers so that fewer workers were needed per unit produced. This greatly increased fixed costs and the capital-to-labor (machine-to-worker) ratio, but also greatly lowered costs on each unit.

Since lowered costs meant prices could also be lowered, an internal logic came into play in the development of Mass Production. As prices were lowered, more people could afford to buy the products, resulting in greater sales and therefore greater production, even lower costs, and prices and so on. A cycle was thus developed that fueled the growth of Mass Production companies.[21] This can be seen from the tremendous growth in Ford Model T sales that accompanied the

Table 2-4   Price and Sales of Model T Fords, 1908–1916

Calendar Year	Retail Price (Touring Car)	Total Model T Sales
1908	$850	5,986
1909	950	12,292
1910	780	19,293
1911	690	40,402
1912	600	78,611
1913	550	182,809
1914	490	260,720
1915	440	355,276
1916	360	577,036

Source: David Hounshell, *From the American System to Mass Production 1800–1932* (Baltimore/London: Johns Hopkins University Press, 1984), p. 224.

continual lowering of its price, as shown in Table 2-4. In 1908, the Ford Motor Company produced slightly more than 10,000 automobiles (of all models), but manufactured over 500,000 Model T's in 1916 as the price dropped from $850 to $360. Total production grew to 2 million in 1923.[22]

This cycle required the development and manufacture of *standardized products*, because any complexities or custom work would upset the production process and result in much higher costs. Although product standardization reached its zenith with Ford, an enduring precept of Mass Production is producing standardized products for homogeneous markets. One of the primary reasons Mass Production (as well as the American System) was developed so extensively in the United States was that the American market was always more homogeneous than the markets of the industrialized countries of Europe. This was the case for a number of reasons, with the homogeneity of demand interrelated with the standardization of output. First, America never had the class distinctions common in Europe; therefore Americans did not have to differentiate themselves from other classes by what they purchased. Along the same lines, income distribution was also more equitable in the United States, resulting in more people clustered around similar needs and desires.

The American market was also much newer, without the long-held traditions common in Europe. Companies with new products did not have to divert their demand from the products of other suppliers, and so did not have to differentiate their products as much and, in particular, did not have to incorporate the idiosyncracies of previous products. Further, the American industrial market grew at a much faster rate than those in Europe. By the time of Ford, it had in fact become the world's first large "common market." This was true not only because the growth rates of both population and income were much greater in the United States, but the relative cheapness of both land and food resulted in higher relative demand for industrial products. A seller's market ensued, wherein companies could more readily impose and consumers more readily accept standardized products. In Europe, meanwhile, limited growth meant businesses had to cater more to customers' tastes to attract them. Because the firms serving the American market were also newer, they did not have the investment in old production methods and could move more easily to the new methods of Mass Production. The low costs of standardized products created by these techniques resulted in low prices that further maintained the homogeneity of American consumers.

As the throughput and scale of the manufacture of standardized products were so important to maintaining low costs, the system of Mass Production became even more dependent on machinery and the division of labor than the American System. The *degree of specialization* of men and machinery clearly differentiated Mass Production from its predecessor. The importance of this distinction deserves an extended quotation from Hounshell, whose detailed study, *From the American System to Mass Production 1800–1932*, examines the development of the two systems. Here is how he describes the implementation of the first assembly line at Ford Motor Company:

On April 1, 1913, workers in the Ford flywheel magneto assembling department stood for the first time beside a long, waist-high row of flywheels that rested on smooth, sliding surfaces on a pipe frame. No longer did the men stand at individual workbenches, each putting together an entire flywheel magneto assembly from the many parts (including sixteen permanent magnets, their supports and clamps, sixteen bolts, and other miscellaneous parts). This was no April Fool's joke. The workers had been instructed by the foreman to place one particular part in the assembly or perhaps start a few nuts or even just tighten them and then push the flywheel down the row to the next worker. Having pushed it down eighteen or perhaps thirty-six inches, the workers repeated the same process, over and over, nine hours, over and over. Martin, Sorensen, Emde and others [Ford production engineers] had designed what may have been the first automobile assembly line, which somehow seemed another step in the years of development at Ford yet somehow suddenly dropped out of the sky. Even before the end of that day, some of the engineers sensed that they had made a fundamental breakthrough. Others remained skeptical. Twenty-nine workers who had each assembled 35 or 40 magnetos per day at the benches (or about one every twenty minutes) put together 1,188 of them on the line (or roughly one every thirteen minutes and ten seconds per person). There were problems, to be sure. Some workers complained about aching backs because of stooping over the line; raising the work level six or eight inches would solve that problem. . . . Some workers seemed to drag their heels while others appeared to work too fast. . . . Soon they found that by moving magnetos at a set rate with a chain, they could set the pace of the workers: speed up the slow ones, restrain the quick. Within the next year, by raising the height of the line, moving the flywheels with a continuous chain, and lowering the number of workers to fourteen, the engineers achieved an output of 1,335 flywheel magnetos in an eight-hour day—five man-minutes compared to the original twenty.[23]

The path to Mass Production led from artisans responsible for producing an entire product by their own means and at their own pace in Craft Production, to groups of (still) craftsmen working together on a defined product or at least a significant component of one in the American System, and finally to workers becoming so specialized that, under the close direction of a supervisor, they performed the smallest of functions, over and over, in the assembly-line production of a single part.

The degree of specialization applied to machinery was similar. In Craft Production, craftsmen used a relatively small set of general-purpose tools to perform all their operations. In the American System, once general-purpose machines adapted to specialized functions provided the means of producing greater numbers of more sophisticated products. But in Mass Production, the entire production process became critically dependent on specialized machines that performed one, and only one, function—often for only one product design, requiring significant retooling for any design changes. The extent of the specialization of machines was heavily influenced by the extent of the specialization of labor, for as the production process was continually broken down, with workers performing smaller and smaller tasks, these tasks became easier to automate.

The entire production process thus became completely dependent on the smooth-running operations of an assembly line of specialized machines and workers to achieve economies of scale and its advantages of greatly lowered costs. If, however, throughput in the factory was not maintained near capacity—if anything went wrong with the machines, workers, or the pace of operations—unit costs would rise rapidly. To prevent this, companies maintained a strong *focus on operational efficiency*, which included the conspicuous use of buffers throughout the factory. Maintaining the productivity of machines and workers each day and increasing their productivity over time—at a predictable rate that became known as the "learning" or "experience" curve—was paramount to company success and consumed an increasingly large cadre of foremen, supervisors, and managers.

From the increased need for control was born the *hierarchical organization with professional managers*. Before 1850, most enterprises were small, family-owned firms, few of which required a full-time manager or much in the way of an administrative structure. With the rise of the American System companies grew larger, required more administration, and as the American System grew into the system of Mass Production, developed hierarchical organizations (first a single hierarchy, then a divisionalized form) to control increasingly complex businesses. By World War I, the day-to-day operations of most large businesses were clearly run not by entrepreneurial families but by professional managers.[24]

These managers often used the precepts of what was called *scientific management*, or *Taylorism* after its famous proponent, Frederick W. Taylor. Strict Taylorism involved meticulous time and motion studies to find and eliminate any and all inefficiencies in workers' activities. This meant eliminating their knowledge and skills as well, as Taylor himself explains:

The managers assume. . . the burden of gathering together all of the traditional knowledge which in the past has been possessed by the workmen and then of classifying, tabulating and reducing this knowledge to rules, laws and formulae which are immensely helpful to the workers in doing their daily work.[25]

While the precepts of scientific management were rarely followed to the letter, they had a tremendous effect on mass producers by focusing managers on planning the work of workers, thereby increasing their specialization, decreasing their skills, and in many cases replacing them with machinery.

The final principle of Mass Production, *vertical integration*, also grew out of the need to control production and was influenced by the rise of large, hierarchical organizations. The tremendous fixed costs of Mass Production required that the assembly line be kept busy to ensure low costs. It followed that an adequate supply of raw materials and components was essential, as was a stable marketplace in which to sell finished products. Therefore, mass producers became concerned not only with production, but also with the entire flow of materials from their raw state through production and distribution. The mass producers became mass suppliers and distributors as well.

This discussion of the principles of Mass Production, then, begins and ends with the principle of flow, which grew from its application to the assembly line to its application to the entire process of reaching consumers with goods. In between, we saw how additional principles were developed and mutually reinforced to create the system of Mass Production as we know it today.

While the diffusion of the American System of Manufactures was due primarily to the machine tool industry, the diffusion of Mass Production owed much to the automotive industry and to Henry Ford and his production engineers in particular. They were very proud of their achievements, wrote books and articles about what they had accomplished in the Ford Motor Company, and opened their factories to technical journalists who communicated what was happening at Ford to the rest of American industry. The other automobile companies soon adopted Ford's techniques, followed by other consumer durable manufacturers and so on into other industries until Mass Production became the dominant mode of manufacture in the United States.

Mass Production as a Paradigm of Management

From its beginnings in the latter half of the nineteenth century, to its flowering at the hands of Henry Ford and his production engineers, to its diffusion throughout American industry in the 1920s and 1930s and its dominance of world industrial production in the years after World War II, the system of Mass Production has propelled the tremendous growth in American economic strength in the twentieth century. In fact, it became virtually the only production system practiced by large U.S. manufacturers, except for internal prototype shops that are still predominantly craft based.

The techniques of the system of Mass Production have not been confined to large manufacturers. All the principles listed in Table 2-3 have been emulated by large service providers such as insurance companies and banks, for which paper became the "unit of produc-

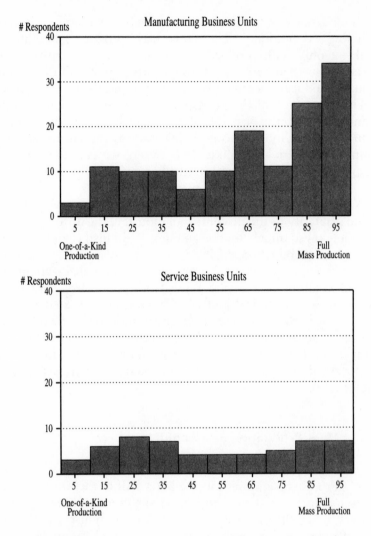

Figure 2-1   One-of-a-Kind vs. Full Mass Production

tion" that flows from one worker to the next in line. And despite the persistence of craft production among small manufacturers, many of them, as well as small service concerns, view mass production techniques as crucial to efficiency and growth.

This can be seen dramatically in Figures 2-1 and 2-2. In a survey of more than 250 executives, managers, and professionals across a variety of businesses,[26] respondents were asked to describe their com-

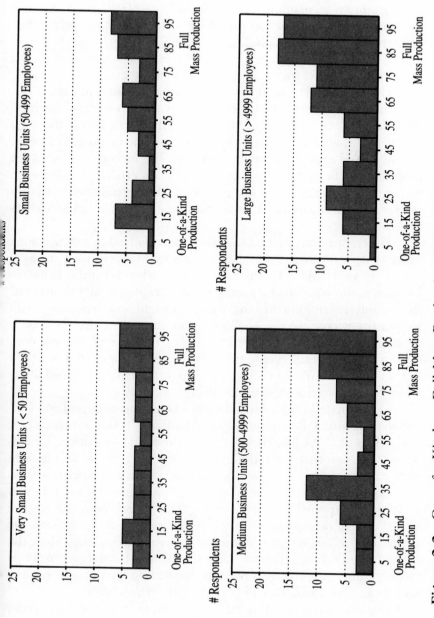

Figure 2-2 One-of-a-Kind vs. Full Mass Production: Size of Business Unit

pany on a continuous scale from "one-of-a-kind production" on one end to "full mass production" on the other. As Figure 2-1 shows, the great majority of manufacturing respondents placed their business units on the mass production end of the scale, with many saying they were 100 percent mass producers. And notice the second part of Figure 2-1: service providers were as likely to say that they used a mass "production" process as a one-of-a-kind process.

The same holds true for small businesses, as seen in Figure 2-2. Like those from service firms, respondents from very small business units with fewer than 50 people were as likely to be on the mass production side of the scale as they were on the one-of-a-kind side. As one would expect, as the business unit size increases, so does the proportion of firms that say they are full mass producers. However, it is clear that the allure of the system of Mass Production exists for service providers as well as manufacturers, and for small as well as large businesses.

The tremendous success of Mass Production led to a view among many American managers and executives that its principles were *the* key to success. Mass Production became what scientific historian Thomas Kuhn has called a *paradigm:* "an accepted model or pattern" that establishes an informational framework and set of rules by which its practitioners view the world.[27] Mass Production has become a paradigm not only of "production" but of *management*, for not only do service providers accept and follow it as well as manufacturers, but (as will be seen) its precepts encompass the entire firm and all its many functions across the value chain.

Unfortunately, the word *paradigm* has become overused and subject to caricature ("Brother, can you paradigm?"). But in this case, it really does fit.[28] As Joel Barker applies the term to business, a paradigm "tells you that there is a game, what the game is, and how to play it successfully."[29] A paradigm can be a powerful mechanism for ordering information and focusing research and practice on a common set of goals. Applied here, the paradigm of Mass Production has the shared goal of *developing, producing, marketing, and delivering goods and services at prices low enough that nearly everyone can afford them.* Since the time of Henry Ford, that has been the "game" to play for many in business, and the principles of Mass Production have taught companies, large and small, how to play the game successfully.

The primary goal of this game is shared, as Piore and Sabel point out, by consumers as well as producers:

In the world of mass production, consumers accepted standard goods; their acceptance facilitated the extension of the market and the reduction of prices, through increasing economies of scale; and the growing gap between the price of mass-produced goods and that of customized goods further encouraged the clustering of demand around homogeneous products.[30]

In this interplay between producers and consumers the paradigm of Mass Production became a feedback loop that creates and reinforces standardized products, mass production techniques, and large, homogeneous markets. The feedback loop provides the informational framework around which practitioners of Mass Production view the world and make the decisions they believe are key to success. It is therefore worth spending some time understanding exactly how this feedback loop operates. The reinforcing principles of this dynamic system of management, in one logical sequence, are as follows:

- A company must make a profit to stay in business. The more profit made, the more successful the business. Simplistically but truthfully, selling the most product at the lowest cost generates the most profit.
- More product can be sold in large, homogeneous markets than in others.
- High product volumes drastically reduce manufacturing costs through economies of scale.
- Demand is elastic; therefore, lowering prices as costs decrease brings even higher volume and greater revenue.
- As prices drop, markets expand. Customer homogeneity expands with them as those on the "fringe" between homogeneous and niche markets succumb to the lower prices.
- Niche markets that remain represent different customer desires and support only relatively low volumes; attempting to go after them merely increases costs. Therefore, ignore them. Leave them to the "little guys."
- To realize the lowest possible costs, hence the largest market, the production process should be as automated as possible. This means high fixed costs but low unit costs, further reinforcing the need for high volumes. New process technology can also be a powerful driver of ever-lower costs—as long as the investment in the current technology has been recouped.
- Efficiency of the production process must be maintained at all times. It requires most of all stability, that everything run

smoothly, with no delays, no interruptions, no surprises. Therefore,

- ○ Inputs must be stabilized: management must control employee wages and supplier prices. This requires a degree of antagonism toward unions, which must not be allowed to control the labor market, as well as toward suppliers that can be played off each other to reduce prices. A high degree of vertical integration may also be warranted to fully ensure the stability and prices of material inputs.
- ○ The process itself must be stabilized: management must exercise control. The product must be as standardized as possible and the manufacturing process broken down into small specified tasks. Workers and machinery must be highly specialized to drive down the time and expense of each individual task.
- ○ Outputs must be stabilized: management must control demand levels not only by ignoring niches but also by using inventory levels to adjust to temporary changes in demand. If, however, demand falls below a level that would affect profits too adversely, workers can be laid off.

- The product life cycle should be lengthened as much as possible, reducing per unit development costs as well as investments in product and process technology, allowing the experience curve to operate to its fullest. Minor changes only add costs and should be avoided. Research and development should focus on new product breakthroughs that can be mass-produced. Marketing and sales should focus on pushing current production out the door.
- The profits made this way allow for a long product development cycle to design and develop product extensions and new products that can be readied for the mass market. A steady stream of new product technology can provide the stable base of products needed to maintain profits over the long run.

Thus the system becomes a feedback loop through new or extended products that can be mass-produced. This feedback loop of reinforcing factors is shown in simplified form in Figure 2-3.[31] The diagram can be read "New products manufactured by a mass production process yield low-cost, consistent quality, standardized goods for large, homogeneous markets; this results in stable demand, causing long product life cycles, which allow for long product development cycles from which new products are created, and so on." The "R" indicates

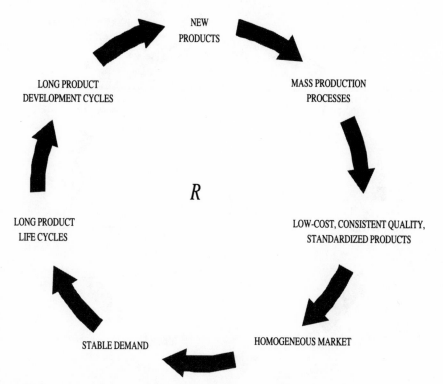

NEW
PRODUCTS

LONG PRODUCT
DEVELOPMENT CYCLES

MASS PRODUCTION
PROCESSES

R

LONG PRODUCT
LIFE CYCLES

LOW-COST, CONSISTENT QUALITY,
STANDARDIZED PRODUCTS

STABLE DEMAND

HOMOGENEOUS MARKET

Figure 2-3 The Paradigm of Mass Production as a Dynamic System of Reinforcing Factors

that this is a *reinforcing* loop, which over time yields products that move more and more toward the ultimate goal of the highest volumes, using the most efficient manufacturing processes with the lowest possible costs for the largest possible markets and at the most stable demand levels.

Figure 2-4 presents the secondary reinforcing loops of the paradigm of Mass Production. These indicate how new developments in product and process technology are key to the continued success of the system. At times, however, the large, homogeneous markets are not stable enough by themselves to maintain the efficiency of the production process. Ignoring niches and using inventory adjustments to stabilize demand are also key to the stability of the entire system.

This, then, is the paradigm of Mass Production. Large or small company, manufacturing or service concern—any company that holds to the paradigm of Mass Production implicitly views the world

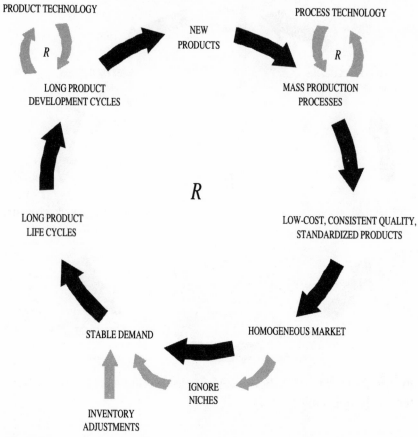

Figure 2-4   The Secondary Feedback Loops within the Paradigm of Mass Production

in this way. The creed of the paradigm can be summed up with the phrase *efficiency through stability and control:* the efficiency of the production process must be maintained through stability in and control of the firm's inputs, process, technologies, and outputs. If this is achieved, all else will follow.

And for its practitioners throughout most of the twentieth century, profits have indeed followed. Let there be no doubt: the paradigm of Mass Production has been remarkably successful for American firms, and for America. Those which held to it first, and managed it best, became the giants of industry, the *Fortune 500* companies. Among their number are Ford, General Motors, U.S. Steel, Standard Oil, IBM, AT&T, Texas Instruments, Du Pont, Xerox, Eastman

Kodak, Procter & Gamble, Goodyear, and General Electric. They, and the thousands of others—large or small, manufacturing or service—that followed in their footsteps made the United States the world's dominant economic power.

Paradigm Lost

As almost everyone today realizes, America's economic dominance is being threatened. Many of the companies mentioned above are in deep trouble. The system that made America great has been challenged by new forms of competition that are increasingly successful. Not only has competition changed, but so have societies, countries, markets, technologies, and consumers. Our world is not the same as the world of the 1910s or 1920s, when Ford pioneered mass production techniques, or even of the world of the 1950s and 1960s, when the United States seemingly cemented its place at the pinnacle of economic power.

Because Mass Production had been so successful for so long in ordering the world and enhancing the profits of its practitioners, it was extremely difficult for managers in the 1970s and 1980s to realize that the world was in fact changing. This was directly due to the dual-edged nature of a paradigm: while it is a powerful tool for ordering information and focusing goals, a paradigm automatically filters out information contradictory to its world view. The seeds of Mass Production's decline have always been present within the system, but they have not and could not be easily seen or understood by its practitioners.

Pure reinforcing loops, as shown in Figures 2-3 and 2-4, are rare; generally, there are natural forces at work within a system to balance it and limit its growth.[32] The *balancing* loops to Mass Production (indicated by a "B") are shown in Figure 2-5 together with other perils that make it a more complete view of the paradigm. This revised view demonstrates what has gone wrong with Mass Production over the past twenty or thirty years.

First, there are limits to the mass production process because of input stability. As one example, to keep the system reinforcing itself, labor costs must keep coming down relative to the price of a product. This can be done with real wage decreases (relative to inflation) or by productivity increases. To the extent that relative and absolute productivity began to decline in the 1970s, the ability of mass produc-

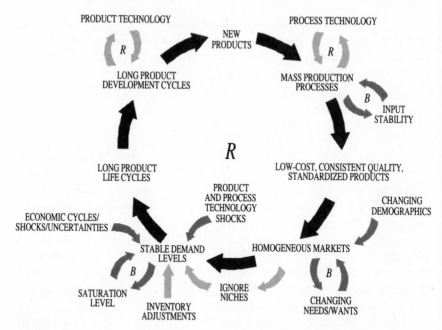

Figure 2-5   Mass Production as a Complete Dynamic System Feedback Loop

tion processes to lower real costs (and therefore lower prices and expand markets) was limited.[33]

Second, the homogeneity of markets is threatened by the changing needs and wants of consumers. Although the causes have been hotly debated, the fact that American consumer tastes have changed—and in particular have diversified into a widening array—is not under question today. Earlier, we saw three reasons why the American market in the late nineteenth and early twentieth centuries was inherently more homogeneous than the industrialized markets of Europe. As we near the close of the twentieth century, these factors no longer exist.

- American society is much less homogeneous with regard to class, race, gender, lifestyles, and national origin. The population as a whole is aging.
- Income distribution is less equal than it was a century ago, creating great differences in disposable income with corresponding disparities in needs and desires.
- The American market, no longer new, is no longer growing much

faster than the rest of the industrialized world. Today, demand for new products frequently has to be diverted from older ones. It is therefore important for new products to meet customer needs more completely, to be of higher quality, and simply to be different from what is already in the marketplace.

These reasons have caused fundamental changes in markets, moving many of them from homogeneous to heterogeneous, a trend that has accelerated over the past twenty years.

The third balancing loop in the mass production system is related to stability of demand. Mass Production depends on stable, steadily growing demand to keep its wheels turning. And in America, that is what producers enjoyed through most of the postwar period until the 1970s. From that point on, the markets in many industries have matured, been saturated and have been buffeted by recessions and oil crises, all with adverse effects on mass producers. What were once sellers' markets have become buyers' markets. Forecasting annual sales and planning production have become more problematic. The feasibility of maintaining multibillion-dollar plants designed to churn out high, predictable volume at low cost seems increasingly doubtful when markets are unpredictable.

Stable demand is also affected by technological shocks. New technology adapted to products can throw a monkey wrench into the demand for older, established products. The demand for home movie cameras and projectors was undermined, diminished, and eventually gutted by the introduction of videotape equipment, a new technology addressing the same purpose and competing in the same market. This scenario has happened over and over again in recent decades. Given the current pace of technological change, product markets will be less and less stable in the foreseeable future.

Similarly, stable demand is also susceptible to process technology shocks: new methods of manufacturing that prove more successful at achieving production goals. The Japanese system of "lean" production, which was specifically created to compete with American mass producers by achieving lower costs at smaller volumes with higher quality, has created just such a process technology shock in the automobile and many other industries. Further, flexible manufacturing systems and computer-integrated manufacturing techniques that have made it more economical to produce a greater variety of products are further shocks to the system of Mass Production.

As this discussion shows, there are serious limits and perils to the system of Mass Production: input instabilities, changing demographics, changing needs and wants, saturated markets, economic cycles, shocks, and uncertainties, and, finally, product and process technology shocks. As these have been encountered in many industries over the past twenty or thirty years, they have caused the breakdown of the otherwise smooth-running system, as *efficiency*, *stability*, and *control* are lost.

When one paradigm fails, it is time to shift to another.

CHAPTER 3

The Emerging System of
Mass Customization

FOR many companies in many industries, the breakdown of Mass Production began in the 1960s, accelerated in the 1970s, and finally burst fully into management consciousness in the 1980s. Because the system of Mass Production became a paradigm of management, it was extremely difficult for managers to realize what was happening. Their world view simply did not provide for these limits, and when the changes could no longer be ignored, their paradigm did not allow for an effective reaction beyond the normal responses that had served so well for so long. Michael Best of the University of Massachusetts has pointed out this exact failure:

The response [to Japanese competition] came too late for whole sectors including motorcycles, consumer electrical products, and steel. Why did it take Western business managers so long to address the issue? One reason is that they lacked categories to explain it. But a second is that even where telling explanations were available they were ignored because they did not offer solutions amenable to existing management instruments of either the firm or the government. In these cases an effective response demanded that managers abandon organizational principles that had earlier made them successful and restructure business enterprises according to entirely different production concepts.[1]

Table 3-1   Features of the Competitive Landscape of the 1990s

• Time-based competition	• Lean production
• Proliferating variety	• Cycle time reduction
• Just-in-time production	• Total quality management
• Regional marketing	• Flattened hierarchies
• Continual improvement	• Computer-integrated manufacturing
• Shortening product life cycles	• Process re-engineering
• Market-driven quality	• Heightened importance of services
• Globalization	• Fragmented markets
• Networked organizations	• Quick response
• Micromarketing	• Flexible manufacturing systems
• Increased customization	• Database marketing

In these industries, what Kuhn calls a "paradigm crisis" has ensued. The old paradigm is unable to explain anomalies or provide solutions for new problems. In the 1990s, it is no longer easy to ignore the changes that have occurred in the past few decades, nor is it easy to discard them as irrelevant or hope that the good old days will return. Table 3-1 lists some of the features of the competitive landscape of the 1990s, features now too near and too large to ignore. A new paradigm is needed that can effectively respond to this new terrain.

What in the World View Is Happening?

These features are prominent in industry after industry. The landscape is completely different from the old world of Mass Production, in which standardized products, homogeneous markets, and long product life and development cycles were the rule, not the exception. Today, a new paradigm of management is emerging, one in which variety and customization supplant standardized products, heterogeneous and fragmented markets spring from once-homogeneous markets, and product life cycles and development cycles spiral downward. Companies and entire industries are making a *paradigm shift*, which Barker defines as "a change to a new game, a new set of rules."[2]

Before fully detailing this emerging paradigm, it is worth spending some time examining more than a few industries in which this paradigm shift is occurring. Once we get inside these manufacturing and service industries, the characteristics of the new world view will become clear.

Automobile Industry

The automobile industry was once prototypical of Mass Production. As the late William Abernathy of Harvard described how it was viewed in the 1970s:

As with the vigorous domestic producers of radios, television sets, textiles, shoes, and a host of other goods a decade or more ago, the automobile industry has entered at last into the mature stage of its life cycle. Its products have become standardized, virtually a commodity distinguishable only in terms of cost, and its production processes have been embodied in equipment that is available for purchase by all comers.[3]

Today, the automobile industry is characterized by a high degree of both product and process innovations. A short list of recent major product innovations includes all-wheel drive and all-wheel steering, air bags, synthetic engine materials, microprocessors controlling more functions, minivans, and automatic overdrive transmissions. Soon to be fully available commercially are heads-up control displays (as in fighter jets), electric cars, infrared night vision displays, and navigation systems. Process innovations have been equally rampant, including a host of such manufacturing automation technologies as robotic welders and painters, and perhaps most important, the large number of process improvements introduced by the Japanese, such as just-in-time production and total quality management.

In short, rather than continuing down the long, slow decline in product and process innovation historically characterizing mature industries, the automobile industry has entered a phase that Abernathy has called "de-maturity."[4] The end result is not only greatly increased product and process innovations but product proliferation and customization previously unheard of in the industry. After increasing throughout the 1970s, the number of distinct car models available increased by more than a third—from 151 to 205—just between 1982 and 1990.[5] In addition, most models have an ever-increasing number of options that allow drivers to tailor cars to their liking. New features in the 1992 model year included a stereo system from Ford that can give the car the acoustic characteristics of a small jazz club, concert hall, and other venues; a suspension system from

Buick that lets a driver choose between a "soft" or "sport" ride; and a set of thirteen different controls from Mercedes-Benz that allows drivers to adjust the car's environment to their personal tastes. The entire process, from order to delivery—*including* production, not just movement from inventory—is heading toward full customization:

In Japan today, Toyota is reportedly offering customers five-day delivery—from the time the customer personally designs his/her own, customised car (from modular options) on a CAD system (in a dealer showroom or in the customer's own home via [a] travelling salesman), through order processing, scheduling, manufacture, testing and delivery.[6]

With Toyota moving production to the United States and its domestic and national competitors trying hard to match it, this unprecedented level of customization may soon characterize the automobile industry in the United States.

Information Technology Industry

These phenomena can also be seen in the information technology industry. In 1964, IBM announced the System/360, the industry's first standardized computer designed by the company to replace its own myriad of models, not to mention those of its competitors. The System/360 ushered in the era of Mass Production in the computer industry, which was thought to have entered a mature phase about 1970, when IBM solidified its already commanding position by announcing the System/370. However, the computer industry refused to be standardized. Digital Equipment Corporation had invented minicomputers in the 1960s, and the 1970s would see the market expansion of a variety of minicomputers, seemingly without slowing down mainframe growth. Similarly, personal computers, invented in the 1970s, exploded in the marketplace of the early 1980s. The trend toward ever-smaller packaging continues with laptop, notebook, and even "palmtop" or "pentop" PCs. Toshiba alone produced more than thirty different varieties of laptop computers between 1986 and 1990, thirteen of them in 1990 alone.[7]

The proliferation of variety in the computer industry is not confined to smaller units over time. The nonscientific market that once consisted solely of mainframes has been fragmented by supercomputers and minimainframes; by technical versus commercial minicomputers; and more recently by superminicomputers, minisupercomputers, servers, and technical work stations. Each new category follows increasingly on the heels of the previous one as product life cycles shorten dramatically.

Further, the applications available on each type of system are becoming more and more customized. While in the 1960s every application was written specifically for—and often by—each customer, by the early 1970s, application packages had become standardized, shrink-wrapped, and mass-produced. That didn't last, either. Vertical packages appeared, as companies in the distribution industry were not the same as those in manufacturing, for example. These vertical markets fragmented further over time, as distribution companies realized they were very different from each other and demanded different applications. Today, the variety extends to a myriad of applications for each four-digit SIC code—and beyond. Further, virtually no application is shipped without a host of features that can be customized by the individual user.

While the information technology industry is not particularly old, having been created in the 1940s or 1950s, its leaders quickly moved to Mass Production as the way to operate. Today, however, the industry is characterized by proliferating variety and complexity, short product life and development cycles, and fragmenting markets.

Telecommunications Industry

The basic trends away from Mass Production are also occurring in service industries, with telecommunications leading the way. For most of the twentieth century this industry—and AT&T in particular—has "mass-produced" telephone services. Massive economies of scale have been achieved by tremendous investments in telecommunications infrastructure stretching across the country, and across the oceans. The incremental (variable) cost of a new home or business accessing this infrastructure was, and still is, virtually nil. Few options were available to the standardized "product" of phone service—options like pulse tone versus rotary and WATS (wide area transmission service) were about it. Demand was exceedingly stable, with product life cycles stretching into decades for communications equipment.

Thanks to the 1984 breakup of AT&T, the situation has changed. Competition in the industry is fierce, the number of innovations is increasing dramatically, and the availability of options and opportunities for customization are skyrocketing. A short list of options available just at home includes Call Waiting, Call Forwarding, caller identification, caller ID blocking, multiple phone lines (with different rings), and voice "mailboxes." The variety and customization on the drawing board (so to speak) are truly mind-boggling, as Mark Emery, director of Advanced Intelligence Network Services Planning for Bell Atlantic, relates: "We have a list of over a hundred new services for rollout to customers over the next few years. Many of these may be brought together to allow each customer to design and implement a unique telephone service."

The underlying hardware technology is undergoing similar changes. No longer can telecommunications companies afford long development cycles in the expectation of even longer product life cycles. Today's hardware has to be produced quickly, for it is replaced quickly. Even fiber optics—the new backbone of the industry—is no longer a standardized product. Corning, the world's leading supplier, has discovered that its customers and their types of usage are unique. Where it used to mass-produce only one type of fiber, it is now providing a specialized variety for each application.

Personal Care Industries

Twenty years ago, when you went into a store to buy personal care items—say, shampoo or soap or cough medicine—you had a relatively small number of brands and varieties to choose from. Since then, the number of varieties has exploded. Shampoo is produced for people with oily hair, dry hair, and (even) normal hair; for particular pH balances; for "environmentally aware" customers; for those who want conditioner added; and so on. The soap market has fragmented along similar lines. Cough medicine is available for your particular *type* of cough: a dry, hacking cough, versus a "sniffily, sneezy" cough (whatever that is), versus a wheezing cough, and so on.

Once, toothbrushes were a pure commodity product whose manufacturers competed almost solely on price. This industry was mature almost from its inception; until the late 1970s, it was marked by only two major innovations: nylon bristles in 1938 and electric toothbrushes in 1961. With the advent of bristle design as a differentiating factor when Johnson & Johnson brought out its Reach brand in 1977, today's toothbrush industry is characterized by constant incremental innovations.[8]

This shift from commodity to variety extends into the personal care of infants as well. Manufacturers used to make one type of disposable diaper, for example, which varied solely in size. In the late 1980s, realizing that girls and boys were different, companies changed the design of diapers to reflect that distinction. In the 1990s, disposable diapers are tailored even further. Procter & Gamble introduced its Pampers Phases line, which has thirteen different diaper designs—not sizes, but thirteen different *product designs*—that reflect the changes in infants as they grow from newborns to toddlers. Kimberly-Clark soon followed with a similar concept called Huggies Baby Steps. These innovations have been occurring with such rapidity over the past five years that industry analysts now consider six months to be a huge lead on the competition.

Proliferating variety characterizes all personal care industries— despite the fact that available shelf space at supermarkets and other retail outlets has not come close to keeping pace with the number of products vying for room on those shelves.

Beverage Industries

Pepsi and Coca-Cola used to slug it out in the soft drink market, with an assorted number of off-brand colas and an allotment of other flavors comprising the rest of the market. Today, not only has "other" grown and commanded an increasing portion of the market, but the basic cola segment has fragmented into diet and nondiet, caffeinated and caffeine-free (not to mention "caffeine-rich" brands like Jolt Cola), with and without fruit juice, and so on. There's not even one Coke anymore—there's Classic Coke and New Coke. On the horizon for vending machines are many variants of canned coffee and tea drinks.

The same is true of liquor, particularly beer. A beer used to be a beer, as Greg Prince, the senior editor of *Beverage World*, has nostalgically related:

> Ah, the good old days. If you wanted a beer, you had a simple variety of types from which to choose.
> If it was hot, you might ask for a cold beer.
> If it was somebody else buying, you might ask for a free beer.
> If it was Ohio, you might ask for a near beer.[9]

Now, that very basic, homogeneous market has been divided into "regular" beer, light beer, nonalcoholic beer, malt liquors, dry beer, holiday beer, and other niches—many filled by new regional "micro-breweries." Why is this happening? Because the industry hit limits to the system of Mass Production in saturation levels, changing needs and wants, and especially changing demographics. In response, brewers have created many niche products to respond to the differing lifestyles, personalities, and "psychographic" characteristics of their customers. Where once the top brands were the same year after year—with the list always topped by Budweiser—these brands themselves have separated into entire families of related but distinct beers. Between March and September of 1991 alone, the five major breweries announced fifteen new brand extensions.

Breakfast Cereal Industry

Like personal care items and soft drinks, the variety in breakfast cereals keeps increasing year after year—with each new variety decreasing the average shelf space (and therefore average sales) of all the others. In 1980, only 88 brands were available in the United States; by 1990, 205 brands were being sold. Among that proliferation, the number of brands able to hold at least a 1 percent share stayed virtually identical: 31 in 1980 and 30 in 1990. During that same period, the share of the best-selling brand—Kellogg's Corn Flakes—fell steadily from 7 to 5.4 percent.[10]

A recent trend has been to create short-lived niche cereals, like those tied to specific popular movies such as *Ghostbusters*, *Batman*, and *Robin Hood*. Generally, the cereals do not last much longer than the movies. But as with beer, most of the new ones seem to be variations on a theme: it's no longer just Cheerios, but Honey Nut Cheerios, Apple Cinnamon Cheerios, and Multi Grain Cheerios. Take your pick. That's why General Mills developed them.

Fast-Food Restaurant Industry

Again, the industries greatly increasing variety and customization are not limited to manufacturing. Service industries are undergoing similar transformations. Remember when fast-food restaurants provided just a quick burger, fries, and a shake? McDonald's symbolized the application of mass production techniques to service industries: its menu, recipes, uniforms, and buildings were standardized, and its production methods were basic assembly-line techniques. This, of course, contributed in large measure to its success: you could go to a McDonald's anywhere in the world and be assured of a consistently good burger and fries.

Burger King tried the same techniques, but could never break McDonald's stranglehold on the number one spot. So it went the customization route: "Have It Your Way!" and "Sometimes You've Gotta' Break the Rules!" became its anti–mass production slogans, which touted the ability to tailor any order to whatever the customer wanted. But it was still primarily a burger and fries.

As McDonald's felt the heat not only from Burger King but other very successful fast-food outlets like Pizza Hut, Domino's, Kentucky Fried Chicken, and Taco Bell, it moved into variety in a big way. First came a special breakfast menu based on the same mass-production formula: Egg McMuffin and hash browns replaced the burger and fries. Then, in the late 1980s, McDonald's began the trend, now encompassing most of the industry, of greatly proliferating the number of menu items. Today, McDonald's has a vast menu: "McDonald's Pizza, chicken fajitas, breakfast burritos, submarine sandwiches, spaghetti and meatballs, bone-in chicken, a grilled chicken sandwich, carrot and celery sticks, fresh-ground coffee, and even bottled mineral water."[11] And these are only some of the more than 150 new items that have been added or are being test-marketed. How has McDonald's done it? Not through Mass Production, but through shortened development and production cycles, flexibility, autonomy, process innovations, and searching for what its customers really want. McDonald's is undergoing a paradigm shift. According to *Restaurant Business:*

The parade of products and promotional items attests to McDonald's accelerated new product and promotional product activity. That flexibility not only occurs in [company headquarters at] Oak Brook [Illinois], but in the field, where owner/operators are dreaming up their own specialties. . . .

[It] is misleading to consider McDonald's a monolith. "People have a vision of McDonald's being identical in 12,000 restaurants," says [president and chief executive officer of McDonald's USA, Edward] Rensi. "It's not. We've got products in Texas that we don't have in Boston. There's a lot going on with McDonald's all the time. Operators around the system may have sub sandwiches, steam-table oatmeal, soup, cappuccino, whatever the environment requires or they're enthusiastic about."[12]

Further, customers can now ask for changes—such as no pickles—to the formerly completely standardized burgers, and get them quickly. Franchisers are encouraged to make whatever changes best suit their local clientele. Employees are being encouraged to take initiative as well. Says chairman Michael R. Quinlan: "Do whatever it takes to make a customer happy."[13]

Why is this happening? Because the fast-food industry hit the limits to the feedback loop of Mass Production, as *Restaurant Business* once again makes clear:

McDonald's has responded to its recent problems with a rapid-fire spate of new products, marketing strategies and public relations overtures over the past 18 months. The unprecedented pace of change by the traditionally deliberate and conservative company indicates management's commitment to boosting its domestic restaurant performance.

The slump is rooted in a combination of factors: vicious price competition in the saturated hamburger segment; a decline in McDonald's price/value relationship due to its price increases; the fact that its investment costs for new restaurants are increasing faster than sales; plus changes in demographics and taste preferences that incline consumers away from its red meat core items.[14]

The fast-food industry, with McDonald's leading the way, is shifting from its tradition of Mass Production to something entirely different.

Insurance Industry

The same is true of the insurance industry. Insurance companies have always taken a "factory-oriented" approach to their business—particularly back-office operations like claims processing. The industry has been so grounded in the methods of Mass Production for so long that it views insurance not as a service but as a product to be manufactured. As the president of First Colony Life Insurance Company relates, "Our strategy continues to be one of manufacturing selected life insurance and annuity products which fulfill a market need. We then distribute those products through independent general agents."[15]

But with demographic change and market fragmentation, the insurance industry has encountered limits to the system of Mass Production. In response, it is moving away from standardized products and mass marketing to flexible, tailored products and niche or micromarketing. This movement is led by companies like The New

England, whose president and chief operating officer, Robert A. Shafto, notes that "clients will increasingly seek tailored solutions to their needs, rather than standard products" and goes on to observe that the industry is discovering that it is a service industry after all: the "industry is learning that the product isn't the product—it is the complete package of information, education, advice, attitude and ongoing service *plus* the actual product that the customer evaluates."[16] To compete in the new realities of the industry, The New England is completely re-engineering its business processes, adding and tailoring new products with shortened development times, increasing services to both customers and agents, and moving the policy approval process closer to customers to drastically cut turnaround time.[17] The New England is leading the insurance industry away from the paradigm of Mass Production.

Banking Industry

Like those in the insurance industry, bankers and brokers use the term "products" to describe their services. They have long focused on mass-producing those products to be successful. Today, they are shifting away from that focus, as Stephen B. White, chief executive officer of Syntonix Corp., has noted: "I believe that the 1990s will bring unprecedented change in the banking industry—a complete paradigm shift. And the survivors will be those who can anticipate the future, look beyond the boundaries of how it has always been, and look at the current situation from a new perspective."[18]

So, like insurance, the banking industry is characterized by fragmented markets, short life cycles, decreasing development cycles, increasingly important innovations, and production moving closer to the customer, with a concomitant decrease in production times with such "products" as the "15-minute mortgage," pioneered by Citicorp, and such services as automatic teller machines. Noted marketing professor Philip Kotler has discussed the paradigm shift going on in financial services this way:

Instead of viewing the bank as an assembly line provider of standardized services, the bank can be viewed as a job shop with flexible production capabilities. At the heart of the bank would be a comprehensive customer database and a product profit database. The bank would be able to identify all the services used by any customer, the profit (or loss) on these services and the potentially profitable services which may be proposed to that customer.[19]

At the forefront of the movement away from standardization and toward customization are companies like American Express, which uses the knowledge gained from the vast number of financial transactions its customers make to tailor the products and services it offers to each and every individual. This movement away from mass marketing, mass production, and mass distribution is widespread throughout the financial services industry.

Paradigm Regained: Mass Customization

Every one of these industries—and many more besides—is undergoing a fundamental shift. No longer do they focus on producing standardized products or services for homogeneous markets. These firms have thrown away the old paradigm of Mass Production, whose focus was efficiency through stability and control. Their world is no longer stable, cannot be controlled, and therefore their operations cannot be kept efficient in the old way. Through the application of technology and new management methods, they have found their way to a new paradigm by creating *variety and customization through flexibility and quick responsiveness*. This is the controlling focus of the new paradigm, *Mass Customization*.

While the practitioners of Mass Production share the common goal of developing, producing, marketing, and delivering goods and services at prices low enough that nearly everyone can afford them, practitioners of Mass Customization share the goal of developing, producing, marketing, and delivering affordable goods and services with enough variety and customization *that nearly everyone finds exactly what they want*. As discussed in Chapter 2, the logic of Mass Production that Henry Ford discovered and put into motion was that lower prices resulted in greater sales, greater sales in higher volumes, higher volumes in lower costs, and lower costs looped back around to allow even lower prices, and so on. Pioneers of Mass Customization have discovered a new logic, one more suited to a world in which stability and control can no longer be maintained. Here, a company that better satisfies its customers' individual wants and needs will have greater sales. With higher profits as well as a better understanding of customer requirements, the company can provide even more variety and customization, which further fragment the market. Because it is outdistancing its competitors in variety and customization, market fragmentation allows it once again to better satisfy its customers' individual wants and needs, and so on.

When this new logic is expanded into a full dynamic system of

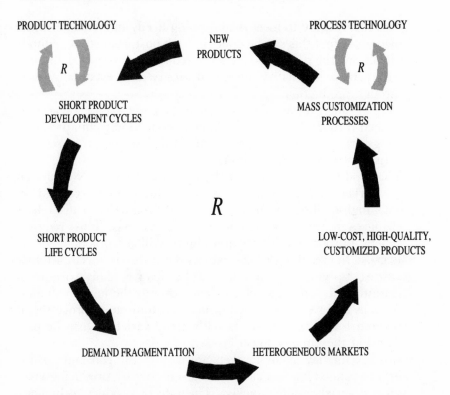

Figure 3-1 The New Paradigm of Mass Customization as a Dynamic System Feedback Loop

reinforcing factors as in Figure 3-1, it becomes clear that what the practitioners of Mass Customization have done is bring the Mass Production feedback loop of Figure 2-3 to a full stop and reversed it.[20] The logical tenets of this emerging system of management, in full, are as follows:

- Demand for individual products has become unstable. What used to be large demand for standard mass-market products has fragmented into demand for different "flavors" of similar products.
- Because demand has fragmented, the large, homogeneous markets have become increasingly heterogeneous. The niches are becoming the market, shifting power to buyers who demand higher-quality goods that more closely match their individual desires.
- Since profits cannot be maintained the old way, it seems preferable to go after some of the niches with the additional variety

desired, then try to meet the changing needs and wants of these niches. At first this can be done through postproduction methods of tailoring the product to niches (often through services), but it is an expensive alternative; increased variety must eventually come through production.

- Creating high levels of variety in production cannot be accomplished through the specialized mass production techniques; creating variety requires flexibility in manufacturing processes, the antithesis of Mass Production.

- The production system must therefore be changed. Now driven by markets and customers, it must produce a number of different, high-quality products via short production runs, short changeover times, and low work-in-process. This requires general-purpose machinery and highly skilled workers.

- Because the resulting new products more closely meet customer desires, a premium price can often be charged. This extra profit margin offsets any loss of efficiency due to the lower volumes. And, as experience is gained in mass customization processes, it is often found that products with many variations can be produced at the same or lower costs.

- Because the new niche markets are smaller and constantly shifting, continued success can be achieved only by producing ever-greater variety more quickly. The rate of product technology change increases dramatically; product development cycles must therefore be reduced just as dramatically.

- Along with shorter development cycles comes shorter product life cycles. Driven by the need to more closely fulfill customer desires, products and technologies are constantly improved upon and replaced.

- The result is less demand for each individual product—demand fragmentation—but increasingly stable demand for the company and its products relative to the old system and to its competitors. Ever-smaller niches to fill with ever-more variety can be sought.

This progression can thus be seen to feed back positively on itself, creating a reinforcing loop of greater variety, through increasing flexibility, more quickly—the exact opposite of Mass Production. To summarize the differences, the new system of Mass Customization is contrasted with the old in Table 3-2.

Technological innovation plays a vital role in the system of Mass Customization. As indicated in Figure 3-1, the application of new

Table 3-2 Mass Customization Contrasted with Mass Production

	Mass Production	Mass Customization
Focus	Efficiency through stability and control	Variety and customization through flexibility and quick responsiveness
Goal	Developing, producing, marketing, and delivering goods and services at prices low enough that nearly everyone can afford them	Developing, producing, marketing, and delivering affordable goods and services with enough variety and customization that nearly everyone finds exactly what they want
Key Features	• Stable demand • Large, homogeneous markets • Low-cost, consistent quality, standardized goods and services • Long product development cycles • Long product life cycles	• Fragmented demand • Heterogeneous niches • Low-cost, high-quality, customized goods and services • Short product development cycles • Short product life cycles

product technologies (such as microprocessors that can embed intelligence in a wide array of products) that increase the adaptability of products can also reinforce greater variety and shorter development cycles. Similarly, the application of new process technologies (such as flexible manufacturing systems and computer-integrated manufacturing techniques) reinforce the system's drive toward greater variety by making it increasingly economical to produce such variety. Indeed, in this new system processes are more important than products. As the figure shows, customers in increasingly heterogeneous markets demand customized products, which creates the need to re-engineer processes for mass customization. Individual new products then flow from these flexible, responsive but long-term and stable processes. In Mass Production, products are developed first and then the processes to manufacture them are created, each process coupled to each product. In Mass Customization, the processes are generally created first and remain decoupled from the ever-changing flow of products.

It is very important to notice two key points about this new paradigm. First, the benefits of low prices owing to economies of scale and other cost advantages of mass production processes are never overcome. That is, companies that can produce at lower costs and charge lower prices still have a competitive advantage; they will be more successful if they can retain low prices while providing the variety demanded by their customers. If this were not true, they could simply go back to Craft Production as their paradigm of management. Whereas the variety and flexibility of Craft Production are required, its costs are too high.[21]

Second, as the feedback loop is reinforced, the niche markets become smaller; they begin reaching down closer to the individual. "Greater and greater variety" blends into "more and more customized." In this regard, the logical conclusion of this feedback loop becomes the same as with Craft Production: individually customized goods and services.

Achieving Mass + Customization

Mass Customization, then, is a synthesis of the two long-competing systems of management: the mass production of individually customized goods and services. The pioneers of this new frontier in business competition are finding that great variety—even individual customization—can be achieved at prices that approach, and sometimes beat, those of mass producers.

In Mass Production, low costs are achieved primarily through economies of *scale*—lower unit costs of a single product or service through greater output and faster throughput of the production process. In Mass Customization, low costs are achieved primarily through economies of *scope*—the application of a single process to produce a greater variety of products or services more cheaply and more quickly. Companies often achieve both, such as economies of scale on standard components that can be combined in a myriad of ways to create end-product variety with economies of scope.

As mentioned above, new technologies are playing a key role. In manufacturing industries, computer numerical control, direct numerical control, and industrial robots greatly increase manufacturing flexibility by controlling parts manufacture through software programming.[22] Flexible manufacturing systems extend this by allowing all members of a family of parts to be manufactured at will and at random. Within a predetermined envelope of variety, there are no cost penalties for manufacturing any one part versus another, yielding a manufacturing system that can quickly respond to changes in demand. Computer-aided design/computer-aided manufacturing allows design modifications and even new designs to be quickly developed with the manufacturing requirements automatically generated from the design specifications. Finally, computer-integrated manufacturing links all the disparate computer-controlled "islands of automation" into a single, integrated system that is fast, responsive, flexible, and very low cost at high volumes. These manufacturing technologies can yield economies of scale and scope simultaneously, what Hamid Noori calls economies of *integration*.[23] Unit costs go down with the greater number of products manufactured because that increases the volume of the entire operation.

Advances in the speed, capacity, effectiveness, efficiency, and usability of information and telecommunications technologies constantly lower the costs of increasing differentiation in service as well as manufacturing industries. The instant application of information throughout a firm's value chain allows it to respond quickly to changes in demand and designs. In addition, whole new classes of mass customized products and services are enabled by such advancing technologies as computerized databases that can respond instantly to individual requests for information, and telephone and entertainment services that can be delivered to individual homes through fiber optic wires.

However, of equal if not greater importance in achieving both low costs and customization are advances in management. The development of just-in-time delivery, lean production techniques, early manufacturing involvement, time-based competition, cross-functional teams, and a host of other advances has increased flexibility and responsiveness and therefore the ability to increase variety and customization without parallel increases in costs.[24] Incorporated within these new ways of managing are four basic innovations that together achieve both mass and customization:

- Just-in-time delivery and processing of materials and components that eliminate process flaws and reduce inventory carrying costs
- Reducing setup and changeover times, which directly lowers run size and the cost of variety
- Compressing cycle times throughout all processes in the value chain, which eliminates waste to increase flexibility and responsiveness while decreasing costs
- Producing upon receipt of an order instead of a forecast, which

lowers inventory costs, eliminates fire sales and write-offs, and provides the information necessary for individual customization

It used to be axiomatic that achieving higher levels of quality meant higher costs; we now know that building quality into processes lowers costs. The same is true of variety and customization; building them into processes can indeed lower costs. To illustrate this, consider changeover times. In mass-producing firms, these occupy a significant portion of production time and therefore dictate long production runs. To determine the exact length of these runs, the concept of "economic order quantity" (EOQ) was developed. As illustrated in the left side of Figure 3-2, the EOQ is the point at which the increasing handling and storage costs begin to outweigh the decreasing setup and run cost on a per unit basis, yielding the lowest total cost per unit. However, when changeover costs are drastically reduced, as seen in the right side of Figure 3-2, the EOQ moves down the curve to a run size of one, resulting in much greater variety at much lower costs. Particularly when customer desires are changing rapidly or demand is uncertain, the cost savings of eliminating changeover time can be tremendous.

While true "lot size of one" production is still uncommon, in both manufacturing and service industries new technologies and new ways of managing are bringing down the costs of variety and customization. Whether the product and process technologies and management techniques exist in every industry to mass-produce goods and services customized to every individual's needs is beside the point. How effectively firms can use the flexible technologies that do exist, create new, more responsive processes and management methods, and use the inherent flexibility of workers to more quickly develop and produce new products and services that more closely match individual tastes is the key to the new paradigm. As Stan Davis, who coined the term "mass customization" in *Future Perfect*, says, "The general message is, the more a company can deliver customized goods on a mass basis, relative to their competition, the greater is their competitive advantage."[25]

A Return to the American System

Mass Customization, like the American System of Manufactures, contains elements of both Craft and Mass Production. As with Craft Production, Mass Customization commonly has a high degree

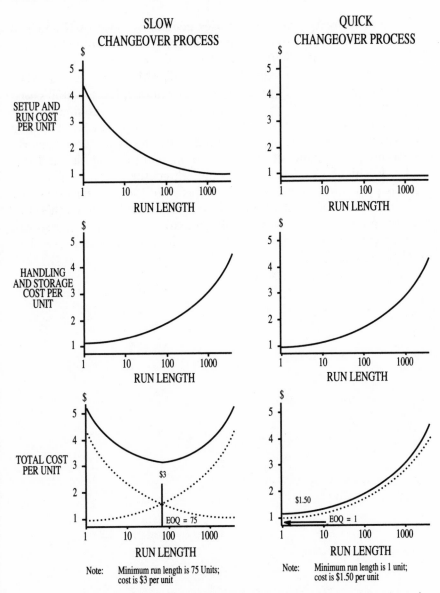

Note: Minimum run length is 75 Units;
        cost is $3 per unit

Note: Minimum run length is 1 unit;
        cost is $1.50 per unit

Source: Adapted from figure from *Kaisha: The Japanese Corporation* by James C. Abegglen and George Stalk, Jr. Copyright © 1985 by Basic Books, Inc. Reprinted by permission of Basic Books, a division of HarperCollins Publishers.

Figure 3-2   The Effect of Reducing Changeover Times on Economic Order Quantities

of flexibility in its processes; it uses general-purpose tools and machines as well as the skills of its workers; it builds to order rather than to plan; and it results in high levels of variety and customization in its products and services. Moreover, like Mass Production, Mass Customization generally produces in high volume, has low unit costs, and often (but not always) relies on high degrees of automation.

In the latter half of the nineteenth century, the American System of Manufactures propelled the United States to its position of world economic preeminence through a combination of flexibility and low costs. In this last decade of the twentieth century, Mass Customization is providing a new basis of competition not only for American companies but for much of the industrialized world.[26] When this shift occurs in an industry, success will come to those companies that can implement the new principles of competition faster and better than their competitors.

CHAPTER 4

Determining the Shift to
Mass Customization

T HE imperative to shift from Mass Production to Mass Customization has not yet been grasped by many of the companies that require it most. This is, perhaps, because Mass Production is indeed a paradigm, a "world view," as Kuhn calls it. As a way of viewing the world around us, a paradigm has a filter that either fits new information into the world view or discards it as irrelevant.[1] A paradigm fits us with "informational blinders," making it difficult to process new information that contradicts the paradigm until its preponderance becomes so great that the whole structure of belief comes crashing down. In business, that is almost always too late.

Managers need to comprehend fully where their firms—and their industries—stand in the shift from the old paradigm to the new. They need to take off the blinders and assimilate previously discarded information into a cogent, realistic view of the world and the direction in which that world is changing. And they need a way to do that systematically. In this chapter, two tools, the Market Turbulence Map and the Variety and Customization Profile, are introduced to allow managers to take a fresh view of their firms and industries to determine if Mass Customization is indeed the direction to take.

The Indicator of Change:
Market Turbulence

The basis for these tools becomes clear in re-examining the discussion in Chapter 3 on how the Mass Production paradigm has broken down. The limiting factors in its feedback loop are the primary points where this has happened:

- Decreases in the levels of *input stability* that can be maintained
- *Changing needs and wants* of customers
- *Changing demographics* of customers
- *Saturation level* of a product within its marketplace
- *Economic cycles, shocks, and uncertainties* that affect the market
- *Technological shocks* that overthrow the current dominant design in the marketplace and replace it with another

All but the first of these are market oriented; i.e., they describe what happens in (or to) a firm's marketplace, causing uncertainty or instability for the firm to the point of creating a turbulent market environment. While companies retain some control over input stability (e.g., by vertically integrating or de-integrating, signing long-term contracts at set prices, collective bargaining, and so forth), they are increasingly losing control over their marketplace. The loss of market control and demand stability knocks out the key props supporting their ability to produce low-cost products and services efficiently.

For example, each of the limits has hit hard in the American steel and automobile industries, two of the most traditional mass-producing industries. Because of the inflexibility and poor responsiveness of both Big Steel and the Big Three auto manufacturers, they have racked up tens of billions of dollars in losses during the recessions of the past two decades. During 1990 and 1991 alone, General Motors lost more than $11 billion as sales declined in its North American operations. In the face of a turbulent environment, mass producers do not have the ability to reduce their high fixed costs, quickly develop new products, or even change over to better-selling models. When market control and demand stability are lost, so is any hope of maintaining efficiency and controlling costs via mass production methods.

This, then, is the primary indicator of the paradigm shift from Mass Production to Mass Customization: the amount of *market turbulence* within an industry and firm. The greater the market turbulence, the more likely that the industry is moving toward Mass Customization, and that the firm *has* to move in order to remain competitive.

"Market turbulence" is an imprecise term but connotes the amount of instability, uncertainty, and lack of control within a firm's marketplace. Think of the turbulence encountered on an airplane: up and down and side to side, uncertain and unpredictable. But most of all it is discomfiting, and as a passenger you can do nothing to make it go away. Such is market turbulence for managers in firms long used to being in the driver's seat on a smooth highway, but who are now swept up in storms of change they cannot control.

Market turbulence could be defined more precisely as the number and magnitude of market events requiring a company's attention per unit of time,[2] just as an airplane trip is perceived as more turbulent the greater the number and magnitude of the plane's movements that passengers notice. Mass producers are ill equipped to notice and respond to a large number of increasingly significant events occurring more frequently in their market environments. Turbulence strikes at the heart of the stability and control so necessary to the system.

Measuring the actual number and significance of events over time may be impossible. To provide a measure useful to managers, Table 4-1 lists a number of factors that, taken together, describe where industries stand on the continuum between low and high market turbulence. By determining where their firms and industries are perceived to stand with these market environment factors, managers can determine, first, the level of overall market turbulence their companies are encountering, and second, whether (and the degree to which) they must shift to Mass Customization. It is imperative to understand each of the factors and how they affect the level of variety and customization in an industry. They are divided into two categories: demand factors and structural factors.

Demand Factors

Demand factors indicate the degree to which a *firm* can control, stabilize, and reduce uncertainty within its markets. The association between these factors and the shift to variety and customization, together with some illustrations, is given below.

Stability and predictability of demand levels. Demand stability, meaning demand without unpredictable up- or downswings (and usually steady, if slow, growth), is the perfect environment for mass

Table 4-1 Market Turbulence Factors

Low Market Turbulence	High Market Turbulence
Demand Factors	
Stable and predictable demand levels	Unstable and unpredictable demand levels
Necessities	Luxuries
Easily defined needs/wants	Uncertain needs/wants
Homogeneous desires	Heterogeneous desires
Slowly changing needs/wants	Quickly changing needs/wants
Low price consciousness	High price consciousness
Low quality consciousness	High quality consciousness
Low fashion/style consciousness	High fashion/style consciousness
Low levels of pre- and postsale service	High levels of pre- and postsale service
Structural Factors	
Low buyer power	High buyer power
Independent of economic cycles	Dependent on economic cycles
Low competitive intensity	High competitive intensity
High price competition	High product differentiation
Low to medium levels of saturation	High levels of saturation
Few substitutes	Many substitutes
Long, predictable product life cycles	Short, unpredictable product life cycles
Low rate of technological change	High rate of technological change

production. It encourages and is encouraged by homogeneous markets; and as long as demand for a product is stable and predictable, then production levels, development cycles, and life cycles will likewise be stable and predictable. On the other hand, when demand fragments into new market segments it becomes unpredictable, smooth production is disturbed, and economies of scale deteriorate. As we saw in Figure 3-1, demand fragmentation is a key characteristic of the Mass Customization paradigm.

When demand for Chrysler's products was declining in the late 1970s, the firm conceived the minivan, which successfully destabilized demand for both station wagons and full-sized vans. This new market soon fragmented in the 1980s into "carlike minivans" (e.g., the Dodge Colt Vista) and "vanlike minivans" (e.g., the Ford Aerostar), and a new category of "tall cars" (e.g., the Honda Civic Shuttle). This fragmentation continues in the 1990s with Mitsubishi's Expo models, which it calls "compact sport wagons." The end result is much less demand stability for individual automobiles and much more variety available to consumers.

Basic necessities versus complete luxuries. Products that fill basic needs (commodities in particular) are more likely to be standardized than are luxuries, which by their nature tend to be more distinctive, higher priced, and unique. For example, there is much more variety and customization available in most four-star restaurants than in most fast-food outlets. Basic clothing needs are met "off-the-rack," while at the luxury end suits and gowns are tailor-made and fitted. Further, the market for necessities will not suddenly go away, which provides a high level of stability. Luxury markets can go away—witness the American boat business when Congress passed a 10 percent luxury tax in 1991.

Easily defined versus uncertain customer needs/wants. If customer needs and wants are uncertain, it is difficult to provide the market with a single product. It is more likely that a number of different products will be created (often by a number of firms) to try to find pockets of need within the market.

Uncertainty of customer needs is common in new markets, resulting in what William Abernathy and James Utterback have called a "fluid pattern of innovation" that leads to diverse product variety.[3] For example, Japanese companies, especially those in the rapidly changing consumer electronics field, often proliferate products in a new market segment (both at one time and by rapidly developing replacement products) because they do not know exactly what the market will respond to.[4] The historical pattern, identified by Abernathy and Utterback and shown in Table 4-2, is that product/ markets move from this fluid pattern of innovation, characterized by a diversity of products, to a transitional pattern in which a dominant design begins to emerge, and finally to a specific pattern of incremental innovation in which products are mass-produced. The breakdown of the Mass Production paradigm in many industries, however, has also broken this pattern, resulting in what Abernathy has elsewhere called "de-maturity," a move away from certainty of needs and standardization to uncertainty of needs and product innovation and proliferation.[5] Whenever there is uncertainty as to what customers want, there tends to be a greater variety of products available.

Homogeneous versus heterogeneous demand. This category gets directly at a key difference between the two systems of management: a mass production company requires its customers to have basically the same desires so they can be filled by standard products, while firms practicing Mass Customization revel in differences in demand that can

Table 4-2 Patterns of Industrial Innovation

	Fluid Pattern	Transitional Pattern	Specific Pattern
Competitive emphasis on:	Functional product performance	Product variation	Cost reduction
Predominant type of innovation:	Frequent major changes in products	Major process changes required by rising volume	Incremental for product and process, with cumulative improvement in productivity and quality
Product line:	Diverse, often including custom designs	Includes at least one product design stable enough to have significant production volume	Mostly undifferentiated standard products
Production processes:	Flexible and inefficient; major changes easily accommodated	Becoming more rigid, with changes occurring in major steps	Efficient, capital-intensive, and rigid; cost of change is high

Source: Adapted from William J. Abernathy and James M. Utterback, "Patterns of Industrial Innovation," *Technology Review* (June–July 1978), p. 40. Reprinted with permission from *Technology Review*, copyright 1978.

be met with greater product variety and customization. The former condition is stable, the latter turbulent.

Rate of change in customer needs/wants. If customer needs are fragmented but evolve very slowly, it may be possible for mass producers to continue with their system of standardized products and services, long life cycles and development cycles, and lower but real economies of scale. If, however, customer needs and wants change quickly and constantly, this system will break down: life cycles shorten, development cycles must soon follow, and economies of scale diminish drastically as retooling becomes more frequent and total volume decreases. Companies that keep up with demand, shorten their development cycles, and figure out how to reduce retooling and changeover costs are finding their way to Mass Customization.

This process can be seen in women's and girls' apparel, which used to be based on a two-season cycle: summer and winter. As consumers became more fashion conscious, spent more money on clothing, and maintained a higher level of "inventory" in their closets, their needs and wants began to evolve more quickly. The apparel and retail industry responded by instituting spring and fall lines, and more recently additional "seasons" to the year, so that new lines of clothing are produced six, seven, and even eight times a year. Companies like The Limited gauge what is selling and what is not during the first week or two of each new season and then change the production schedules of their suppliers in order to ride the current wave.[6]

Price consciousness. Price-conscious customers place great demands on a firm's cost structure and profit margins. These customers are less loyal and readily switch between brands if they can find a better deal. Except for truly dominant firms that can outcompete anyone and everyone on costs and survive prolonged price wars, this makes a firm's demand more unstable, its forecasts and schedules more uncertain, and its market environment more turbulent. One of the available strategic responses in this environment is to move from standardized to nonstandardized products and services.[7]

Quality consciousness. Higher quality expectations of customers also ups the competitive ante for businesses. Quality itself can become a dimension along which variety is increased, and it can also be used to allow customers to see what were once standardized goods in a new light. Further, the definition of quality has changed in the last decade or so from statistically meeting specifications and tolerances to satisfying the expressed and latent needs of customers. Total quality management programs aimed at the latter definition are clearly moving many firms to provide greater variety and customization to better meet their customers needs.

Fashion/style consciousness. Few things can induce variety in an industry more than a base of customers intent on following the latest fashions. That is certainly why there is so much variety in the apparel industry. Fashion consciousness directly penalizes mass production firms because of their inherent inflexibility in the face of changing demand. It is axiomatic that what comes into fashion goes out of fashion. Firms flexible enough to change designs and production quickly in this sort of turbulent environment have a distinct advantage over those that cannot.

Level of pre- and postsale service. The level of service demanded by customers is directly related to how much customization they desire, as service is inherently customized to what a buyer needs at a given time. Producers and marketers of standardized goods can still differentiate them by the amount and type of service provided. For example, in the computer industry, most hardware system models sold by any particular manufacturer are fairly standard; the primary differences in what customers receive are gradations of features like processor speed and the amount of memory or disk space. However, each system is customized by the software, the number and type of terminals, how it is set up and used, and a host of other factors. This customization is a presale service; the ongoing (postsale) adjustment and maintenance of the system is necessarily customized to the extent that the system is.

As can be seen from this discussion, the demand factors listed in Table 4-1 help determine the turbulence of a company's market, and therefore indicate how much variety and customization it will need to provide. It is important to note that many of these factors can be manipulated by a firm. For example, the firm could retreat from the more turbulent segments in which it competes in order to stabilize demand and be able to determine customer needs more easily.[8] Or it could ignore niche products or label them "inferior" or "noncompetitive" when they may actually be gaining market share. The Hertz Corporation, for example, reportedly maintained at one point that it was gaining market share in the car rental business when it was quickly losing share to off-airport competitors like Enterprise Leasing. Hertz simply did not count off-airport rentals as part of the same business it was in, even though airline passengers were using them.

While this is to some degree a natural thing to do, manipulating these factors becomes insidious to the extent that it hides the fundamental paradigm shift from being seen within a firm. Although factor manipulation can delay the effects of the shift, it cannot forestall them forever. Companies that recognize this will not so much manipulate the market to regain stability as revel in its uncertainties to gain significant advantages over competitors.

Structural Factors

Structural factors reflect the basic nature of an industry and are therefore less subject to manipulation by individual firms. They may be manipulated by trade associations and governments, but this, too, is a dangerous game that will likely have the effect of decreasing the competitiveness of firms within the industry, making them even more vulnerable to the shift in paradigms when its full effects eventually arrive.

The association between each of the structural factors[9] listed in Table 4-1 and the shift to variety and customization is given below.

Buyer power. The greater the power of buyers in an industry, the less companies can control their environment and the more turbulent it becomes. When firms hold all the advantages (e.g., when there are a few large firms and many small buyers), they tend to standardize products, increase economies of scale, and maintain higher margins. In other words, they act the part of typical mass-producing companies.

Significant buyer power, however, decreases the chances that the Mass Production system will work because companies have to respond more to what their customers need and want. This often results in significant price competition—if low prices are what the buyers most desire. But it also results in more variety and customization as firms differentiate their products—especially when buyers value variety at least as much as price. This is the case in a large number of consumer markets in which "the customer is king" and can easily switch among readily available competing brands like toiletries.

Articles not highly valued by consumers (like toilet paper) are characterized by price competition less than by product differentiation, while articles more highly regarded by consumers (like shampoo) are characterized by both price competition *and* product proliferation.

There is one seeming exception to this situation that needs to be addressed: the case of standards. When firms hold the power, they differentiate their products in such a way as to "lock in" their customers with high switching costs, making it difficult for them to change brands. This is particularly troublesome to customers when a number of products are interrelated within a system, such as plumbing or wiring within buildings, or computer systems within networks. These kinds of products simply have to fit or work together for the system as a whole to work. Therefore, as customers gain power, they can demand that standards be created and enforced to their benefit, with a corresponding loss in variety.

Often, however, this simply leads to change in the locus of differentiation: manufacturers differentiate their products along new dimensions to re-create high switching costs, and new companies use the standards as a way to enter a field of competition with instant credibility. For example, as customers in the computer industry gained power in the 1980s, many demanded that the UNIX™ operating system be made a standard. As UNIX gained significant success a loss of variety ensued, as some proprietary operating systems have essentially "gone out of business." However, no two UNIX systems are alike; manufacturers have naturally differentiated them with features and services to make their own offerings more appealing. More important, a host of startups has used the UNIX standard as an easy way to enter the computer system business, and a host of applications has appeared for UNIX. So, with the operating system standard, the locus of variety changed from operating systems to system hardware and to application software and services. This is not an isolated example. The same thing has happened with the DOS operating system standard for personal computers, with the VHS videocassette standard, and, on the low-tech side, with plumbing fixtures.

Degree of influence of economic cycles. The degree to which firm and industry sales are influenced by economic cycles of recession, recovery, and expansion also indicates how much control individual firms have over their market environments. As discussed in Chapter 3, when these firms lose their ability to control and stabilize their demand, they can no longer maintain the system of Mass Production. Further, economic or other external shocks that localize and intensify recessionary impacts to particular industries can have tremendous destabilizing effects. Piore and Sabel trace the breakdown of the Mass Production paradigm in large measure to five external shocks to the system over the past twenty-five years: the social unrest of the late 1960s and early 1970s, the international movement to floating exchange rates in 1971, the two oil shocks of 1973 and 1979, and the worldwide economic recession of 1980–1982.[10] These extremely turbulent events penalized mass producers by creating tremendous uncertainty, destabilizing both their demand and production inputs, and greatly increasing their costs. At the same time, these events *rewarded* those companies flexible enough to handle the uncertainty and provide the variety of products that would see them through the crises.

Competitive intensity. The number of competitors in an industry, how strongly they compete, and the extent to which they battle for market share can have a great impact on where the industry stands on the spectrum between Mass Production and Mass Customization. Companies within industries that maintain a "club" atmosphere— where everyone is relatively happy with its position and/or afraid to rock the boat—have little incentive to innovate and proliferate products. They enjoy the stability so necessary for mass production. In the United States, the automobile and oil industries occupied this position before the onslaught of global competition, as did the trucking industry before deregulation in the late 1970s and early 1980s. High competitive intensity, on the other hand, can result in (as well as be caused by!) uncertain demand, the need to differentiate, and the search for niches to fill—all signs of market turbulence. It is not happenstance that the globalization of markets and the blurring of industry lines—the greatest contributors to increasing competitive intensity over the past twenty or thirty years—have coincided with increased turbulence and the breakdown of the system of Mass Production.

Price competition versus product differentiation. As discussed, price consciousness among customers and high buyer leverage both lead to high market turbulence. However, if companies respond to these forces by pure price competition, there will be little variety and customization in that industry. This is the case of any number of commodity products, from wheat to copper to toothpicks. Customers will pay nothing extra for differentiation, buying only from the lowest-priced producer. However, in noncommodity industries, the extent to which firms respond with product differentiation strategies will increase the amount of variety and customization in the industry.

Level of saturation. Market saturation brings an immediate end to positive feedback in the system of Mass Production. Many consumer durables reached their saturation points in the 1960s and 1970s. By 1970, refrigerators, television sets, radios, and electric irons had reached 99 percent of U.S. households; washing machines, toasters, and vacuum cleaners were found in more than 90 percent; and by 1979, there was one car for every two people in the United States.[11] Companies that want to continue to grow in a saturated market can do one or more of the following:

1. Invade foreign markets with current products.
2. Create alternative uses for current products to "break through" a natural saturation limit.
3. Create extended products for alternative uses.
4. Increase the rate of innovation to decrease the time to replacement.[12]
5. Meet customer needs more closely—i.e., increase the amount of variety or customization—to gain a larger share of new and replacement sales.

Each option inherently increases variety, the first in foreign markets, the second two in related markets, and the last two in the current market. The order of the five alternatives also traces the paradigm shift: the first two or three are the only viable responses of those still stuck in Mass Production; the use of the last two or three shows the responses of a company moving toward Mass Customization. One such company is Mars, maker of M&M's and other candies. Precisely because it hit a saturation level in candy consumption in the late 1980s (at about nineteen pounds per year per person), Mars greatly increased the variety in its products, introducing more new ones in 1990 than it had in the previous twenty-five years.[13]

Not all companies make this shift as easily. Many cannot let go of their tightly held paradigm and eventually retreat from markets, reducing variety as they go. For these companies, saturation limits seem to be a trip wire in the decision to retreat, as it forces them to realize that their management system no longer works under that condition. It seems better to them to conserve their resources for battles in less saturated—and less turbulent—market segments.

Vulnerability to substitute products. The logic here is simply that the more vulnerable a firm's products are to substitutes, the more time the firm is going to spend on exactly meeting customer needs and therefore the more the variety and customization that ensues. Investing with securities brokers, for example, used to be one of the few ways that people could invest their money for high returns. Over the past twenty years, a number of substitute products to direct securities investing have become increasingly important, including real estate partnerships, money market and equity mutual funds, and various new insurance policies. During this period, the bankers, brokers, and insurance firms that make up the financial services industry have created a blizzard of new "products" to enhance their competitive positions in the face of so many substitutes.

Product life cycle length and predictability. Long and predictable product life cycles, defined as the time from the first shipment of a product to its replacement or withdrawal,[14] are an integral part of the Mass Production system. They reinforce and are reinforced by stable demand and homogeneous markets. By the same token, decreasing and unpredictable product life cycles indicate the reversal of the system, an increase in market turbulence, and the need for increased innovation that signifies the need to move toward Mass Customization.

Rate of product technology change. One of the primary reasons why product life cycles are decreasing in many industries is that the rate of change in product technology is *increasing*. This is to some degree the natural consequence of growth in any economy: as the economy grows, more dollars are put into product research and development. This increases the amount of product technology becoming available, although not necessarily its rate of change. But increasing amounts of money are also put into research and development of process technologies and into increased applications of capital that allow new products to be developed more quickly and manufactured more productively. These factors together increase the rate of product technology change.

Mass Production is heavily dependent, however, on a slow rate of technological change. A slow, steady rate is stabilizing, allowing process investments to be recouped. A fast rate is inherently destabilizing, wiping out heavy investments in production tooling and increasing the uncertainty of not only production investments but R&D investments as well.

In his 1970 book *Future Shock*, Alvin Toffler described how great the rate of technological change had become.[15] Since that time it has only accelerated. In particular, the still-growing application of information technology across the value chain has intensified the rate of technological change.[16] Those industries that have seen this rate increase the most will tend to be those industries that have been unable to maintain the system of Mass Production.

The Market Turbulence Map

The preceding discussion of the demand and structural factors of market turbulence was somewhat simplified. In reality, a high degree of turbulence in any single market environment factor would rarely, by itself, denote a shift to Mass Customization. What matters most is the *overall level* of market turbulence as defined by the total set of environmental factors and *how fast* the set as a whole is changing from low to high levels of turbulence over time.

Managers can use these factors to map their firms' current position and compare it to the past. Figure 4-1 provides a Market Turbulence Map, a template, which can be employed as a tool to indicate the need to shift to Mass Customization. For ease of use, the continuum between very low and very high market turbulence is placed on a scale between 0 and 100. With the questionnaire discussed below and provided in the Appendix, managers can mark each factor to indicate how turbulent it is perceived to be. Different marks can be used for the past (and a future projection, if desired) to develop a picture of the firm's market turbulence over time.

In practice, it is useful for analysis to reorder the market environment factors from the greatest to least change in turbulence. Ranking makes it easy to see which factors have changed the most as well as which are presently the most turbulent. This can be seen in Figure 4-2, the Market Turbulence Map for 1980 and 1991 for one large high-technology company.[17] This company's need to shift to Mass Customization is demonstrated by the high degree of overall market

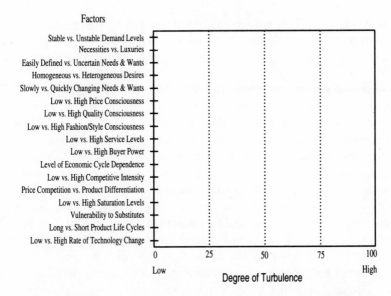

Figure 4-1 Template for Market Turbulence Map

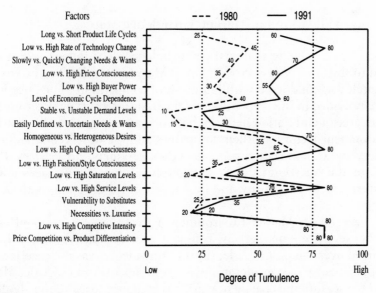

Figure 4-2 Market Turbulence Map: Example of a Large High-Technology Company

turbulence in 1991 as well as greatly increased turbulence over time. Overall market turbulence in 1991—the average of all the individual factors—is 61 on the 100-point scale, an increase of 50 percent since 1980.

Of course, the responses of individual firms to turbulence differ dramatically. Instead of making the shift, firms can try to manage within the paradigm of Mass Production by focusing on fewer products, retreating from the more turbulent segments of the market, serving its shrinking group of homogeneous customers, and so on. Strategies like these have resulted from the guidance of many consultants and authors to "stick to your knitting" and "focus" on only those major segments in which you can be number one or two in market share. While these are valuable admonishments in the appropriate context, interpreted too broadly or in an inappropriate context, they can only lead to defeat in the face of market turbulence.

Market turbulence can indicate the *need* for the paradigm shift and in general whether an industry is moving toward higher levels of variety and customization, but it cannot establish whether any particular firm is actually doing it.

Validating the Market Turbulence Map

To validate that market turbulence does indeed indicate a need to shift from Mass Production to Mass Customization, extensive research was conducted with hundreds of companies.[18] The questionnaire provided in the Appendix was the basis for a survey determining the degree of correlation between how managers perceived the market environment factors for their companies and the observed amount of variety and customization present in their products and services. Part One of the questionnaire, "Demographic Information," asks about the respondent's company and business unit for grouping with other respondents.

Part Two, "Market Environment Perceptions," asks about each of the seventeen market environment factors and how they have changed over the past decade. (Future turbulence was not ascertained simply because of considerations for respondents' time.) A decade is used to measure the change in market turbulence to avoid the "boiling frog phenomenon," in which small changes accumulated over time into large changes go unnoticed. The time frame needs to be long enough that distinct differences in the market environment factors

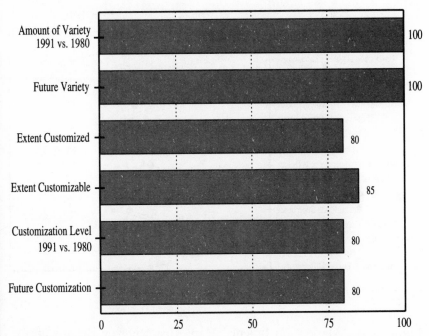

Figure 4-3   Variety and Customization Profile: Example of a
Large High-Technology Company

can be discerned. The questions in Part Two allow the Market Turbulence Map to be constructed.

Part Three, "Product Perceptions,"[19] inquires about the products
or services of the business unit. The key questions here provide a profile
of the amount of product variety and customization in the business
unit's past, present, and future. This Variety and Customization Profile can be graphed to show the level of variety and customization, as
portrayed in Figure 4-3 for the company whose Market Turbulence
Map was shown earlier. As its profile shows, this business unit has
greatly increased the amount of variety and customization in its products during the 1980s and plans to continue to do so in the future.
This was expected from the large increase in its market turbulence.

Finally, Part Four, "Process and Organization Perceptions," asks
six questions about the business unit's processes and organization.
The end of each section of the questionnaire has a few open-ended
questions to give respondents the opportunity to provide more detail
on their particular circumstances.

The survey involved 255 respondents representing 227 business
units within 164 companies across a wide variety of industries. (Com-

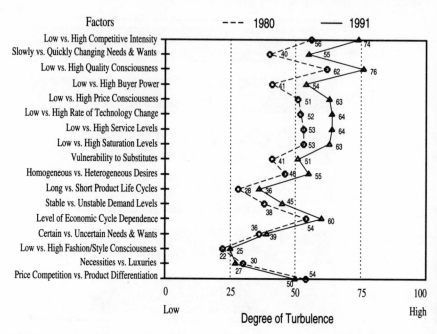

Figure 4-4   Market Turbulence Map: Mean Survey Results of All Respondents

plete demographic information is provided in the Appendix.) The mean results of each question about the level of market turbulence in 1991 and in 1980 for this survey are shown in the Market Turbulence Map of Figure 4-4. The market turbulence for the average business unit did indeed increase, as expected, between 1980 and 1991. Averaging the seventeen factors for 1980 yields an overall market turbulence of 44, which grew to 53 by 1991, an increase of 9 points. This is perhaps less of an increase than might be expected, but it is the average of a large number of responses with a wide degree of variation between individual business units. The business unit with the greatest increase (a large provider of telecommunications services) saw its turbulence increase 39 points, from 27 to 66. Twenty-three business units experienced a decrease in turbulence, including one from 63 to 49 (which was, interestingly, a supplier of telecommunications products).

The average Variety and Customization Profile for all the respondents is shown in Figure 4-5. As expected, there has been a *tremendous* increase in variety and customization since 1980, a trend that the respondents project will continue at virtually the same pace. The

All Respondents

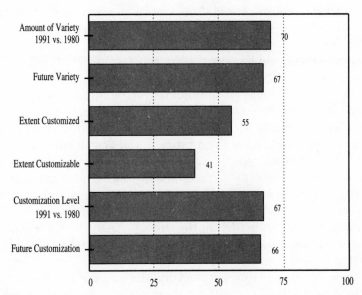

Figure 4-5   Variety and Customization Profile for All Respondents

customization has manifested itself more in products *customized* by the firm as opposed to *customizable* by the customer.

These two results—a general increase in market turbulence together with a general increase in variety and customization—do not by themselves demonstrate that the two increases are correlated. To validate that these are indeed correlated events, I performed least-squares regression analysis[20] to determine the best linear fit of the measures of market turbulence given in the Market Turbulence Map when correlated against the six measures of variety and customization given in the Variety and Customization Profile. While more complete data are provided in the Appendix, the major point that the analysis demonstrates is that every measure of variety and customization is positively correlated to the market turbulence in 1991 and to the change in market turbulence. All but one of these correlations is statistically significant at the 95 percent confidence level.[21] Moreover, the majority of the correlations are significant at a confidence level of *99.99 percent.* Therefore, the data strongly validate that increased market turbulence correlates with increased variety and customization.

In general, an increase of one point in either the static or dynamic level of market turbulence will—on average—correspond to an increase of one-half to one full point in the various indicators of the paradigm shift.

Two caveats should be noted. First, this research deals only with the perceptions of its respondents; it did not attempt the impossible task of measuring changes in the number of significant events each company faced over the past decade or actual changes in variety and customization. That the latter has increased in a large number of industries is demonstrated both empirically and anecdotally throughout this book. Second, positive correlations do not by themselves indicate causality, but only a relationship. That increased market turbulence was the prior cause of the increase in variety and customization can be reasonably argued by analyzing in detail all of the statistical information provided in the survey. Analysis of five industry groups—information technology, automotive, telecommunications, defense, and commodities—further bolsters the case. The results of these detailed analyses are beyond the scope of this book, but are summarized in the Appendix for those readers who wish to delve further.

The purpose of the Market Turbulence Map and Variety and Customization Profile are to provide easy and quick tools that managers can apply with some confidence to analyze their industries to determine if they, too, should undergo the shift from Mass Production to Mass Customization. From the results of this survey, it is evident that this is the case.

When this shift occurs, a host of changes follow. Analysis of additional product, process, and organization questions included in the survey found these changes to fit well with the system of Mass Customization. The most important finding was that respondents in firms producing more variety and customization than in the past believe they have higher quality products *at lower costs* than they used to have.[22] In addition, on average the respondents indicate that their firms:

- Acknowledge the greater importance of responding quickly to customers' changing needs, of product innovations to their success, and of incremental versus breakthrough innovations;
- Do a much better job of meeting their customers' complete needs and wants;
- Have shorter product life cycles and product development cycles;

- Are moving away from mass production processes toward more one-of-a-kind production;
- Have much more production flexibility than they used to; and
- Have undergone more drastic changes in organizational structure and processes to accomplish the increased variety and customization that both causes and is caused by all these activities.

This is all in perfect accord with the feedback loop presented in Chapter 3 that describes the new system of Mass Customization.

Using the Market Turbulence Map

Managers whose firms still operate within the Mass Production model can analyze their own industries and determine if they and their firms should shift to Mass Customization.

This can be done by distributing the questionnaire reproduced in the Appendix to key executives and/or knowledgeable managers and professionals across a broad cross section within the company. From their responses, a Market Turbulence Map can be drawn, from which the level of turbulence in the firm's market environment—now and over the past decade—can be determined. It would also be possible to project the level of turbulence into the future. Graphing the Variety and Customization Profile will indicate how much the levels of variety and customization have changed in the firm's products and services over the past decade. Combined with analysis of the entire set of questions, the extent to which the firm and its constituent parts have already shifted to Mass Customization can be determined.

PEC Corporation of Stuart, Florida, has developed a personal computer software package called **Q&View™ for Mass Customization** to automate the process. It allows many people to answer the questionnaire at their leisure and then can aggregate the responses for analysis of the firm or business unit. The Market Turbulence Map and Variety and Customization Profile, as well as other graphs for more detailed analysis, are automatically generated. In addition, the complete survey database of more than 250 responses can be browsed through for comparisons within industries, similar-size companies, and so forth.

If using the entire survey seems onerous, focus on only the most important of the seventeen market environment factors. Table 4-3 provides a ranking of the individual market environment factors in importance to their ability to indicate increased variety and customi-

Table 4-3 Individual Market Environment Factors Ranked by Importance

Market Environment Factor	Importance
Slowly vs. Quickly Changing Needs & Wants	0.750
Long vs. Short Product Life Cycles	0.626
Low vs. High Rate of Technology Change	0.610
Homogeneous vs. Heterogeneous Needs & Wants	0.559
Low vs. High Service Levels	0.440
Low vs. High Quality Consciousness	0.406
Low vs. High Competitive Intensity	0.357
Level of Economic Cycle Dependence	0.242
Stable vs. Unstable Demand Levels	0.231
Necessities vs. Luxuries	0.228
Price Competition vs. Product Differentiation	0.217
Low vs. High Price Consciousness	0.204
Easily Defined vs. Uncertain Needs & Wants	0.197
Few vs. Many Substitutes	0.180
Low vs. High Buyer Power	0.162
Low vs. High Fashion/Style Consciousness	0.156
Low vs. High Saturation Levels	0.022

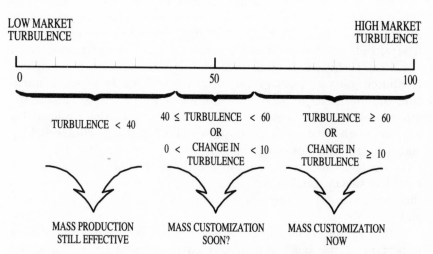

Figure 4-6 Indicating the Paradigm Shift from Mass Production to Mass Customization

zation.[23] Averaging (or weighting) the first seven factors alone would provide clear indications of the need to shift.

In any case, the following guidelines (summarized in Figure 4-6) may be used to determine the appropriate action:

- If current market turbulence in an industry is more than 60 points or if the *change* in turbulence in the past decade has increased by 10 or more points, the industry is undergoing the paradigm shift *right now*.
- If current turbulence is between 40 and 60 points, or if the level has begun increasing and is expected to continue to do so in the future, the industry is on the threshold of the paradigm shift.
- If current turbulence is below 40 and has not been increasing, mass production remains a viable approach.

In the latter case, many managers will find that creating standardized goods and services for stable, homogeneous markets can still work. But as the next two chapters show, there are good reasons for abandoning the worst facets of the system of Mass Production even if the need to shift to Mass Customization is not compelling. By doing so, they may find over time that it becomes natural and relatively easy to begin adding more variety and customization. As that becomes effective and ingrained in their organizations, they will be the ones creating market turbulence for their competitors.

CHAPTER 5

The Old Competition:
How Mass Production Companies Faltered

MARKET turbulence has been the major cause of the shift from Mass Production to Mass Customization in many industries. But what has caused market turbulence?

There are two primary reasons why industry after industry has gone from stable to turbulent environments over the past twenty or thirty years. First is the number of sweeping changes in modern society, changes that have completely altered the landscape of both American and global markets. Second, as will be seen in Chapter 6, over the same time frame equally sweeping changes have occurred in the ways in which firms compete—not just in America but globally. Feeding off the changes in society, new forms of competition have discovered the power of Mass Customization and created turbulence in the market environments of every firm with which they compete.

Another feedback loop is operating here. Societal changes created a turbulent environment in which it became difficult for mass producers to be successful. Smaller, more flexible, and usually foreign companies—what many are aptly calling the New Competition[1]—exploited the opportunity provided by the inability of the mass producers—the Old Competition—to adapt to this turbulence and began providing more variety and customization. This created yet more market turbulence, which reinforced the strategies of the New

Competition until they truly discovered the paradigm of Mass Customization.

In short, turbulence in society as a whole created the climate in which Mass Customization could be most effective. Mass Customization, in turn, increased the levels of market turbulence and set in motion the self-reinforcing feedback loop of more variety, higher levels of customization, and greater turbulence. To understand this feedback loop more fully, let's examine the societal changes that first set it in motion.

Changes in Modern Society

During the 1960s and early 1970s, a number of events and changes affected consumers, producers, markets, and societies in ways that altered the nature of industrial competition. Here are just a few:

- Great social unrest, including Vietnam War demonstrations and the civil rights movement;
- The first of the baby boomers became adults;
- Rising affluence and, perhaps, growing separation of socioeconomic classes;
- The acceleration of technological change;
- The end of the fixed exchange rate system;
- The first oil shock;
- Disintegration of the nuclear family (itself a disintegration of the extended family), with increasing rates of divorce, unwed mothers, absent fathers, and crime;
- The first generation raised on TV;
- Saturation levels among consumer durables like appliances and automobiles;
- High inflation combined with high unemployment; and
- The ecological and consumer rights movements.

The list could go on. These sweeping changes have had profound effects on modern society, effects discussed in countless books over the past few decades.

The effects of these changes on society have been no less profound on business firms. Taken together, they swept away the underpinnings of Mass Production, for they struck at the system's craving for efficiency, stability, and control by causing the inherent limits to the system of Mass Production to come into play.

Mass producers could not maintain stability of demand in the face of both high levels of saturation and the tremendous economic shocks and uncertainties of the time. They could not control their vast, homogeneous markets when changing demographics, social unrest, and a host of other trends splintered these markets into ever-smaller fragments. And they could not maintain the efficiency of their own production processes when the price and availability of energy, materials, and labor could no longer be forecast with adequate certainty.

Perhaps if these changes had come at another time, the Old Competition could have better adapted to them. Ten or twenty years earlier they might not have been mired so deeply in the system as a paradigm of management and, therefore, could more easily have seen what was happening around them. But this was not the case. Mass producers of the 1960s were pleased with their tremendous postwar success and smugly assumed that it would continue indefinitely. They felt, in fact, that the "problem of production" was largely solved and that they could shift their focus to financial, marketing, and other facets of the firm.

This overconfident and perhaps arrogant attitude rendered the typical mass-producing firm ill prepared to meet the challenges of the post–1960s world. Even this overconfidence was misplaced, for the problem of production had not, in fact, been solved.

The Detrimental Effects of
Mass Production

As the system of Mass Production became a paradigm of industry, its practitioners focused on similar objectives and created relatively standard approaches to dealing with common situations like labor, suppliers, investment decisions, and customers. These objectives and approaches flowed naturally from the paradigm and created many positive consequences for both companies and society. The benefits included the low costs that made many products affordable to the masses, time-saving products that granted more hours for leisure activities, and the technological fruits of heavy investment in research and development.

However, there were other, just as natural, consequences of Mass Production that, while they solved problems within the system, were in reality harmful to the long-term health of firms and to society. As we will see more fully in the next chapter, the detrimental effects

Table 5-1   The Old Competition: The Production Function

Focus
- Production or operational efficiency

Primary Benefit
- Low variable costs with low (affordable) prices in quantity

Detrimental Effects
- Growth in overhead, bureaucracy, and real costs
- Production inflexibility
- High inventory costs
- High cost of variety
- Separation of thinking and doing
- Lack of investment in worker skills
- Poor management/employee relations
- Poor relative quality
- Relative productivity decline

of Mass Production provided the New Competition with clear opportunities. Even without the natural limits to the feedback loop coming into play, mass producers would have been challenged by the new-style producers, most notably Japanese, who have expended considerable effort in resolving each of the detrimental effects.

This chapter discusses the detrimental effects of the system of Mass Production in terms of the four most influential functions of the modern corporation: production, research and development, marketing, and finance/accounting. With this discussion, a more complete picture emerges of the prototypical mass production firm.

The Production Function

As shown in Table 5-1, the focus of the manufacturing (or service production) function of most mass producers has been on *operational efficiency*. This was one of the principles of Mass Production given in Chapter 2, one which Siegfried Giedion, in his study of the history of mechanization, calls "the dominant principle of the twentieth century."[2] It can be defined as the amount of materials processed (for continuous process industries) or the number of products or parts produced (for batch manufacturing industries) per labor or machine input time. The driver of operational efficiency is the economy of scale realized with larger run sizes on fixed or decreasing pools of direct workers and machines. In the short term, capital and labor investments are fixed costs, while the raw materials and/or parts that go into the final product are variable costs that increase proportionally to the amount of final product. The average cost per unit can be driven down dramatically simply by increasing the scale of operations—as long as those operations are efficient. To increase efficiency, mass producers focused on reducing the amount of time required for direct labor or machine operations. And they were generally very successful.

Low average costs drove down the costs and prices of mass-produced goods. Products became more affordable, especially to those with lesser incomes, and everyone gained. This has been the primary benefit of the focus on operational efficiency. However, this focus has also caused a number of detrimental effects (listed in Table 5-1). First, operational efficiency is concerned only with *direct* labor and machinery; that is, with those workers and machinery that are physically adding value to the goods produced. To increase operational efficiency, *indirect* labor and machinery, as well as other costs, were often added to ensure that the production lines ran smoothly. This took many forms: industrial engineers to monitor the lines and recommend improvements; work-in-process and other buffers to ensure uninterrupted production; and managers and supervisors to coordinate the vast network of machines and labor.

As companies moved into multiple product lines, the detrimental effect of *growth in overhead, bureaucracy, and real costs* escalated. Between 1899 and 1929 alone, the ratio of wage earners to salaried employees decreased from 12.9 to 5.6.[3] Alfred Chandler relates this to Mass Production's principle of flow, for "a high volume of flow demanded organizational innovation. It could be achieved only by creating an administrative hierarchy operated by many full-time salaried managers."[4] Chandler further maintains as a basic proposition that "once a managerial hierarchy had been formed and had successfully carried out its function of administrative coordination, the hierarchy itself became a source of permanence, power, and continued growth."[5] Mass Production propagated bureaucracy, and associated overhead proliferated as well. Management accounting systems typically did not fully or properly allocate this overhead, resulting in growing total costs and misinformation as to the real costs of any one product line.

The focus on operational efficiency also led to *production inflexibility*. Disruptions to the production process had to be eliminated, and along with them went the flexibility to produce nonstandard products or to respond to special orders without severely driving up costs. Long runs with only infrequent changeovers (because they were so expensive) were required to gain economies of scale. *Inventory carrying costs*, already high, were driven higher still as components for products not currently running were placed in inventory after being purchased or assembled. Further, the range of a firm's customers demanded the entire range of the firm's products—not what was currently running on the line—resulting in significant finished goods inventory to spread out the consumption of long production runs. Because of the very *high cost of variety* that resulted from this situation, variety was in fact limited.

Another, more insidious consequence of the focus on operational efficiency was the treatment of workers as mere components of the production process—essentially, as if each worker was another machine that had to be planned, coordinated, told what to do, and monitored for any deviations from specifications. Following directly from the precepts of the scientific management movement, the *separation of thinking and doing*, of planning and acting, was probably the most harmful of all the detrimental effects of Mass Production.

The definition and responsibility for the improvement of all work activities, as well as the flow of production, was taken away from workers and placed under the control of managers, industrial engineers, and planners of all sorts. The sole responsibility of workers was to follow simple directions—to the letter. Workers were managed like machinery: they could be worked harder or longer. The idea of working *smarter* had no place in this mechanistic system. Thus, another detrimental effect was the *lack of investment in worker skills*.

But workers were more trouble than machines, and they made more errors. The best situation of all, as Harvard professor Rosabeth Moss Kanter relates, would be to eliminate as many workers as possible:

In turn-of-the-century organization theory and its "scientific management" legacy, individuals constituted not assets but sources of error. The ideal organization was designed to free itself from human error or human intervention, running automatically to turn out predictable products and predictable profits.[6]

Workers, naturally, did not cooperate in this. A tug of war for control of the shop floor resulted. On the one side were management teams that would exploit, de-skill, and try to eliminate their employees—

and not share any profits gained; on the other side were the employees, increasingly banded together in unions, who would restrict output and even sabotage machinery to demonstrate that they were being
pushed too hard.[7] As a result, *poor management/employee relations* have
been the rule in firms following the paradigm of Mass Production.

Not unrelated to this situation are the final detrimental effects of
the production function: *poor relative quality* and *relative productivity
decline*. The advent of the American System of Manufactures and its
transformation into the system of Mass Production produced tremendous advances in both quality and productivity. But by the 1960s
and 1970s, these advances seemed to all but stop, leaving the system
vulnerable as the New Competition surged ahead in both quality and
productivity.

What caused the relative decline in two factors of such importance to production? The mistaken belief in the absolute trade-off
between operational efficiency and quality was a primary culprit.
Operational efficiency meant the assembly line had to keep moving
at all costs (a telling phrase in this instance!). It was supposedly
cheaper to let defects pass through and then "inspect quality in" at
the end of the line, rather than let the assembly workers "manufacture
quality in" from the beginning. This not only resulted in poorer
quality, it was less productive and not even cheaper—just more "op-
erationally efficient." Workers were ill equipped to improve quality
or productivity on their own. The separation of thinking and doing
and lack of investment in worker skills saw to that.

The tug of war between management and labor was restrained
somewhat through an uneasy alliance of shop-floor control that solidified after World War II. This system of control was based on two
concepts: job classifications, which described and codified the tasks
of ever-more specific jobs, and seniority rights, which allocated those
jobs. Job classifications hurt productivity in particular: workers whose
jobs required less than a full day's work could not be shifted to duties
outside their classification, and many production workers could be
idle for hours waiting for a maintenance worker to perform a simple
task such as changing a motor belt. Seniority rights hurt quality as
years of service, not making quality products, influenced promotions
and layoffs. Both concepts greatly hurt the flexibility of U.S. companies in the face of the quickly changing competitive landscape of the
1970s and 1980s.

Another factor behind the relative decline in productivity and
quality was the belief that both were already "good enough"; that the

production problem had been solved and attention could be turned elsewhere; and that customers were satisfied with current quality and would not pay any more for increasing it. This view became prevalent in the heyday of Mass Production, the decade or so after World War II, when a shortage of goods in the rapidly expanding American economy allowed mass producers to let quality slip without negative market consequences. The added time spent replacing rejects, reworking defects, and fulfilling warranty claims all hurt productivity as well.

The "pattern bargaining" concept was a third factor in the decline of quality and productivity, especially in the automobile industry. Detroit automakers agreed to allow the United Auto Workers to hammer out a contract with one car manufacturer, then use it as a pattern for the others. The intent was to remove labor from the competitive equation, so that in effect the UAW wouldn't have to compete with itself. While it made sense at the time, both sides forgot one important factor in the equation: foreign producers *could* and *did* use labor for gaining competitive advantages in productivity and quality.

In summary, the single-minded focus on operational efficiency resulted in a host of damaging consequences not only to firms, but to their employees and to society. The very foundation of America's rise to world economic dominance from the 1850s onward—its ability to produce high-quality goods at lower costs—was being lost.

The Research and Development Function

If production was America's foundation for economic preeminence, invention and innovation created the frame around which all else was constructed. As discussed in Chapter 2, a key characteristic of the American System of Manufactures was the continuous stream of technological improvement that nineteenth-century entrepreneurs and their workers accomplished. While there were many great American inventions in this period (the McCormick reaper, the Whitney cotton gin, the Colt revolver, the Singer sewing machine, and the Remington typewriter, to name a few), the borrowing of English inventions and their subsequent improvement was far more important to America's success. An English contemporary, trying to establish a new armory as an eduction center as much as a production facility, lamented that "the American machinist takes every opportunity of becoming acquainted with our inventions and scientific litera-

Table 5-2 The Old Competition: The Research and
Development Function

Focus
• Breakthrough innovations

Primary Benefit
• Great technological advances

Detrimental Effects
• Lack of incremental innovations
• Separation of innovation and production
• High costs and long cycle times
• Loss of customer focus
• Fewer process innovations
• Relative technological decline

ture, while the great majority of persons in this country are compara-
tively careless on this point."[8]

With the advent of the system of Mass Production and "big
business" in the twentieth century, however, inventions and innovations moved out of the hands of entrepreneurs and workers and into
the specialized hands and minds of scientists and engineers in R&D
laboratories. The first centralized facility was probably General Electric's General Research Laboratory, established in 1900. GE was soon
followed by most of the giants of industry; by the 1930s, 115 of the
200 largest companies had established central research laboratories.[9]

With the locus of innovation moving from production to centralized laboratories, the focus moved from the continuous technological
improvements of the American System to the *breakthrough innovations*—major new technologies or products—of Mass Production (see
Table 5-2). The reasons for this movement are directly related to the
system of Mass Production as a paradigm of management. First, the
detrimental effects of the focus on operational efficiency in production
discussed above ripped away the abilities of workers to contribute
their ideas and handiwork to the development of innovations. Second,
the need to standardize products and lengthen production runs meant
that changeovers and retooling had to be done as infrequently as
possible. This discouraged and impaired the ability to make incremental improvements both to the product and to the process of its
manufacture. If the tremendous costs of shutting down and retooling
the line were going to be incurred, it had better be for something
major—a breakthrough, not an incremental improvement.

The benefit of this new focus on breakthrough innovations was, of course, that many breakthroughs were indeed achieved, resulting in *great technological advances* in almost every facet of modern society. Any list of the greatest inventions of the twentieth century would include such wonderful American inventions as television, nylon, transistors and semiconductors, computers, lasers, and plastics. Companies aimed for innovations like these that of themselves would provide a significant and sustainable competitive advantage—innovations that would allow them to "break through" the pack of competitors and stand alone with a new product that could be mass-produced at great profits. And very often they won the gamble.

There is no doubt that sustaining the great prowess of the United States in research and development is crucial to its continued prosperity. Increasingly, however, American companies are not the ones profiting from American inventions. In the nineteenth century America profited by imitating and improving English inventions. Now, Japan, Germany, and a host of other countries are the imitators, taking American inventions and improving them, as the MIT Commission on Industrial Productivity has pointed out:

The United States is still unarguably the leader in basic research. The scale of its scientific enterprise is unequaled, and it is second to none in making new discoveries. Yet U.S. companies increasingly find themselves lagging behind their foreign rivals in the commercial exploitation of inventions and discoveries. Transistor radios, color television, videocassette recorders, and numerically controlled machine tools are just a few examples of products now dominated by foreign manufacturers, even though the major enabling technological advances were first made in the United States.[10]

The reasons for this stem from the American focus on breakthrough innovations.

First, and most obvious, this focus resulted in a severe *lack of incremental innovations* in both products and processes. The balance between continual and punctuated innovations tilted too far to the one side, arresting the regular, ongoing development of many products and of the mass production process itself.

Second, the focus on breakthrough innovations did to research and development what the focus on operational efficiency did to production: it separated thinking and doing. Management assigned the task of innovation (thinking) to scientists and engineers in ivory tower laboratories, physically removing them from manufacturing plants, where management had assigned the task of production (doing) to unskilled laborers. As with the production function itself, the *separation of innovation and production* may have been the most destructive of the detrimental effects.

In *The Breakthrough Illusion*, Richard Florida and Martin Kenney persuasively argue that corporate management in fact treated research and development in much the same manner as they treated production:

> By the 1960s signs of stress were visible, and by the 1970s this once-powerful system began to unravel. . . . The increasingly specialized and hierarchical division in the R&D lab was the first, and in many respects the most fundamental, problem that emerged. For a time the "founding fathers" of corporate R&D . . . avoided the extreme functional specialization of Taylor's approach and created a more cooperative environment in their labs. But the R&D lab was gradually subjected to the same techniques of "scientific management" used in other parts of the corporation. There were two dimensions to this: (1) R&D labs were divided into various functional specialties, and (2) they were strictly segregated from later-stage, scaleup, and production activities.[11]

The corporate product development process was modeled after assembly lines, beginning with research and development, which passed along ideas to a product development group, which developed products and "threw them over the wall" to manufacturing, which made the products as best it could before transferring them to marketing to sell. Each "work station" in this process was itself composed of specialized employees paid to play their part but not to interact with the whole. This was once again the responsibility of the management hierarchy.

The third detrimental effect within research and development followed: *high costs and long cycle times*. With a loss of communication between each phase in the process, little was known about the problems and concerns of the following phase, and little thought was given to the people who would buy the product. That is not to say that the people in each group were not doing their best; these are simply the natural consequences of separating innovation and production. Product development aims at turning the ideas of research into realistic products; manufacturing develops a process for producing the product. Suboptimization, redesigns, delays, too many people—all can be rampant in companies organized functionally, raising costs and lengthening development cycle times. Turf battles often result, with each group blaming problems and delays on the others. In this environment, the customers and their needs and wants usually get lost. *Loss of customer focus* results. The corporation is always looking inward, management trying to coordinate the morass it caused and employees concerned only with their own immediate function. The mass market awaiting new products becomes a given, always assumed to be there and always needing whatever eventually comes off the assembly line. This leaves the company open to attack from those who truly understand and can fulfill the needs and wants of customers.

The focus on breakthrough innovations also left companies open to attack from those determinedly improving their development and manufacturing processes. Because breakthrough innovations were primarily oriented at product technologies, *fewer process innovations* were a direct result. As will be seen in the next chapter, the New Competition understood the value of process innovations and thereby achieved unprecedented flexibility and responsiveness.

The final detrimental effect of the breakthrough innovation mentality is *relative technological decline*. Separated from production, research and development could not create the incremental innovations so necessary to move product and process technologies along, and production itself was ill equipped to do so. High costs and long cycle times tended to reduce the number of technologies that could affordably be investigated and nurtured. The dislocation of communication between research, development, manufacturing—and customers—often resulted in ideas and inventions that could not readily be commercialized, products that could not economically be manufactured, and goods too few people wanted. As Florida and Kenney say, "R&D came increasingly to be viewed as an expensive but necessary gamble, in which the costs of countless losses could be covered by one big 'home run.' "[12] But these "home runs" no longer occur with regularity or a sense of certainty. It is no wonder that so many mass producers turned to "the selling concept" in the 1960s and 1970s.

The Marketing Function

As seen in the description of the paradigm of Mass Production given in Chapter 2 (Figure 2-3, for example), its key components within the marketing function are low-cost, standardized products sold to homogeneous markets resulting in stable demand. Standardized products are required for the operational efficiency of the production process; demand stability is required not only for efficiency but to allow

Table 5-3   The Old Competition: The Marketing Function

Focus
- Selling low-cost, standardized products to large, homogeneous markets

Primary Benefit
- Stable, predictable demand

Detrimental Effects
- Disregard for many customer needs and wants
- Disgruntled, disloyal customers
- Opening of market niches
- Segment retreat and avoidance
- Lack of exports

---

funding of breakthrough R&D projects. Both of these can be achieved only with large, homogeneous markets.

Thus, as outlined in Table 5-3, the focus of the marketing function within mass-producing companies has been on *selling low-cost, standardized products to large, homogeneous markets*, and its primary benefit to the firm was *stable, predictable demand*. Accordingly, marketing was really the servant of production, not of the customer.[13] Marketing assumed that what customers wanted most of all was a great price. Henry Ford discovered that this approach can lead to a cycle of lower costs enabling lower prices, with those lower prices leading to greater volume that enables even lower costs. Texas Instruments perhaps best exemplifies this approach in recent times, as marketing professor Philip Kotler points out:

Texas Instruments, the Dallas-based electronics firm, is the leading American exponent of the "get-out-production, cut-the-price" philosophy that Henry Ford pioneered in the early 1900s to expand the automobile market. Ford put all of his talent into perfecting the mass production of automobiles to bring down their costs so that Americans could afford them. Texas Instruments puts all of its efforts in building production volume and improving technology in order to bring down costs. It uses its lower costs to cut prices and expand the market size. It strives to achieve the dominant position in its markets. To Texas Instruments, marketing primarily means one thing: bringing down the price to buyers.[14]

This approach worked for Ford Motor Company, Texas Instruments, and countless other mass producers—for a while. While customer needs could usually be galvanized around low-cost, standardized products during a market expansion phase, it became harder to accomplish as the products matured. A natural effect of the marketing function's focus has been the *disregard for many customer needs and wants.* Customer desires for anything beyond what was provided in the standardized set of products were disregarded, not sought out, or assumed not to exist.

For example, American automakers have long complained about the "intractability" of the Japanese market, that it is so hard to gain any significant market share because of Japanese industry and government practices. While this complaint has validity and is shared by companies in many different industries, Detroit has done little to redesign its cars for this market.[15] This became common knowledge during President George Bush's January 1992 trip to Japan, when he was accompanied by automobile and other executives. Because the Japanese drive on the left side of the road, they have always had the steering wheel on the right side of the car rather than the left. So, naturally, Japanese automobile companies have always produced right-side steering for their domestic market and left-side steering for exports to America and elsewhere. That requirement has apparently been too much for Detroit's production systems; it has long disregarded even this most obvious of customer needs in Japan. In response to questions on just this issue, the CEO of Ford remarked:

You've got a market of 7.8 million units in Japan, and imports total 2.9%. That says something about the Japanese market. All the manufacturers in the world can't be that bad. . . . The cars we sell from the U.S. have left-hand drive. But would right-hand drive really make a big difference? A lot of manufacturers have right-hand-drive capability, but look at those total imports into Japan. Right-hand drive alone won't make that much difference.[16]

No, but it is a start. What other needs of the Japanese marketplace are being ignored if this most obvious one goes unmet?

When low costs alone could not keep their markets stable, mass producers have typically resorted to pure selling.[17] Manufacturers removed from the end customer by one or more layers of wholesalers, retailers, or dealers concentrated their selling efforts on these channels and have used massive advertising, price promotions, or whatever else worked in "unloading" their merchandise. When the trend toward smaller cars began in 1969, rather than design and build them smaller, the American automakers focused on selling what they were making. As the president of General Motors said that year, "Never has the need for aggressive salesmanship and good management been more critical."[18] Five years later, when it became obvious that consumers were moving away from large American automobiles to smaller Japanese models in droves, the response of the chairman of General Motors was the same: "We've got a selling job to do with the dealer, and he has a job to do with the customer."[19] When all else fails, use the "hard sell," as Kotler describes:

From the moment the customer walks into the showroom, the auto salesperson "psychs him out." If the customer likes the floor model, he may be told that there is another customer about to buy it and that he should decide now. If the customer balks at the price, the salesperson offers to talk to the manager to get a special concession. The customer waits ten minutes and the salesperson returns with "the boss doesn't like it but I got him to agree." The aim is to "work up the customer" and "close the sale."[20]

The job of these salespersons, as with all mass producers, is not to figure out what the customer wants so much as to sell what the manufacturer has already built. Custom orders used to be more prevalent in the American automobile industry, but as they have perceived foreign competition to be about quality and efficiency, the perceived need for greater operational efficiency in the 1970s and 1980s led the automakers to push their dealers to sell only what they already had on the lot. The dealers, in turn, pushed prospective customers to forgo desired options that were not on the floor models, and to accept options on the floor models that they would have preferred to do without. A sales general manager retiring from one of the automakers said with pride, "If I've accomplished nothing else in my years here, I have succeeded in stamping out special orders!"[21]

Hard-sell tactics used to sell lower-quality, less-innovative goods that were not what the customer wanted led to *disgruntled and disloyal customers*. People do not like hard-sell tactics, but they will tolerate them to acquire something they really want. If what they purchase turns out to be not *quite* what they wanted, their dissatisfaction with the product is magnified by their dissatisfaction with the sales tactics. The same holds true for retail advertising. Customers "duped" by ads and promotions into buying poor-quality merchandise will think twice before buying from that same manufacturer or retailer again. And word spreads quickly.

The basic problem was that the focus of the marketing function of mass producers was not on *marketing*—it was on *selling*, on "pushing product." Selling is a necessary part of the marketing function, but marketing is so much more, as management guru Peter Drucker observes:

There will always, one can assume, be need for some selling. *But the aim of marketing is to make selling superfluous.* The aim of marketing is to know and understand the customer so well that the product or service fits him and sells itself. Ideally, marketing should result in a customer who is ready to buy. All that should be needed then is to make the product or service available.[22]

Of course, few companies—mass producers or not—ever executed so well that all they needed to do was make their product or service available and customers lined up to buy. However, the focus of mass producers on selling standardized products to homogeneous markets made it particularly difficult for them to practice true marketing, to truly understand and fulfill customer needs.

This led to the *opening of market niches* that smaller, more flexible competitors were happy to fill. The New Competition could attack the Old by filling these niches with higher-quality, more-innovative products that better met the needs and wants of customers "at the edges" of the homogeneous market. This was the perfect attack against mass producers that didn't want to change their standardized products to service the edges of the market anyway. They let other companies have what they felt were "leftovers," secure in the belief that they couldn't be beat in providing the low costs the majority of the market wanted. However, the New Competition didn't rest with filling the niches, but resegmented the full market into more and more niches, and eventually attacked the mass producers head on. The Japanese started by serving niches in industries they now dominate, including automobiles, cameras, watches, and consumer electronics.

The mass producers in these industries facilitated this gradual Japanese takeover by practicing *segment retreat and avoidance*. When the New Competition entered an industry, the established mass producers at first took little notice of them, as they were merely servicing market segments that the mass producers were ignoring. These segments were typically at the low end of the total market, offering lower profit margins. As the New Competition expanded the niches they were filling, resegmented the markets, and added innovations and product variety at lower costs than the Old Competition, typical mass producers retreated from those segments and avoided direct confrontation. They simply figured that the profit margins at the low end and edges of the market were not worth the fight and that their development and manufacturing prowess was unassailable. What they failed to realize was that the New Competition did indeed have the development and manufacturing—not to mention marketing—skills to continue the onslaught through segment after segment until they fully covered the market.[23]

As one example among many, the Japanese entered the U.S. market for television sets in the 1960s with small black and white models, a segment U.S. producers were ignoring. General Electric and the others at first avoided direct competition because they did not consider this to be a segment with much potential. As the Japanese progressed into larger black and white segments, the U.S. companies retreated from producing smaller sets and, eventually, from the entire black and white marketplace. They still felt safe in this, however, as color televisions were the wave of the future and beyond the capabilities of foreign producers. But the Japanese kept on, and over a twenty-five-year time frame the American producers retreated right out of the marketplace. All television sets are today manufactured by either Asian or European producers—although more often than not manufactured right here in America.[24]

The final detrimental effect of the Old Competition's focus on selling low-cost, standardized products to large homogeneous markets is a *lack of exports*. While many mass producers (including GM and Ford) have made exporting a priority, it has been estimated that less than 10 percent of America's manufacturing companies export at all.[25] Why? Because the United States is the largest, most homogeneous market in the world. Exporting would mean modifying the standardized product—"localizing" it—which would only drive up costs and take attention away from where the profits could really be made.

This has had a number of spin-off effects that have made American producers less prepared for today's environment of globalized markets and increased variety and customization. First, being totally dependent on the U.S. marketplace, companies that do not export are more susceptible to demand instability in that marketplace. Second, lack of exports leave free reign for the New Competition to use their own home markets as a base of high profits to subsidize American market penetration. Third, producers gain little experience in understanding the needs of diverse sets of customers or in providing increased variety and customization to meet those needs.[26]

It all adds up to firms that are poorly positioned in today's rapidly changing environment. While the marketing function's focus on selling low-cost, standardized products to large, homogeneous markets had its benefits, it resulted in a number of detrimental effects that provided perfect opportunities for the New Competition. Unfortunately, what was going on in finance and accounting did not help much, either.

The Finance/Accounting Function

Accounting reports have existed for thousands of years, but prior to the Industrial Revolution, these merely recorded market transactions. Accounting records allowed the owner of the "firm" to determine if he sold more goods to customers than he paid to his suppliers, and by how much. The nature of firms changed with the Industrial Revolution and with it the nature of the accounting systems firms employed. In *Relevance Lost: The Rise and Fall of Management Accounting*, Professors Thomas Johnson and Robert Kaplan describe this change:

As a consequence of the Industrial Revolution and the ability to achieve gain through economies of scale, it became efficient for nineteenth-century enterprise owners to commit significant sums of capital to their production processes. In order to gain maximum efficiency from their capital investment, owners hired workers on a long-term basis, rather than bearing the costs and risks of continual spot contracting. The long-term viability and success of these "managed" organizations revealed the gains that could be earned by managing a hierarchical organization, as opposed to conducting all business through market transactions. . . .

The emergence more than 150 years ago of such organizations created a new demand for accounting information. As conversion processes that formerly were supplied at a price through market exchanges became performed within organizations, a demand arose for measures to determine the "price" of output from internal operations. Lacking price information on the conversion processes occurring within their organizations, owners devised measures to summarize the efficiency by which labor and material were converted to finished products, measures that also served to motivate and evaluate the managers who supervised the conversion process. . . . Thus, management accounting developed to support the profit-seeking activities of entrepreneurs for whom multiprocess, hierarchical, managed enterprises were more efficient than conversion processes through continual transactions in the marketplace.[27]

The very existence of the finance/accounting function in firms arose from the need of owners (and later, management) for cost information upon which to base production decisions. Throughout the

Table 5-4 The Old Competition: The Finance/Accounting
Function

Focus
- External financial reporting

Primary Benefit
- Profits

Detrimental Effects
- Short-term managerial focus
- Lack of long-term investment in capital, people, and technology
- Poor supplier relations
- Misleading information
- Diverted attention of management toward diversification and conglomeration

---

reign of the American System, and including the early years of the
system of Mass Production, cost management information played a
critical role in the success of companies. It was not developed by
finance majors or MBAs (there were none) but by the entrepreneurs
and engineers for whom it created value.[28] However, as Mass Production came into its own as a paradigm of management, the role of cost
management changed, as did its relevance to managerial decisions.
According to Johnson and Kaplan:

By 1925, American industrial firms had developed virtually every management accounting procedure known today. . . .
    After 1925 a subtle change occurred in the information used by manag-
ers to direct the affairs of complex hierarchies. Until the 1920s, managers
invariably relied on information about the underlying processes, transactions, and events that produce financial numbers. By the 1960s and 1970s,
however, managers commonly relied on the financial numbers alone. Guided
increasingly by data compiled for external financial reports, corporate management . . . has "managed by the numbers" since the 1950s.[29]

Thus, at least since the 1950s, the focus of the finance/accounting
function in the typical mass producer has been on _external financial
reporting_ (see Table 5-4). Accounting systems have been focused on
providing the information required by the Internal Revenue Service,
government regulators, and Wall Street. Top management, meanwhile, used those systems in meeting the expectations of Wall Street,
driving their corporations toward short-term financial gain.
    The primary benefit of this focus has been the profits generated
by these corporations. There is no denying that the system of Mass

Production has been very successful and profitable for American corporations. In the stable environments of years past, focusing on external financial reporting did not result in many detrimental effects, as the mass producers had lower costs and could outcompete everyone else. The natural consequence was a tendency toward a *short-term managerial focus*, but during the heyday of the Old Competition there were enough profits around to fund long-term research and development and maintain capital investment.

Over time, that has become less and less the case. Wall Street's craving for quarterly financial performance and corporate America's compliance has created its own feedback loop—one that has driven the time horizon of top management down to shorter and shorter lengths. In a seminal *Harvard Business Review* article in 1980, Robert Hayes and the late William Abernathy described this as "the new management orthodoxy." After detailing American economic performance during the 1960s and 1970s, they state:

The conclusion is painful but must be faced. Responsibility for this competitive listlessness belongs not just to a set of external conditions but also to the attitudes, preoccupations, and practices of American managers. By their preference for servicing existing markets rather than creating new ones and by their devotion to short-term returns and "management by the numbers," many of them have effectively foresworn long-term technological superiority as a competitive weapon. . . . We believe that during the past two decades American managers have increasingly relied on principles which prize analytical detachment and methodical elegance over insight, based on experience, into the subtleties and complexities of strategic decisions. As a result, maximum short-term financial returns have become the overriding criteria for many companies.[30]

With companies rewarding short-term financial success, it is not surprising, as Hayes and Abernathy decry, that financial managers with little or no operational experience have risen to command positions. They knew the "tricks of the trade" to make the short-term financial numbers look better: "Managers discovered that profits could be 'earned' not just by selling more or producing for less, but also by engaging in a variety of nonproductive activities: exploiting accounting conventions, engaging in financial entrepreneurship, and reducing discretionary expenditures."[31] Not to mention cuts in long-term investments in capital and people required to maintain technological superiority.

The result for many American companies has been a *lack of*

long-term investment in capital, people, and technology. Decreasing competitiveness has been the direct consequence.

Long-term investment is not the only thing hurt; so are the relationships companies have with their suppliers. The financial focus of the typical mass producer has resulted in *poor supplier relations* as corporations pit one against the other, trying to squeeze out every ounce of cost. And when recessions hit, suppliers are squeezed even more. This, in turn, forces suppliers to lower their own quality and long-term investments, which has come back to haunt mass producers in today's environment. Many companies are today working hard to change their supplier relationships, but the extreme adversarial relationships of the past make it doubly difficult.[32]

The issue of costs surrounds what is perhaps the most detrimental effect of the finance/accounting function's focus on external financial reporting: *misleading information.* As noted earlier, since the 1920s, accounting systems have been geared toward the needs of the external financial community, not the needs of decision makers within the firm. There are numerous reasons for this. Johnson and Kaplan cite the lack of innovation in the accounting field, the lack of perceived value in maintaining two systems for the two different needs, and the cost of maintaining two systems prior to the advent of computers.[33] While today's information processing capabilities make it cheaper and easier to design and maintain two separate accounting systems, companies rarely do it.

The need for separate systems is clear from the distortions to basic information that result from using a traditional financial system for decision making. The most misleading information results from the typical accounting system's use of direct labor to allocate the costs of overhead to products—as if the direct labor caused the overhead. This moves management attention from the overhead itself to reducing direct labor, which often has already become a small portion of the total costs. And as it becomes a smaller portion, the total costs of the product become even more distorted as overhead sways on less and less labor. Johnson and Kaplan give the example of one company that tracked direct labor, materials, and overhead accounts:

The distribution of overhead, which represents 60 percent of the costs attributed to the product, is based on direct labor cost, even though labor is the smallest of the three cost categories. Despite the errors introduced by allocating 60 percent of the costs based on a cost category representing only 11 percent of costs, the factory accountants, and their computers, have reported the costs data out to five significant digits. Given the arbitrary allocation of overhead, it is unlikely that the first digit of the five is correct![34]

In many cases, tremendous amounts of industrial engineering talent are spent trying to reduce a few minutes of direct labor, actually increasing total cost rather than reducing it. And when a manager does reduce overhead, he or she rarely gets full credit for it as the savings are immediately distributed among all departments by the allocation procedure.

Other distortions arise because of the accounting system being geared to financial reporting. First, inventories are viewed as assets rather than materials that generate carrying costs but may or may not produce revenues in uncertain markets. Second, the timing of monthly and quarterly reports is out of sync with production problems, which are generally weekly or daily events. Third, the costs for sales and general administration are not included as part of product costs by the financial rules, so wide variability in these costs across products is completely missed. Fourth, sunk costs—those which are already committed and cannot be influenced by any short-term decisions, such as pension costs—are arbitrarily allocated to the product costs used for decision making, even though they have no relevance. Finally, long-term investments like employee education, parts of research and development, and process improvements have to be treated as costs of the period in which they are incurred rather than as investments to be spread out over the time in which they will bear fruit. Therefore, to meet the financial targets for the period, divisions and companies simply eliminate or delay these long-term investments.[35]

With all these distortions arising from the use of financial reporting systems for managerial decisions, it is no wonder that so many decisions have been so wrong. Profitable product lines have been eliminated or sold off because misallocated overhead led management to believe their costs were much higher than they really were; efficient plants have been closed because they were overburdened with the sunk pension costs of workers who were older than the company average; and long-term investments necessary to maintain competitive position have been left unmade because the quarter's results were not looking good enough.

The misdirected focus on external financial reporting also led top management to search for other avenues by which to achieve the financial gains expected by Wall Street and its stockholders. When not enough internal projects could be found to meet the return on investment (ROI) hurdle rates required by finance, companies had to look elsewhere. Thus, particularly since the mid-1960s, many companies have sought to acquire firms with higher ROIs than their own. Undoubtedly, many mergers and acquisitions have paid off for all concerned, but particularly as the acquisitions move farther afield of the company's line of business and become exercises in conglomeration, the natural consequence of these activities is the *diverted attention of management to diversification and conglomeration*, rather than attending to the needs of the core business and the competencies required to maintain competitiveness.

A "wave" of mergers occurred between 1965 and 1975. Eighty percent were conglomerations[36]—the purchase of a totally unrelated business—with a resulting diversification not only of stockholder risk but of top management attention. In the 1980s, after the New Competition became a powerful force in America, another "wave" was created, this time in the form of leveraged buyouts (LBOs). The end result was the same, according to CEOs themselves:

The leveraged-buyout binge of the 1980s was exciting while it lasted, but more than two-thirds of U.S. chief executives believe that the economy has suffered as a result. Among the most serious consequences, they say: LBOs sapped R&D spending and capital expenditures by diverting the money to debt repayment and investment banking fees. Management's attention was squandered on short-term financial concerns, and long-term planning languished. Any good that may have come from the takeovers was outweighed by the extremes to which Wall Street pushed the trend.[37]

Diversification and conglomeration were not only caused by top management's focus on external financial reporting and short-term financial gains, they reinforced that focus by causing CEOs everywhere to worry about their own short-term performance lest their companies, too, become targets for someone else. This self-reinforcing feedback loop was in full force just as the Old Competition was succumbing to the New in industry after industry.

The Old Competition

In summary, while what can now be labeled "the Old Competition" was tremendously successful for many years, that is no longer the case. The methods and practices by which mass producers achieved success—their focus on operational efficiency, on breakthrough innovations, on selling low-cost standardized products to large homogeneous markets, and on external financial reporting—became outmoded when the fundamental changes of modern society hit in the 1960s and 1970s. Further, each focus carried with it a number of detrimental effects that undermined the typical mass producer from within, just as the sweeping changes were knocking the legs out from under the firm from without.

Thus was the stage set for the arrival of the New Competition.

CHAPTER 6

The New Competition:
How Mass Customization
Companies Succeeded

Sweeping Changes in Modern Competition

Chapter 5 began with a brief discussion of the changes that have occurred in modern society. This chapter discusses the equally sweeping changes that have occurred in industrial competition over the same period. The fact that these changes have happened at about the same time is no coincidence. The far-reaching events and changes of the 1960s and 1970s brought instability, uncertainty, and lack of control to the great mass producers of the post–World War II era. The detrimental effects of their system left them ill prepared for such changes, unable to adapt to an increasingly turbulent environment, and wide open to attack by newer, more flexible forms of competition.

The New Competition did not succeed by figuring out how to mass customize goods and services. Rather, it succeeded by figuring out how to outperform the mass producers across the value chain. By focusing each business function on themes more appropriate to a world of market turbulence, the New Competition turned the detrimental effects of Mass Production into positive effects for firms, their workers, and for society. Although the New Competition did not foresee the changes of the past thirty years, it was organizationally prepared for them. This equipped it to discover the paradigm of Mass

Customization, which flowed naturally from its collective responses to the changing environment. That is how the New Competition succeeded.

Just what is this "New Competition"? For our purposes, the term refers to three forms of competition which, while very different, share fairly common goals within each function of the value chain and, therefore, share the benefits of those goals.

Japan, Inc.

The first form is the one that gets most of the press: predominantly large Japanese companies leading networks of suppliers and cooperating with both the national government and domestic competitors—what is often referred to as "Japan, Inc." In reality it is not only Japanese companies that operate this way; a host of Asian countries are copying the Japanese playbook. The so-called Gang of Four (Hong Kong, South Korea, Singapore, and Taiwan) is fast approaching the position of Japan ten or twenty years ago, with the Gang of Five (India, Indonesia, Malaysia, the Philippines, and Thailand) following in their footsteps.

There are three prominent explanations for the explosive growth of Japan since the late 1940s, when it was a ruined country. The first view, which became popular in the late 1970s, is that Japanese society and culture are inherently different from those of the Western world. These differences—homogeneity of culture, consensus decision making, paternalistic management style, and so on—have resulted in unique partnerships between management and employees, firms and the government, and competitors and suppliers. Such partnerships, in turn, have resulted in an exceptional form of competition uniquely positioned to take advantage of Western shortcomings.[1]

The second view, which became prevalent a few years later, argues that these partnerships involve sinister cartels and conspiracies against Western competitors.[2] Here, the Japanese government conspires with domestic firms to keep foreign competition out of Japan. Then it supports small groups of companies (cartels) within targeted industries with funds, research, and engineering talent so that they can flood Western countries with subsidized goods. This leaves many Western companies feeling as if they are not up against a single competitor they can get their arms around, but a formidable wall of nationalistic companies and government agencies—a sinister force—that thwarts fair competitive practices.

The third and most recent view focuses on Japanese management methods, strategies, and successful execution.[3] In this view, Japanese companies explicitly chose strategies that best fit their environment, made those strategies flexible and responsive to competitor moves, and then simply executed the fundamentals of competition exceptionally well.

Each of these views, in fact, has valid points. The place of culture in Japan's success cannot be denied—although large paternalistic corporations with consensus decision making and lifetime employment really affect only a third of Japanese workers.[4] Similarly, Japan's industrial policies are particularly adept at using market mechanisms (as opposed to bureaucratic fiat) to target specific industries for exports and protect many industries from imports. The benefits of partnerships between companies and their employees, their suppliers, and to some degree their competitors, are also obvious, although it seems that common sense rather than conspiracies drives these partnerships.[5] Finally, the strategies of individual Japanese firms to first enter and then take over markets (as well as the superb execution of those strategies) have been critical to the success of the giant, well-known Japanese corporations—although the contribution of smaller Japanese companies to the success of the large industrial firms is less generally known.[6] Whatever the underlying factors, a large number of formidable competitors have risen from the ashes of World War II, propelling Japan to the number two rank in world economic power.

As James Abegglen and George Stalk describe it in *Kaisha: The Japanese Corporation*, Japanese strategies have gone through four phases during this journey.[7] First, immediately after World War II, Japan focused on gaining cost advantage through low wages. It began by concentrating on labor-intensive industries like textiles, garment manufacturing, shipbuilding, and steel. But the success of this strategy was its own downfall as Japanese wages quickly recovered with the improving economy. Wage rates nearly doubled during the 1950s and almost tripled during the 1960s.[8]

According to Abegglen and Stalk, as increasing wage rates reduced its ability to compete on that basis, Japan moved to competitive advantage based on economies of scale. Beginning in the late 1950s, Japanese companies, particularly in shipbuilding and steel, greatly expanded their operations, substituting capital for labor. Many industries that were not amenable to economies of scale, such as garment making, encountered declining competitiveness as wages continued to rise.

The third phase practiced by Japanese companies focused on

manufacturing. While competitive advantage based on low wages and scale economies rebuilt the Japanese economy, it was the improvement of the process of manufacturing within particular segments of automobile, consumer electronics, construction equipment, and other industries that catapulted Japan to near the top of the economic pack. The segments selected were generally at the least profitable end of the product line or in areas ignored by larger American producers. Using these as a beachhead, the Japanese moved up and out to capture increasingly larger portions of the marketplace. It was during this phase that Japan, Inc., concentrated on Mass Production, specifically on bettering the techniques and processes of American mass producers.

The fourth phase that many Japanese companies have entered is, of course, Mass Customization. These Japanese companies discovered that the increased flexibility and quick responsiveness developed in besting their American counterparts at Mass Production allowed them to greatly increase levels of variety and customization in their product lines.[9] Although they did not use the term, Abegglen and Stalk identified the movement toward Mass Customization back in 1985:

The vision of the future of most kaisha manufacturers is one of increased product complexity. Product complexity has to be increased to hold existing customers and to attract new customers. The managements of Japan's kaisha have set their goals as increased flexibility, because with it comes increased capability to meet the demands of the market place. There will probably always be the Japanese factory that spits out, uninterrupted, 200,000 video cassette recorders a month, but more Japanese manufacturers are finding ways to produce smaller volumes of more varieties without the increase in costs so often observed in the past and still found in the West.[10]

This is one form of the New Competition.

Flexible Specialization

A second form has been identified by Michael Piore and Charles Sabel. As mentioned in Chapter 2, the system of Mass Production never really eliminated Craft Production as a way of organizing work and workers. Piore and Sabel recognized a number of industrial communities that have risen from historical roots in Craft Production, and found that despite having no single firm that provides organizational guidance and control (or economies of scale), these communities of small companies are together capable of handling today's unstable environment. Each firm specializes in certain portions of the community's value chain, while the community as a whole remains flexible in responding to changes in the marketplace.

Flexible specialization is a descendant of the system of Craft Production. It revolves around the industrial community's response to change, as Piore and Sabel explain:

Flexible specialization is a strategy of permanent innovation: accommodation to ceaseless change, rather than an effort to control it. This strategy is based on flexible—multi-use—equipment; skilled workers; and the creation, through politics, of an industrial community that restricts the forms of competition to those favoring innovation. For these reasons, the spread of flexible specialization amounts to a revival of craft forms of production.[11]

Through their flexibility and unique specializations, these communities can outcompete mass producers by manufacturing a great variety of products to meet small market niches. These products are customized to a great extent and generally command a premium price, but without premium costs.

Flexible specialization was first identified in what became known as "the Third Italy." It is this portion of central and northwestern Italy that has driven the Italian economic resurgence of the 1970s and 1980s, through which it has become the fourth-largest industrial country.[12] As Sabel describes:

It is a string of industrial districts stretching from the Venetian provinces in the North through Bologna and Florence to Ancona in the South, and producing everything from knitted goods (Carpi), to special machines (Parma, Bologna), ceramic tiles (Sassuolo), textiles (Como, Prato), agricultural implements (Reggio, Emilia), hydraulic devices (Modena), shoes, white goods, plastic tableware, and electronic musical instruments (Ancona). But the example of the Third Italy is conquering the first two [Italys] as the organisational practices of the industrial districts spread to Turin (factory automation) and the Canavese (software and computer equipment) in Piedmont, the Milanese provinces (furniture, machine tools) in Lombardy and Bari in the South.[13]

These areas are true districts in the sense that political and/or social associations exist to service the entire community. These associations, which range from productive associations and labor unions to industrial parks and collective service centers, provide essential services that allow each firm to specialize in a portion of the value chain, and often provide additional economies of scale that allow the community to compete with mass producers, most often by collecting and disseminating crucial information to the industrial community.[14]

Other examples of flexible specialization can be found throughout Europe, including textile, garment manufacturing, furniture, machine tool, and shipbuilding districts in Denmark; the metalworking community of Sweden; and textile, garment manufacturing, textile machinery, machine tool, automobile component, and metalworking industrial districts of Germany.[15] That the same types of industries keep showing up on these lists is no coincidence, for these are the industries that remained within the system of Craft Production while most others were moving to Mass Production over the past century.

Craft production techniques also survived in Japan, where the recent success of the machine tool industry has been based on craft principles. While the relatively small firms comprising this industry in Japan make extensive use of manufacturing automation, they are not vertically integrated; each specializes along a narrow range of machine tools and can quickly move production from one product line to another because of the flexibility of both its employees and its processes.[16]

Flexible specialization can also be found in the United States. The U.S. steel industry fell on hard times in the 1970s and 1980s; the large, integrated mass producers were extremely hard hit, losing billions of dollars and laying off thousands of employees. However, a group of producers developed electric-arc technology to eliminate blast furnaces, resulting in a loose confederation of "minimill" plants that produce specialty steel near their markets. Minimills thrive by being very flexible and innovative.[17]

One of the most prominent examples of flexible specialization is Silicon Valley in California, named after its many semiconductor firms. Semiconductor firms founded in the 1960s and 1970s, like Intel, National Semiconductor, and Advanced Micro Devices (AMD), were very much focused on mass-producing standardized components for the mass market of computer and electronics manufacturers. As a result, they became rigid, less willing to pursue new technologies, and have ridden the tides of a cyclical industry. However, in the 1980s, a new wave of semiconductor firms—companies like Cypress Semiconductor, Atmel, Chips & Technologies, LSI Logic, and Weitek—has risen and followed the approach of flexible specialization, as AnnaLee Saxenian reports from her extensive research of Silicon Valley:

These start-ups have pioneered a flexible approach to semiconductor production—one which appears well adapted to the market conditions of the 1980s. These new firms have unbundled production in order to spread the costs and risks of developing state-of-the-art semiconductors, and they have adopted flexible design and manufacturing technologies which allow them to remain highly focused and responsive while avoiding the price wars which periodically plague commodity production.

While the region's established firms . . . produced standard, general purpose semiconductors such as commodity memories and microprocessors for mass markets, the newcomers typically specialize in short runs of high value-added components, including semi-custom and custom chips as well as standard parts targeted at narrow niche markets.[18]

Los Angeles appears to be at the center of a number of technology-based industrial communities, including movies, television, video games, and music recording.[19] The movie industry is an interesting example, as the "golden age" of motion picture production—from the 1920s to about 1950—was very much based on the system of Mass Production. Called the studio system, a small number of vertically integrated firms controlled movie production from start to finish, using standardized formulas and (seemingly) interchangeable actors to put out picture after picture, on budget, one after another, to a waiting mass market. The onslaught of television and a Supreme Court ruling that forced the studios to divest themselves of theaters made the industry environment more unstable and uncertain, resulting in the decline and eventual death of the studio system. Today,

motion pictures are now only rarely made by a single major studio. . . . Instead, the major studio acts primarily as a financial investor, and an independent production company organizes the production. This company may exist solely to produce one film. Production inputs—pre-production services, set design and construction, electrical work, sound mixing and master, film processing, and so on—are provided by a large number of specialized firms, the services of which are contracted by the independent company.[20]

Whatever one may think of the "quality" of movies today, there certainly is an explosion of variety to suit most every taste. In combination with the many different vehicles for entertainment and the various avenues by which they reach consumers, the result of flexible specialization across the various fields of entertainment is the increasing ability of individual consumers to choose for themselves exactly what they want to see and hear, when they want to be entertained, and where.

What are the common elements among these examples of flexible specialization? There appear to be four characteristics that identify this kind of industrial community:

- *Flexibility plus specialization.* The firms comprising the community specialize on particular facets of the total value chain, from raw materials to consumer purchases. The community as a whole is flexible in using different companies at different times to fill ever-changing market needs. One year, the product designs of one company may be very successful, and it then subcontracts production to others whose designs were not as successful. The next year, the opposite may happen. The only leader of the community is the marketplace.

- *Permanent innovation.* Flexibility is achieved through the continual adaptation and mastery of technologies both old and new. Firms within the community depend on each other for technological advances in their own areas of specialization. In addition, since the productive output of the community is always changing, companies focus more on the processes by which the products are made and on the process innovations necessary to continually adapt to the changing market environment.

- *Skilled workers.* Technology alone is not enough; flexibility is achieved through the high degree of skills commanded by the community's workers. Like the technology, workers must be flexible, multiskilled, and adaptive.

- *Community structure.* Through wage agreements, work traditions, and other political and social means, industrial districts can provide the right environment for innovation, and at the same time provide an essential "sense of community" to workers and management, both within individual firms and across the broader community.[21] Barriers to entry are erected to protect limited community resources; competition that spurs innovation is encouraged; and competitive forces that detract from innovation, such as "sweat shop" wages and working conditions that merely drive down prices, are discouraged.

Through these characteristics, in an increasing number of areas around the world, flexible specialization communities are providing the means by which firms can collectively respond to changing customer requirements with increased variety and customization.[22]

The Dynamic Extended Enterprise

One form of the New Competition is familiar to the average American, much more so than the kaisha of Japan or the flexible specialists of Europe and elsewhere. It is the American corporation. Not all American corporations, and certainly not *only* American corporations, but many "traditional" companies have made their way to the new system of Mass Customization and are focusing on providing increased variety and customization.

Typical of these New Competition firms are high-technology companies like Motorola, Corning, Computer Products, and units of IBM, which have discovered that technology alone no longer secures their "rightful" share of the market, but that the needs and wants of individual customers have to be fully met. Included are regional Bell operating companies like Bell Atlantic and BellSouth, which since the breakup of AT&T in 1984 have discovered that they have a huge "pipe" into every home and office through which they can offer a myriad of customized services to individual users. Large financial and insurance concerns like Citicorp's Credit Products Group, American Express, The New England, and Progressive Insurance have discovered that their customers can no longer be aggregated into large market segments, but that competitive advantage comes through the identification and fulfillment of the needs of individual customers. Finally, this form of the New Competition encompasses smaller enterprises like Lutron Electronics, Azimuth Corporation, Bally Engineered Structures, and TWA Getaway Vacations, which have discovered that they can deliver individually customized goods and services at prices formerly confined to much larger corporations.

Large or small, these corporations have discovered the power and advantage that lie within the paradigm of Mass Customization. They also found that in order for them to achieve that advantage, two things are essential. First, they had to re-engineer their processes and organizations to provide the flexibility and quick responsiveness required in this new environment. Both processes and organizations—the means by which goods and services are produced and customers are reached—have to be dynamic and continually improving to identify and fulfill the ever-changing needs of customers. Second, these enterprises realized that they cannot go it alone. Mass Customization can be achieved only through the committed involvement of employees, of suppliers, of distributors and retailers, *and* through the involvement of end customers themselves in both the identification and fulfillment of their wants and needs. For these reasons, this form of the New Competition can be called *the dynamic extended enterprise*.

The Positive Effects of Mass Customization

The three forms of the New Competition—Japan, Inc., flexible specialization, and the dynamic extended enterprise—differ greatly from one another, yet also have marked similarities.[23] Most important among these—as will be seen in this section—they provide variety and customization through flexibility and quick responsiveness. The ways in which they achieve this may differ, but the goal remains the same. Each form of the New Competition focuses on similar themes in each of the primary functions of the value chain. Each theme differs, sometimes only subtly, from those of the prototypical mass producer, but their natural consequences differ remarkably from the detrimental effects of Mass Production. The positive effects of Mass Customization are what allow the New Competition to reverse the feedback loop and move toward the volume production of individually customized goods and services.

As in the last chapter, the focus and both the positive and detrimental effects of each function of the value chain are discussed below. It is doubtful that any one firm fully exemplifies all of the characteristics. But collectively, these characteristics best describe the New Competition facing traditional mass producers today.

The Production Function

As shown in Table 6-1, the focus of the manufacturing or service production function of the New Competition is on *total process efficiency*. This encompasses much more than the mass-production focus on operational efficiency, for the latter concentrates production resources on making as efficient as possible only those activities which are *operating* on or transforming the product. As Michael Best defines it,

Process efficiency includes both productive and unproductive time. Unproductive time is the time materials spend in inventory or other non-operational activities such as handling, moving, inspecting, reworking, recording, batching, chasing, counting, and repacking. . . . *Process* throughput

Table 6-1   The New Competition: The Production Function

Focus
• Total process efficiency

Positive Effects
• Low overhead and bureaucracy
• Optimum quality
• Elimination of waste
• Continual process improvement
• Low inventory carrying costs
• High labor productivity
• Integration of thinking and doing
• High utilization of and investment in worker skills
• Sense of community
• Low total costs
• High production flexibility
• Greater variety at lower costs

Detrimental Effect
• Demanding, stressful environment?

---

efficiency is the ratio of the time a product is being transformed to the time it is in the production system.[24]

Focusing on the efficiency of the total process limits costs incurred outside of operational activities—in other words, the positive effect of *low overhead and bureaucracy* naturally results. There is no need to increase these factors solely because operational efficiency and unit costs would improve with greater capital or more overseers. That strategy can lead to lower variable costs, but higher total costs once the overhead and bureaucracy are factored in; this is particularly true when demand falls short of projections.

With the Japanese especially, the focus on total process efficiency goes hand in hand with concerted efforts at seeking *optimum quality* and *eliminating all waste* in the process. For the Japanese a defect is a "treasure," because its discovery uncovers a process shortcoming that, when corrected, yields higher quality and less waste for all subsequent production runs. *Continual process improvement* flows from this view of defects and quality, as well as from finding and the *elimination of waste* in the process. Rather than viewing inventory (work-in-process as well as final) as a buffer and hedge against the uncertainties of the process and the market, the New Competition views inventory as waste that adds costs and inefficiency. In addition to the immediate effect of *low inventory carrying costs*, the focus on total process efficiency results in the entire production process being viewed as a series of steps, each of which adds either value or costs. If you reduce to the point of elimination all steps that do not add value, process efficiency soars.

One measure of this is work-in-process (WIP) turnover: the ratio of total sales to the value of work-in-process inventory. In the late 1970s, when American automobile manufacturers were operating about 10 WIP turns a year, Japanese carmakers were between 50 and 200; by 1982, Toyota was turning over its WIP inventory more than 300 times.[25] *Labor productivity*, another positive effect, is estimated by Abegglen and Stalk to increase by 35 to 40 percent with every doubling of WIP turnover through "just-in-time" or "lean" production methods that eliminate waste.[26] A key reason that productivity improves as less and less inventory is used—and as less and less *time* is involved with the total process—is that more opportunities are available for the workers to learn about what they are doing and to improve the process.[27] Indeed, extensive labor productivity and continual process improvements can be achieved only through the concerted efforts of production workers themselves. For mass producers this was the exclusive fiefdom of managers, industrial engineers, and planners. The New Competition's focus on total process efficiency results in joint management/worker involvement in defining and improving the process: the *integration of thinking and doing*.

By integrating thinking and doing, the New Competition involves everyone in the continual improvement of the production process and its total efficiency. It provides opportunities for education and training, including cross-training in multiple skill areas. The New Competition thus maintains *high utilization of and investment in worker skills*, which reinforces the positive aspects of the entire system. Another key to this reinforcement is the *sense of community* that Piore and Sabel identified as so important. It begins with good management/ labor relations and extends outward to suppliers, distributors, and other companies involved in the total production chain. The New Competition realizes that everyone involved in that chain is responsible for customer satisfaction, which occurs only through working together as a community.

The end result of the focus on total process efficiency, particularly in times of uncertainty and changes in market demand, is *low total costs* and *high production flexibility*. Total costs are lowered because of low overhead and bureaucracy, the improvement in quality, the elimination of wastes and low inventory carrying costs, and the relative productivity of the workers. In addition to the flexibility of multi-skilled workers, the high production flexibility of the New Competition also results from its use of machinery. As with Craft Production and mechanization, the New Competition uses automation to enhance worker skills rather than replace them.

Each of the preceding positive effects of the New Competition's focus on total process efficiency has contributed to either reducing costs or increasing flexibility and responsiveness. This culminates in the final effect of realizing *greater variety at lower costs* than the Old Competition was ever able to achieve. Through these effects, the New Competition has learned how to mass-customize products and services.

If there is a downside to this approach to the production function, it may be the creation of a *demanding, stressful environment* for management and workers. Running a lean operation that eliminates all waste leaves little time for anything else. While the typical assembly line worker in a mass-producing company may be bored by repetition, the worker in a mass-customizing company may encounter stress with his increased responsibilities and decreased idle time.[28] Further, while the individual plant worker may have more responsibilities and autonomy to improve the process, that process must still be strictly adhered to and quickly performed.[29] Some will choose not to work in an environment with these characteristics, and all managers should be aware of the possibility and ensure that stress is kept to a minimum.

Meanwhile, competitive advantage is kept to a maximum. Because the New Competition focuses on total process—as opposed to operational—efficiency, it is able to beat mass producers at their best game: the production function.

The Research and Development Function

Today, the New Competition also outcompetes the Old in research and development. While the Old Competition has always focused on breakthrough innovations—the "big bang" product that can be mass-produced to millions of waiting consumers—the New focuses on *continual incremental innovations,* as given in Table 6-2.

The R&D function tends to be heavy on the "D"—product development, or more accurately, product development, improvement,

Table 6-2 The New Competition: The Research and
Development Function

Focus
• Continual incremental innovations

Positive Effects
• Continual improvements, eventual technological superiority
• Integration of innovation and production
• Frequent process innovations
• Low costs and short cycle times
• Mutually beneficial relationships with other firms
• Better fulfillment of customer wants and needs

Detrimental Effects
• Lack of breakthrough innovations?

and refinement. In Japan, for example, nearly 90 percent of the average R&D budget goes to development.[30] Research is strongly goal oriented—focused on the improvement of a particular product line or concept—as opposed to the less directed basic research conducted in the United States.

The industrial sector of Japan was rebuilt in the 1950s and 1960s by acquiring and applying technologies of the United States and Europe. Japan at the time was not thought to be a competitive threat. In addition, its markets were small and distant and somewhat difficult to penetrate, so American and European corporations thought nothing of selling and licensing their technology.[31] These technology transfers have since come back to haunt their inventors, as the Japanese have excelled at the *continual improvements* that have brought them *eventual technological superiority* in technology after technology, including semiconductors, video and music recording, television, automobile engines,[32] and so on. Flexible specialization districts are similarly technologically vibrant communities. New technologies are brought into the communities (often through collective monitoring and identification mechanisms) and quickly disseminated to the benefit of all.

While the Old Competition's complete focus on breakthrough innovations caused it to separate the sites of innovation and production, the New Competition's focus engenders the *integration of innovation and production*. Incremental innovations can best be achieved not by ivory-tower scientists but by those closest to the action of product and process development. This is well illustrated by the success of one of the leading steel minimill producers, Chaparral Steel. According to an MIT study:

Chaparral has achieved tremendous improvements in productivity by making a myriad of small changes on a continuing basis. Now the world's lowest-cost producer in its market segment, Chaparral reached this position by scouring the world for good ideas, experimenting with those ideas in the operating furnace, implementing those that worked well, and generally encouraging everyone involved in the enterprise, including production and maintenance workers and foremen, as well as engineers, to keep their eyes open for ways to make the process run faster and better. According to Chaparral spokesmen, the company's willingness to use its plant as an R&D facility—there are, in fact, no separate R&D laboratories —has been a key ingredient in its success.[33]

In most companies, production workers hold the potential for a tremendous amount of knowledge that, if cultivated and allowed to bloom, can yield tremendous incremental improvements in both the methods of production and products themselves.[34] Product development functions that are physically close to and integrated with production functions can greatly benefit from the proximity and interaction.[35] In this way, the New Competition achieves not only technological product superiority but *frequent process innovations* that yield technological superiority in manufacturing and development processes.

A related positive effect that flows from the focus on continual incremental innovation is *low costs and short cycle times*. Breakthrough innovations require enormous resources and a long time to bring to fruition. Much more frequent product innovations and introductions can be made at much lower development costs. This is especially true if the technology has already been developed and proven elsewhere.[36] Nowhere is this more noticeable than in the automobile industry, in which a development cycle of three to four years has allowed the Japanese to come from behind in technology incorporation and pull far ahead of U.S. automakers, whose development cycle was five to six years during the 1980s. In 1983, GM announced Saturn, a new company that would use Japanese-style production techniques to produce high-quality, competitive automobiles within three to five years. While Saturn still holds promise for moving GM in the direction of Mass Customization, it did not sell its first automobile until 1990. Meanwhile, Honda, which announced its luxury division, Acura, in

1983, had produced three major versions by the time the first Saturn rolled off the line.[37]

Much of the advantage in cost and time can be attributed to the New Competition's *mutually beneficial relationships with other firms*. The focus on incremental innovations not only encourages using technologies from wherever they can be found, it also encourages the adoption of whatever innovations will bring products to market faster and focuses the entire production chain on meeting customer wants and needs better and more quickly. Among Japanese automobile producers, suppliers share 30 percent of the total engineering effort, versus 6 percent among American producers.[38] Greater and more cooperative supplier involvement has been found to account for about one-third of Japan's advantage in engineering costs and four to five months of their development time advantage.[39] Flexible specialization communities are entirely based upon cooperative relationships between all of the firms. Similarly, dynamic extended enterprises develop a network of firms that supply, consult, and perform product and process development.

No matter what form the New Competition takes, its focus on incremental, continual improvement provides the basis for *better fulfillment of customer wants and needs*. When customer desires are a moving target, time-consuming attempts at breakthrough innovations are extremely prone to miss the mark (and the market). With smaller, incremental steps, companies can more quickly follow the moving target. That also places the New Competition in the ideal position from which to develop products that will *lead* the market and move it into areas that anticipate customers' latent wants and needs.

The downside of the focus on incremental innovations has been a *lack of breakthrough innovations*, but that may be coming to an end for a number of reasons. First, the accumulation of a number of incremental innovations can soon yield the equivalent of a single breakthrough. For example, Sony's and Matsushita's continual improvements in VCRs to what was an expensive, cumbersome American device yielded a completely different product that bested RCA's attempt to leapfrog in technology, the videodisk. Second, as the New Competition masters new technologies, it becomes the best in the field and can therefore no longer depend on others for breakthroughs. It *must* add that capability for continued prosperity, as indeed Sony and Matsushita are now doing by hotly pursuing, along with Philips, the next wave of video technologies. This is the same progression made by the entrepreneurs of the American System, who first imi-

tated British technology, then innovated adaptations, and finally over-
took England with their own inventions. Increasingly, the New Competition is synthesizing the capability for *both* incremental and
breakthrough innovations:

- The new dynamic extended enterprises generally bring their own
  extensive research and development functions to bear, moving
  them from a focus on breakthrough innovations to more of an
  appropriate synthesis.

- Although it is still a prevalent belief that Japan has no technological creativity, that simply is not true. As Abegglen and Stalk
  have noted:

  It is foolish and foolhardy to take refuge in stereotypes about the Japanese as "copiers." They are already a major force in world technological
  competition. . . . Western competitors were caught by surprise when
  the kaisha achieved cost and quality levels fully competitive in many
  industries. Will Western competitors be surprised again as technological
  parity, and leadership, is achieved?[40]

  Japanese companies are driving toward that leadership through
  both incremental and breakthrough innovations. They have
  greatly increased their expenditures on research in the last decade, and are focusing more creatively on new products and new
  technologies. Today, they are far ahead of the United States in
  research expenditures/revenue and in patents, which are concentrated in areas that can quickly yield commercial products.[41]

- It is not yet clear whether flexible specialization communities
  are moving toward a synthesis of incremental and breakthrough
  innovations. However, smaller firms are tremendous innovators
  and develop many breakthrough innovations;[42] these communities may move in this direction over time for the same reasons
  the Japanese have.

Another reason the New Competition may be increasing its capability for breakthrough innovations is that it masters not only one
technology, but an array of technologies and technological skills. Increasingly, it can synthesize multiple technologies together to create
totally new products and processes, and with them new markets.[43]
Examples include Yamaha's electronic pianos (acoustic + digital electronic technologies) and Sharp's pocket televisions (video + LCD +
miniaturization technologies). In an article discussing the "corporate

Table 6-3   The New Competition: The Marketing Function

Focus
- Gaining market share by fulfilling customer wants and needs—first domestically, then in export markets

Positive Effects
- Filling the niches
- Ability to respond quickly to changing customer needs
- Market takeover
- High sales domestically and through exports
- Technology-intensive products

Detrimental Effects
- Too enamored of technology?

imagination" that this synthesis requires, Gary Hamel and C. K. Prahalad state that "almost every Japanese company we are familiar with has high-level, cross-company project teams whose mission is to leverage the company's worldwide resources to create new businesses."[44]

In summary, the New Competition's focus on continual incremental innovations has resulted in a number of positive effects that have brought its practitioners to the forefront of technology. Their research and development functions bring them a distinct competitive advantage, and can no longer be counted on to avoid breakthrough innovations.

The Marketing Function

As set forth in Table 6-3, the focus of the marketing function is not on selling what the New Competition has, but on *fulfilling customer wants and needs*. It knows that this is the best way to gain *market share*, for low costs alone are no longer enough. Further, with the globalization of the world's markets, market share is viewed from a world perspective: the New Competition attacks market share *first domestically, then in export markets*. This was captured in the editorial introduction to an article on market share in *Tokyo Business Today*:

Japanese companies are characterized by a desire for increased market share rather than short-term profits. Marketing strategy is based on the concept that a company will be successful only if it can secure a favorable share of the market. This aggressive approach proved extremely effective when Japanese companies started to expand into overseas markets: they were able to win a sizable share of those markets in a relatively short period. . . .

Japanese businesses work constantly to improve and develop new products that attract consumers. Companies that ignore this fundamental concept—that fail to develop products that suit consumer's needs—will not survive the race.[45]

One could argue that the focus as stated in Table 6-3 is too complicated to be a single "focus," but all three facets play an important part in explaining and understanding the success of the New Competition. The most defining characteristic, of course, is the identification and fulfillment of the individual wants and needs of each customer. The more closely any company can match the exact desires of each customer with a product, the greater its competitive advantage. The New Competition lives on that advantage.

Both the Old and New Competition worship at the altar of market share, but there is a key difference. The Old Competition wants market share of only a certain kind: stable, homogeneous, relatively easily served, and generating an acceptable rate of return on investment. To maintain their stability, control, and financial hurdle rate, its proponents are more than willing to let smaller, niche-oriented firms into the game to be buffers against cyclical downturns. They may even *define* the market as only that portion which is relatively stable and homogeneous. For some retailers, the "market" is in-store sales; catalogue sales don't count. For some rental car companies, the "market" is airport rentals; off-premise rentals don't count. For some watch manufacturers, the "market" is jewelry store purchases; discount stores don't count. And so on. This attitude leaves the way open for the New Competition to gain market share by *filling the niches* left by the Old. This strategy requires that the entrepreneurs be flexible, nimble, and very customer oriented. It meshes very well with their strengths in production and research and development, which provide the New Competition with the *ability to respond quickly to changing customer desires*. Often, these companies are not sure what niche a new product will fill. But because marketing is so good at capturing customer feedback and development is so good at incremental changes, they will put out a product to see what happens. After they listen to the "voice of the customer," they will make incremental improvements and introduce another product—or two or three. Through this process—what has been called "expeditionary marketing," "product churning," and "market prototyping"—the New Competition successfully deciphers the desires of various niches and satisfies them.

It rarely stops at filling existing niches, however. First, that very act expands the sizes of the niches, creates new ones, and in general fragments the broader marketplace as more customers find their true desires better met by the New Competition. Thus begins the process of *market takeover*. Kotler, Fahey, and Jatusripitak in *The New Competition* have described the stages by which this takes place:

- Stage I: Market Opportunity Identification. Identifying those segments of the market which are not being adequately served by the incumbents.
- Stage II: Development of Market-Entry Strategies. Comprehensive entry strategies are devised, based on distinctive advantages which can be demonstrated in the marketplace.
- Stage III: Market-Takeover Strategies. These strategies change over time to match the firm's changing conditions with the focus on market-share expansion.
- Stage IV: Market-Share Maintenance Strategies. The New Competition does not rest on its laurels, but creates strategies geared to further market share success by the continuous monitoring of changing customer desires.[46]

All three forms of the New Competition pursue similar strategies through their focus on exporting their products and technologies. In virtually every case, before embarking on global expansion these firms first ensure that they have a secure base in their home market—the third component of the New Competition's marketing focus. They realize that gaining market share in export markets takes time and may generate little or no profit for years; the domestic market has to provide the profits for their ventures. The Japanese are abetted in this not only by government policies but also by the typical mass producer's reluctance to modify its products for the Japanese market, which may cause it to forgo that market altogether. The positive effect of the New Competition's marketing focus is *high sales domestically and through exports*.

For several reasons, the three forms of the New Competition also tend to market *technology-intensive products*, even if they were not considered to be so when first pursued (such as automobiles, watches, and musical instruments). First, the New Competition's R&D focus on continual incremental improvement naturally extends product technology. This can push the most mundane of products, over time, into the arena of high technology. Toto Ltd., for example, markets a number of high-tech toilets, including paperless versions, ones that keep the seat warm in winter, and others that analyze urine for medical problems.[47] Second, new technologies provide the best possibilities for serving market niches and fragmenting larger, more homogeneous markets.

A potential detrimental effect of the marketing function's focus, for which some companies have been criticized, is becoming *too enamored of technology*, thereby losing sight of the customer. Is there really a market for Toto's high-tech toilet? Or bathtubs from American Standard that can be set to fill at a certain time, have visual displays of water depth, and built-in surveillance systems?[48] Do people want a washing machine (from Matsushita) with optical sensors to determine the size and dirtiness of the load and microprocessors to select which of 600 different cleaning cycles will clean that load best?[49] It seems likely that many of these exotic product features will find a sizable market, and some will not, but who knows for sure?

The New Competition isn't prescient; it does not know for sure what will and will not sell. But it will continue to succeed if it continues to focus on gaining market share through fulfilling the wants and needs of individual customers, both domestically and through exports.

The Finance/Accounting Function

To support the New Competition's drive for market share through continual incremental innovation in R&D and total process efficiency in production, the finance/accounting function focuses not on external financial reporting, but first of all on *manager-useful information*. To thrive in an environment of constant change and instability requires information that is generated expressly for the decision at hand, not information created for another purpose entirely and then massaged on a "best can do" basis. In these firms, top management demands that the finance/accounting function present them with useful information.

Perhaps even more important is providing *worker-useful information* (see Table 6-4). For the New Competition, finance/accounting is truly a function whose mission is to support and reinforce the strategies of the firm, not supplant them. While return on investment (ROI) figures may be used, they play second fiddle in the accounting sys-

Table 6-4 The New Competition: The Finance/
Accounting Function

Focus
• Manager- and worker-useful information

Positive Effects
• Sound long- and short-term decisions
• Long-term supplier interdependence
• Low costs, high profits
• Long-term investment in capital, people, and technology
• Attention to core competencies

Detrimental Effects
• Stockholders ignored?

---

tem to nonfinancial measurements that reflect where management wants the firm to go.[50] According to one of the few studies of accounting practices in Japan, for instance:

Companies seem to use accounting systems more to motivate employees to act in accordance with long-term manufacturing strategies than to provide senior management with precise data on costs, variances, and profits. Accounting plays more of an "influencing" role than an "informing" role. For example, high-level Japanese managers seem to worry less about whether an overhead allocation system reflects the precise demands each product makes on corporate resources than about how the system affects the cost-reduction priorities of middle managers and shop-floor workers. As a result, they sometimes use allocation techniques that executives in the United States might dismiss as simplistic or even misguided.[51]

When a company's strategy includes reducing direct labor and increasing automation, direct labor may indeed determine the allocation of overhead. However, if the strategy is focusing on reducing the number of parts in a product, particularly nonstandard parts that tend to increase indirect labor, then the company may allocate overhead based on the number of parts, or add an overhead surcharge for any custom parts. Similarly, if management wants to focus on reducing throughput time in the factory, then direct labor hours may be replaced by a measure that incorporates indirect labor for non-value-added activities. Thus, the accounting system supports the strategy by straightforwardly influencing engineering and manufacturing decisions. And, as in the very beginnings of accounting in the American

System of Manufactures, this is helped by the fact that the system is often run not by accounting experts but by engineers.[52]

These practices result in *sound decisions*, both *long-term* decisions made by top management and *short-term* decisions made by middle management and the workers themselves. This is true not only in much of Japan, but also in flexible specialization communities where entire firms are narrowly focused on the particular strategies required to compete in their marketplaces. Dynamic extended enterprises are among the first of many American firms that are also turning toward accounting systems that provide information useful for decisions, as opposed to only for external financial reports.[53] It is perhaps more than mere chance that the CEOs of the Old Competition have typically come from the finance side of the business, while the heads of Japanese firms are typically engineers. The heads of flexible specialization companies usually worked their way up from operations, and even the American dynamic extended enterprises seem to be more often than not led by engineers and those from operations: e.g., George Fisher of Motorola, Ray Smith of Bell Atlantic, Michael Quinlan of McDonald's, and Leslie Wexner of The Limited.

A key cost strategy of the New Competition, particularly in Japanese companies, involves the concept of "target cost." Instead of designing a product and then determining its costs, target costs are based on what the marketplace will bear, and these are allocated to each component of the product and to the departments or suppliers responsible for those components. Once these groups estimate the cost at which they think they can build the component, the "battle" begins, as reported in *Fortune* by Ford S. Worthy:

The battle is an intense negotiating process between the company and its outside suppliers, and among departments that are responsible for different aspects of the products. The sum of the initial estimates may exceed the overall target cost by 20% or more. By the time the battle is over, however, compromises and tradeoffs by product designers, process engineers, and marketing specialists generally produce a projected cost that is within close range of the original target.[54]

Further, once the target cost is met, the focus remains on reducing that cost with each new product generation or as competitors improve their products and processes to lower their costs.

Unlike the battles between the Old Competition and its suppliers, which has been more often than not adversarial and acrimonious, the battle between the New Competition and its suppliers is within the context of *long-term supplier interdependence*. Target costs are not "thrown over the wall" to suppliers any more than they are to internal departments. Rather, companies work with their suppliers to achieve target costs and reductions over time and are willing to support them with engineering help, process innovations, and even extra time when necessary. During downturns, suppliers are still asked to reduce costs and profits even further, not with a threat but in a sense of shared distress among a community of companies.

The Old Competition worried much more about profits than about costs. The pertinent equation was:

$$Cost + Profit = Price$$

That is, after the product was designed and the cost determined, the finance/accounting function would add the "customary" profit required to reach the ROI hurdle, and that would be the price. If that price was unacceptable in the marketplace, the product would be scuttled or sent back for redesigning. For the New Competition, the pertinent equation is:

$$Price - Cost = Profit$$

The price at which the product can succeed in the marketplace is determined first, then the costs required to make a necessary profit are targeted and allocated. The result is *low costs* and, if the competition cannot match those costs, *high profits*.

But the profit on individual products may not need to be particularly high or even what one would normally think as acceptable if those products help achieve the company's strategic goals. This is particularly true when long-term market share or proliferating variety is the goal, as Worthy describes for Coca-Cola's Japanese subsidiary:

Coke is the leader in Japan's soft drink market, which is enlivened by more than 1,000 new products each year. Ninety percent of them fail to last more than a year, and a traditionally minded American cost accountant could certainly prove in advance that most will go under. Yet Coke churns out new sodas, fruit drinks, and cold coffees at the rate of roughly one product a month; its business in Japan is very profitable. While Coke requires each new product to clear a profitability hurdle, the height of the hurdle varies— markedly, it appears. As a Coke executive there says: "We know that some of these strange products will survive only a month or two, but our competitors have them, so we have to have them." Some are going to be hits.[55]

Here, the finance/accounting function fully supports the firm's expeditionary marketing tactics.

By focusing on both manager-useful and worker-useful information, the finance/accounting function in the New Competition also provides the means by which the right long-term decisions are made. A natural consequence is the *long-term investment in capital, people, and technology* required to maintain strategic competitiveness. The New Competition does not fall into the trap of shortsightedness, nor do its accounting systems encourage it. Its accounting systems focus management and employees alike on the tasks at hand: improving process efficiency in production, meeting customer wants and needs in development, and gaining share in marketing. This results in both management and worker *attention to core competencies* that mean success in the marketplace.

What managers and workers are not focused on is the stockholders of the corporation; a potential detrimental effect is that *stockholders* may simply be *ignored*, and along with them short-term financial results. For example, in one study of American and Japanese executives, the number one and two corporate objectives for American firms were found to be return on investment and capital gain for stockholders; in Japanese firms, the top objective was increase in market share, while gain for stockholders barely registered at all.[56] Summarizing the importance of long-term perspectives on Japanese accounting practices, another study found:

The national emphasis on long-term performance has had a strong influence on management. This far-sighted approach is in direct contrast to U.S. methods, wherein stockholder earnings per share receive a large part of management attention. In Japan it is not clear how company performance is measured, who measures it, and how or to whom it is reported. Japanese companies, for example, are not required to issue quarterly financial reports to stockholders.[57]

American firms that have found the new paradigm of Mass Customization often talk about the "stakeholders" of the firm, which include employees, suppliers, and customers, not just the stockholders. Even in flexible specialization communities, where management and often workers *are* the stockholders, the focus remains on the long-term health of the company and the community, not on short-term gains.

The New Competition

In summary, the new forms of competition that have arisen in the global marketplace over the past thirty years did not set out to produce high variety or customization at low costs. Rather, each form—whether Japan, Inc., flexible specialization communities, or dynamic extended enterprises—was simply trying to find its way to competitive advantage in a world increasingly characterized by a high degree of market turbulence. By either trying the system of Mass Production and realizing its deficiencies or by realizing that their small size blocked off that avenue of competition, these firms, communities, and even nations moved beyond the paradigm of Mass Production. They turned around each of the detrimental effects of Mass Production by focusing on total process efficiency in production, continual incremental innovation in R&D, gaining market share by fulfilling customer wants and needs (first domestically, then in export markets) in marketing, and by focusing on managerially useful as well as worker-useful information in finance/accounting.

From these central goals flowed many positive effects that gained competitive advantage for the New Competition. Most of them were the exact opposite of the detrimental effects of Mass Production, as

Table 6-5 The Old vs. the New Competition:
The Production Function

The Old Competition	The New Competition
Focus	*Focus*
• Production or operational efficiency	• Total process efficiency
Primary Benefit	*Detrimental Effect*
• Low variable costs with low (affordable) prices in quantity	• Demanding, stressful environment?
Detrimental Effects	*Positive Effects*
• Growth in overhead, bureaucracy, and real costs	• Low overhead and bureaucracy
• Production inflexibility	• Low total costs
	• High production flexibility
	• Elimination of waste
• High inventory carrying costs	• Low inventory carrying costs
• High cost of variety	• Greater variety at lower costs
• Separation of thinking and doing	• Integration of thinking and doing
	• Continual process improvement
• Lack of investment in worker skills	• High utilization of and investment in worker skills
• Poor management/employee relations	• Sense of community
• Poor relative quality	• Optimum quality
• Relative productivity decline	• High labor productivity

Table 6-6 The Old vs. the New Competition:
The Research and Development Function

The Old Competition	The New Competition
Focus	*Focus*
• Breakthrough innovations	• Continual incremental innovations
Primary Benefit	*Detrimental Effects*
• Great technological advances	• Lack of breakthrough innovations?
Detrimental Effects	*Positive Effects*
• Lack of incremental innovations	• Continual improvements, eventual technological superiority
• Relative technological decline	
• Separation of innovation and production	• Integration of innovation and production
• High costs and long cycle times	• Low costs and short cycle times
• Loss of customer focus	• Better fulfillment of customer wants and needs
• Fewer process innovations	• Frequent process innovations
	• Mutually beneficial relationships with other firms

can easily be seen in Tables 6-5 through 6-8, which repeat the information in this and the last chapter for ease of comparison.

The New Competition is not infallible, but it has been able to outperform the Old in an era of sweeping societal changes. By turning around the detrimental effects of Mass Production, the New Competition provided the foundation of flexibility and quick responsiveness required to greatly increase variety and customization. Eventually, it discovered the paradigm of Mass Customization and began purposefully seeking out the wants and needs of individual customers, reducing product development and life cycles, fragmenting market homogeneity, and finally seeking out new processes of Mass Customization and re-engineering around them.

The very act of shifting to the paradigm of Mass Customization further increases market turbulence for everyone else. The sweeping changes of modern society caused one level of turbulence in most industries, but for those industries in which the New Competition has become a force, market turbulence has been exacerbated. The position of the old mass producers thus becomes even more tenuous. In these industries, the alternative to slow decline and eventual surrender is to re-engineer the corporation for a turbulent world, joining its competitors in the new frontier in business competition, Mass Customization.

Table 6-7   The Old vs. the New Competition:
The Marketing Function

The Old Competition	The New Competition
Focus • Selling low-cost, standardized products to large, homogeneous markets	*Focus* • Gaining market share by fulfilling customer wants and needs—first domestically, then in export markets
Primary Benefit • Stable, predictable demand	*Detrimental Effects* • Too enamored of technology?
Detrimental Effects • Disregard for many customer needs and wants • Disgruntled, disloyal customers • Opening of market niches • Segment retreat and avoidance • Lack of exports	*Positive Effects* • Ability to respond quickly to changing customer needs • Filling the niches • Market takeover • High sales domestically and through exports • Technology-intensive products

Table 6-8   The Old vs. the New Competition:
The Finance/Accounting Function

The Old Competition	The New Competition
Focus • External financial reporting	*Focus* • Manager- and worker-useful information
Primary Benefit • Profits	*Detrimental Effects* • Stockholders ignored?
Detrimental Effects • Short-term managerial focus • Misleading information • Lack of long-term investment in capital, people, and technology • Poor supplier relations • Diverted attention of management toward diversification and conglomeration	*Positive Effects* • Low costs, high profits • Sound long- and short-term decisions • Long-term investment in capital, people, and technology • Long-term supplier interdependence • Attention to core competencies

PART **II**

Exploring the New Frontier
in Business Competition

CHAPTER 7

Developing a Strategy
for Mass Customization

FOR an expanding number of industries, the world is an increasingly turbulent place. Customer wants and needs are changing and fragmenting. Product life cycles are getting shorter; keeping up with technological change is becoming more difficult. Basic requirements for quality and service levels go up as the competition gets tougher every year. But these and all the other factors that contribute to market turbulence are not just changing—the rate of change actually seems to be accelerating.

As seen in Part I, firms mired in the system of Mass Production find that increased turbulence is difficult both to comprehend and deal with. Firms that do nothing in response to increased turbulence will find that their product life cycles and development cycles are hopelessly longer than those of their competitors, that they fall behind technologically, and that they can no longer effectively meet their customers' wants and needs. As these firms become less competitive, as they inevitably will, some will simply decide to retreat from the more turbulent segments of their marketplace.

Strategic Responses to a Turbulent World

Doing nothing and segment retreat are clearly losing "strategies," if they can be considered strategies at all. Retreating to higher margin and less turbulent segments may provide temporary solace, but the New Competition will not forgo them forever. It is only a matter of time.

The proper strategic response is to enter the new frontier in business competition and shift to Mass Customization as a way of doing business. There are three basic ways to do this: incrementally over time, more quickly via business transformation, or by creating a new business firmly planted in the new territory. As shown in Table 7-1, each is more appropriate for some organizations than for others.

Incremental movement is most appropriate for companies whose market turbulence, while increasing, is still low enough and increasing slowly enough that they are still able to be somewhat effective under the old ways of doing things. This gives them time to make incremental changes that, while not geared toward marked improvement in competitive advantage, are also not going to be disruptive or have a large potential downside if not done well. It also assumes that competitors are not already in the process of transforming their businesses to be geared around the system of Mass Customization. If competitors are indeed making great strides in this direction, it will be only a short time before market turbulence will increase dramatically for companies proceeding incrementally. Later in this chapter, the Toyota Motor Company will provide the example of a prototypical Japanese company that improved incrementally over many decades, eventually discovering that its flexibility and responsiveness gave it a distinct advantage over its American competitors that were mired in the old system of Mass Production. Toyota and its Japanese competitors have greatly increased the market turbulence of the Detroit automakers because they shifted incrementally to Mass Customization.

Incremental movement also results when individual groups within a company shift to Mass Customization without the participation of the company (or business unit) as a whole. To begin down this path is very appropriate for middle- and lower-level managers, as well as nonmanagers, who have been unable to gain consensus from top management on the need for change across the business unit or do not have enough influence to try. Successes at lower levels on specific projects can often be touted throughout the enterprise, creating a snowball effect that gains the consensus necessary to change the organization as a whole. The story of the IBM unit in Rochester, Minnesota, illustrates how various groups separately implementing

Table 7-1 Entering the New Frontier

Strategic Response	When Appropriate	Company Examples
Move Incrementally	• Market turbulence low and not increasing dramatically • Competitors not transforming for Mass Customization • Middle- and lower-level managers and employees who want to change but cannot affect the business as a whole	• Toyota Motor Company • IBM Rochester • Bally Engineered Structures, Inc.
Transform the Business	• Dramatic increase in market turbulence • Competitors already shifting to Mass Customization • Only if instigated or fully supported by top management	• Motorola Pager Division • Société Micromécanique et Horlogère (SMH) • Computer Products Inc.
Create a New Business	• Businesses based on new, flexible technologies • New ventures in large corporations • Most any new business	• France Télécom (Minitel) • Azimuth Corporation • Personics Corporation

many of the concepts of Mass Customization can be brought together to focus the rest of the organization as well.

Incremental change, instigated and consistently pushed by top management, can over time result in the complete transformation of a business. Bally Engineered Structures, Inc., demonstrates how a company can transform its products, processes, and organization over nearly a decade of constant and consistent incremental change.

Indeed, business transformation can be accomplished only when top management is fully and cohesively behind the change, whether it instigated it or agreed to the need on the basis of lower-level encouragement. Quick transformation is not only most appropriate but is imperative for companies that have had dramatic increases in market turbulence or whose competitors are themselves re-engineering to compete effectively in a turbulent world. As the examples of Motorola's Pager Division and Société Micromécanique et Horlogère will show, it is unfortunate but quite typical that a crisis is generally necessary to precipitating business transformation. Unless companies truly hit bottom, coming to the full realization that business as usual will no longer cut it in their industry environment, they rarely will voluntarily undergo the upheaval that comes with business transformation. Computer Products, Inc., illustrates that this upheaval can be a painful but necessary step on the way to transforming a company.

In many industries, the companies that do not wait until they hit bottom, or that need only proceed incrementally but instead transform quickly, will gain spectacularly. Because of the history of an organization, its existing culture, and the natural desire to avoid not only pain but significant change of any kind, it is difficult to transform without a crisis. Therefore, new businesses that do not have this baggage can often come into an industry—or create an industry—and gain tremendous advantage by mass-customizing products or services.

Most new businesses that fully embrace Mass Customization from the start derive their advantage primarily from technology, either proprietary or off-the-shelf. As the example of France Télécom and its Minitel videotex service demonstrates, large existing organizations can create new businesses themselves—a new industry, really—based on new information and telecommunications technologies. New businesses that are not based on technology can also create a Mass Customization strategy. Azimuth Corporation, which mass-customizes commercial graphics, illustrates that technology alone is rarely enough to provide a sustained competitive advantage; companies must search for strategic leverage through their people, processes, and organizations. Personics Corporation, which mass-customizes music tapes, further illustrates that embracing Mass Customization is no guarantee of business success.

Personics, Azimuth, and the other companies listed in Table 7-1 are described in more detail below to show how companies are responding strategically to market turbulence and the ability to mass-customize products and services. Each organization is different from the others; each has started from a different point, is moving at a different pace, and is using different techniques to make the shift to Mass Customization. But they are all responding strategically *to* market turbulence, or by being the first in their industry to shift, are strategically *creating* market turbulence for their competitors.

Move Incrementally

For many firms, the shift from Mass Production to Mass Customization begins slowly, incrementally, often unknowingly. When market turbulence increases and the limits to the system of Mass Production are encountered, increasing variety and customization is the natural response of successful firms. The shift to Mass Customization begins in earnest when a firm realizes that what it is experiencing in the marketplace and what it is doing internally are fundamentally different from previous conditions. Once a firm realizes that the current situation is not temporary and stops making the standard excuses for poor performance—"Once this next product comes out . . . ; As soon as we work all the bugs out of our process . . . ; Once the marketplace settles down . . . ; As soon as this recession is over . . . ; If only the playing field were level . . ."; and so on—then and only then can it begin to have a coordinated strategy that encompasses all the changes that must occur for it to operate within the system of Mass Customization.

The strategy of incrementally providing more variety and customization—even at higher costs—is often sufficient to keep a firm in the ball game. If turbulence isn't increasing too greatly, if the competition isn't moving too quickly to transform itself, if the firm's present market position is still solid, then incremental improvement in the variety of the company's products and services, to its processes, and to its organization may be enough to maintain its competitiveness for quite a while. As demonstrated in Chapter 6, the New Competition did not itself set out to proliferate variety and expand levels of customization. Rather, by focusing organizational functions on themes more appropriate to modern times and by incrementally improving all the functions across the value chain, it created flexible and responsive processes and organizations, thereby discovering that it could mass-customize products and services. This took Japanese companies decades.

Toyota Motor Company. Toyota provides an excellent illustration. When the company announced its goal to produce passenger cars in 1933, its founder, Toyoda Kiichirō, declared: "We shall learn production techniques from the American method of mass production. But we will not copy it as is. We shall use our own research and creativity to develop a production method that suits our own country's situation."[1] After what would today be described as a massive benchmarking effort, focusing on the Ford Motor Company, Kiichirō and his head of production, Taiichi Ohno, set out to create the Toyota Production System. After several false starts were made in the 1930s, the system's design finally came together after World War II. The production system's slogan became "small lot sizes and quick setups" because that was more suitable to the low volumes of the smaller Japanese market.[2] In the late 1940s, setups for large processes took two to three hours, and reducing that time met with quite a bit of resistance on the factory floor. Incremental improvements were made, but progress was slow. It took until the mid-1950s to reach the hour mark, with most processes achieving a fifteen-minute setup by 1962 and three minutes by 1971.

Throughout that period, Toyota produced a small number of models with few options. But with similar incremental improvement in its product development functions, by the 1970s it could produce a new model every three or four years (versus five years or more for American manufacturers). Finally, with its development and production processes fine-tuned to be able to develop new models quickly and changeover frequently, Toyota began to proliferate model variety. The "voluntary" agreements to limit exports to the United States of the 1970s and 1980s helped a great deal; they had the natural effect of forcing the company to move upscale to more expensive models and options to continue its sales growth via higher prices per vehicle. Adding variety and customization became even more of a focus, resulting in more models, more innovative styling and features, and shorter product development and product life cycles. Toyota pulled ahead of its domestic rivals during the 1970s and 1980s, and challenged GM for the title of world's largest automobile manufacturer.

By the late 1980s, Ohno could articulate Toyota's strategic focus in terms of time: "All we are doing is looking at the time line . . . from the moment the customer gives us an order to the point when we collect the cash. And we are reducing that time line by removing the non-value-added wastes."[3] Reducing time not only in production setups, but throughout the value chain is key to Mass Customization, and a major area for incremental improvement at Toyota.

Today, Toyota offers five-day delivery of custom-ordered cars in Japan. Although it is not yet in a position to truly mass-customize automobiles, the company has come a long way from copying American mass-production techniques to fully embracing the tenets of Mass Customization as its way of doing business. It did this through continual incremental improvements over thirty or forty years.

IBM Rochester. This slow but proven approach is also appropriate for middle- and lower-level managers and employees whose operations do not affect enough of a business to institute companywide transformational change. They can start with their own function and make whatever changes better meet their customers' individual wants and needs. By slowly and successfully pushing and pulling changes through the value chain, they can tout successes and thereby gain the executive support necessary to make change happen across the organization. If the conditions are right—that is, if market turbulence is not increasing too rapidly and competitors are not moving more quickly—this can be a fine start.

The IBM business unit in Rochester, Minnesota, 1990 winner of the Malcolm Baldrige National Quality Award, is a good example. One reason cited by the Baldrige examiners in bestowing this award was the development laboratory's process for listening and reacting to customers and business partners (those that provide applications and services tailored to different customers).[4] While initially instigated by top management's vague desire to involve customers in the development process of the Application System/400™ midrange computer, this activity was designed and implemented (starting in 1986) by a small group of IBM personnel. Until then, a high wall had surrounded development programmers and engineers. Talking to customers, or anyone in the marketing organization, was viewed as taking too much time from the task of product development. One of management's tasks was to ensure the insulation of the developers.

A new process, dubbed "early external involvement," changed all that.[5] During the development of the AS/400™, hundreds of business partners and customers provided feedback directly to programmers and engineers on functions that were still being developed. This resulted in a number of key incremental improvements to the product and to the development process. First, the quality of the AS/400 system was greatly enhanced as hundreds of defects were found by the participants prior to the system's release. Second, the product development process was hastened by providing developers with a forum in which to air their problems and questions and gain immediate feedback; decisions were reached sooner and with better consensus. Third, as a basic part of their involvement, non-IBM business partners and IBM systems engineers readied thousands of applications that could be announced and shipped with the system and gained expertise in services like installation, training, system customization, and special programming. When combined with the system, these applications and services create complete offerings that tailor the general-purpose AS/400 for particular industries and customers. Additional benefits included tremendous trade-press exposure at the system's announcement and, perhaps most important, the feeling of pride and system ownership gained by the customer and business partner participants. With their participation in its development, the AS/400 became *their* system, and gave them not only a monetary but an emotional stake in its success.

What was once a side activity performed by a temporary, cross-functional team is now an integral part of IBM Rochester's development process,[6] and comparable activities are prevalent in many other IBM sites. Meanwhile, a second incremental improvement activity has similarly focused Rochester manufacturing on tailoring systems for individual customers. In the mid-1980s, customers who purchased a System/36, a predecessor to the AS/400, received different pieces of the system at different times from different IBM manufacturing locations. The printer would come one week from Lexington, display terminals the following week from Raleigh, the system itself at yet another time from Rochester, and so on, until all the pieces finally arrived and the customer could call IBM to put it together. This uncoordinated distribution process caused quality problems as well as customer frustration.

In 1986, IBM decided to fix these problems by standardizing around a few configurations and consolidating all the pieces at the Rochester manufacturing plant. As an added service, the System/36's were preloaded with the operating system and all the various pieces were tested before being put together in one shrink-wrapped package for delivery on a single pallet to the customer. Called Total System Packages, or TSPs, these were very successful. Customers loved the service, and TSPs saved IBM money through fewer quality defects, by company sales of more standard configurations, and by its customer engineers spending less time installing the system. IBM offered discounts of about 5 percent to encourage customers to buy TSPs, which still left it a small profit on the service.

But over time, customers demanded "specials": they wanted one printer substituted for another, a system with more memory, one more or less display terminal, and so on. With the greater variety of models and options available with the AS/400, which IBM began shipping in September 1988, the plant found it was incrementally adding more configurations and options to the TSP offering every year, and was shipping more items outside of the shrink-wrapped package. It discovered that customers had different needs and were willing to pay a small premium to get exactly what they wanted.

After years of adding incremental variety to the Total System Packages, IBM Rochester created a Customer Solution Center in 1991 and added a fee-based service to customize any system most any way a customer wanted. This represents a team effort between the manufacturing plant, development laboratory, and the customer service division that has re-engineered manufacturing and distribution processes—and invented a few new ones—to provide a quick and constant flow of customized solutions. The tailoring includes the installation of not only the operating system with the very latest revisions (a service more than 90 percent of customers request), but whatever application and data the customer wants from his own shop or from one or more business partners, even whatever non-IBM equipment the customer wants connected to his system. Everything is already installed and thoroughly tested at the Customer Solution Center so that an IBM customer engineer is rarely needed at the customer site. And the processes are able to handle changes in customer requirements up to the very last minute. IBM makes a profit, charging less than 1 percent of the total system price for these services.

With this level of improvement, IBM soon added what it calls "Plug 'N' Go" offerings targeted at small businesses in niche markets that have never before purchased a midrange computer. When a customer orders a system, IBM Rochester tailors it and sets it up so that the customer literally has only to plug it in and turn it on.

One key to the success of this program and its quick development (it only took six months from concept to market) was the early involvement of the business partners that provide the tailored Plug 'N' Go applications. This involvement was accomplished through the same group that began early external involvement for the initial release of the AS/400, converging separate activities into a more powerful force for shifting to Mass Customization. A second key factor in Plug 'N' Go's success was that each business partner used a new program called the Application Program Driver (APD) to develop its application. The driver is a flexible tool that provides standardized modules for common application functions, such as menus, security, batch jobs, backup, and integration with AS/400 office functions (electronic mail, calendars, and so forth). Each business partner can pick up the standardized modules, customize them, and add its own software programs, quickly developing an application that "looks and feels" like any other application developed with APD.

IBM Rochester's movement toward Mass Customization has helped the AS/400 become the only minicomputer to gain market share in the industry since its announcement in 1988. Each incremental improvement in different functional and cross-functional areas has moved the entire business unit further away from its earlier conception of its business as providing general-purpose, standardized systems for what was thought to be a homogeneous marketplace of small- and medium-size businesses. Today, IBM Rochester has a vision of where it is taking the AS/400 in the 1990s that includes Mass Customization as a stated principle. Its vision statement attests that "the niches *are* the market and the ultimate niche is the individual customer. . . . Therefore, [IBM Rochester] must provide solutions that fit by enabling more customization." According to its vision, IBM Rochester's future systems—the basic hardware and software, not just the applications and services surrounding them—must be mass-customized to fit the wants and needs of individual customers.

While strategic elements are already defined or in place, IBM is still a long way from achieving its vision, with many technical, functional, and organizational barriers to be overcome. But through a path of incremental improvement in processes and products—adding flexibility and responsiveness in its processes, gaining variety and customization in its products and services, and finally creating a vision and strategy that focus the entire organization on what needs to be done—IBM Rochester is far ahead of its competitors.

Bally Engineered Structures. IBM Rochester is still just beginning its change process. Given enough time, it is likely to find that incremental movement can meld into transformational change. Bally Engineered Structures, Inc., of Bally, Pennsylvania, illustrates this well.

Today, Bally mass-customizes a wide variety of structures: walk-in coolers, freezers, insulated outdoor structures, refrigerated warehouses, environmentally controlled rooms, cold storage buildings, and blast chillers. The company's modularized and modifiable panels and accessories can be put together in a virtually limitless number of ways to meet the needs of individual customers. And every product Bally ships is precisely manufactured to each customer's specifications; except for companies like McDonald's, which requests fifteen "standard" walk-in refrigerators for its fifteen standard buildings, it never ships the same product twice. Bally has been rewarded with slowly growing market share leadership in an industry hit hard by recession.

The most interesting piece of the story at Bally, however, is not the product, but how the firm arrived at this point and where it is headed. Bally has undergone tremendous change to achieve its level of Mass Customization. It has taken nearly a decade (so far), for the company has changed through incremental movement. To appreciate its improvement requires understanding its history.

Bally Engineered Structures was established in 1933 as a custom-engineering and job-shop manufacturer of building structures. By the 1970s, the industry had matured and price competition became the way of doing business. Bally's founders moved the company from a job-shop orientation to that of a mass producer. Where one customer's order used to be handled all together as a job, it now made everything to plan, determining the number of panels to be produced each month and decreeing long runs with few setups.

Bally showed steady profits and maintained its market share during this time, and was eventually purchased by Allegheny International. In 1983, Tom Pietrocini was brought in to run the unit. Pietrocini found a sleepy, ordinary company that was profitable but flawed. Its cost structure was much higher than that of its competitors, and innovation in product and process was stagnant. Further, market saturation plagued the industry, causing a long, steady decline in revenues that averaged about 2 percent a year. Competition was driving prices down, putting extreme pressure on Bally's cost and profit structure. It quickly became clear to Pietrocini that at its current course and speed, Bally was slowly going out of business—even though it was still technically the market share leader.

Pietrocini decided that radical changes were needed to turn Bally around. He wanted to differentiate Bally's products again, to more closely meet customers' individual needs, to deliver faster than anyone else, to reduce costs, and to develop new products based on Bally's distinctive competencies in panels, panel locking, and refrigeration. He wanted Bally to be a world-class manufacturer.

In beginning what he calls "the journey," Pietrocini decided not to try to change everything at once, nor did he announce a grand and glorious vision for Bally's future. Pietrocini didn't even touch the manufacturing process, but began attacking all of the administrative processes that flowed around it, impairing, delaying, and standardizing an otherwise excellent manufacturing process. These administrative processes so encumbered manufacturing that it was taking five to seven weeks to produce standardized products that required only four days of manufacturing process time.

Pietrocini decided to focus on continuous incremental improvement in Bally's administrative processes using the ninety-day plan as his primary tool. Every ninety days, Pietrocini would bring his management team together and ask, "What can we change for the better?" Once the "what" was determined, he let the employees closest to the problem figure out the "how." Ninety days later, Pietrocini would get everyone together again and ask, "Did we make the right decision ninety days ago? What could be done better? What can we change now?" Now that this process is ingrained in the culture, the driving force is no longer management but employees.

For Bally, empowerment was only one condition for success; the second was information pertinent to the task at hand. As Pietrocini relates, "To achieve the economical viable business of tomorrow, each individual employee must not only be empowered, but also have access to relevant information to change the way work is performed." To that end, Bally installed an IBM System/36 in late 1983, running a manufacturing package. Over time, this put information in the hands of the workers who needed it. Pietrocini's developing vision for the company coalesced into one in which all the manufacturing and administrative processes were integrated by the information available on the computer. To Pietrocini, the challenge in manufacturing is "to transform data into information and then apply it to the workplace." But rather than simply automating the existing processes—as so many companies have done with computers—Bally used its system to completely re-engineer administrative processes.

Particular attention was placed on reducing cycle time, eliminating waste, and providing more customization. Since 1983, there has been a more than tenfold increase in Bally's "envelope of variety." To support Bally's thrust into customization, the sales and ordering processes have been completely redesigned. Each order changes an average of two and a half times before the panels are finally manufactured. Because of the complexity of the structures, this would entail eighty-six distinct steps—all done serially—and take up to two and a half weeks. So, for a structure that in the end required only four days of manufacturing time, as much as five to seven weeks could be spent just in processing change orders.

Using artificial intelligence software available on its AS/400, which replaced the System/36, Bally was able to capture the decision rules of its configuration experts, eliminate all of the checking and rechecking that took place, and reduce the number of steps each order change required.[7] Today, this process, which takes fifty-six mostly parallel steps—including feeding the new configuration directly into a computer-aided-design (CAD) system—is almost always done in less than four hours. The CAD system automatically generates a drawing that can be faxed directly to a sales rep in the customer's office for verification, then feeds all the data to the manufacturing software to generate the bills of material. Pietrocini says that the process improvement "changes the whole dynamics of selling in this industry," allowing Bally to design custom structures essentially while the customer waits. And thanks to the knowledge-based tool, the configuration experts are spending their time creating new types of structures.

When these or any other experts are needed in the sales process, their help is easily obtained. The AS/400 maintains a database of everyone in the company along with their skills and experiences, so exactly the right person can be found and contacted quickly by telephone or electronic mail. This provides an "experience database" available to the entire company.

Another tool in Tom Pietrocini's bag has been continual organizational changes. He flattened the organization, reducing the number of reporting levels from seven to five, but also reorganized particular areas whenever necessary to focus on a problem. For example, production inventory control was eliminated because, as the chief financial officer, Tom Weaver, notes, "they were always in their office, not out on the floor." Today, production planning is part of the sales function (perfectly appropriate for a make-to-order business) while production scheduling is done right on the floor. In other cases, people are brought together to work as a team on a project, then disbursed into new organizations once the project is completed.

This is one of several ways Bally is breaking down the "functional silos" that existed. In an all-union shop, it is also breaking down the belief that years of service should determine pay. Wage increases are now based on the skills, knowledge, and ability to adapt that each employee demonstrates.

This is important in a company where, according to Weaver, "Workers were robots; we made them that way, and we wanted it that way." Now that times have changed, it has been tough to empower employees because the concept is totally foreign to them. It helped when half of the foremen were moved out of manufacturing. The five remaining foremen no longer have time to supervise all 180 employees. Instead, the workers themselves are responsible for planning and supervising their own work, while the ex-foremen are leading the new product development effort.

The "integration of thinking and doing" on the factory floor, similar to what happened four to five years earlier in the front office, is integral to Bally's efforts to redesign the manufacturing process. Although continued improvements are still expected in administrative processes, the five- to seven-week cycle time has been reduced to five days, while the manufacturing process still takes the same four days it took in 1983. This is the next step in Bally's journey of continuous improvement, and it is already proceeding much faster in manufacturing than it did in administration.

During 1991, through quality improvements and cost reductions, Bally reduced its break-even point by close to 50 percent. Unfortunately, the 1991–1992 recession really hurt the entire industry, and Bally has yet to achieve the profits it eventually expects from this improvement. Much of the cost reduction has been achieved by layoffs, but these have been accepted by the workers and their union as the inevitable consequences of being in a tough business, particularly during a recession.

Pietrocini tells his employees that he doesn't want people who just do as they are told, like those of his competitors; he wants "knowledge workers" who can apply their "brain capital" to improving the business, continuing the journey toward world-class manufacturing. Pietrocini's vision for Bally's has shifted from CIM (computer-integrated manufacturing) to CDIN, or "computer-driven intelligence network," which will one day link not only Bally's knowledge workers, but its sales reps and suppliers into one network for sharing information across the entire value chain.

Throughout its incremental transformation into a mass customization company, Bally Engineered Structures maintained its market share leadership with 12 to 15 percent of the $400 million (and declining) industry. In 1983, Tom Pietrocini expected that the transformation would take "a couple of years." When the management team took the company private in a 1987 leveraged buyout, they thought it would be just a few more years before they turned the corner. Now they and their employees realize that it is a never-ending journey, one that will last as far as they can see into the future as Bally maintains its focus on reducing every element of cost in the factory, on improving its quality, flexibility, and responsiveness to its customers, and on increasing the envelope of variety within which it can mass customize refrigerated and other structures.

Bally has already come a long way. Its products command a 5 to 8 percent premium in the market, and it can manufacture customized structures and deliver them two to four times faster than competitors' more standardized versions (the more complicated the structure, the better Bally's differential). Tom Pietrocini is dedicated to continually improving Bally's performance, making life tough for his competitors, and creating a great deal of turbulence in his industry.

Proceeding incrementally. By beginning and proceeding incrementally, both Bally Engineered Structures and the Toyota Motor Company have transformed themselves from mass producers to mass customizers. IBM Rochester is still in transition, but it began its incremental movement several years after Bally and decades after Toyota. Because of their relative position in their respective industries, because their market turbulence was not dramatically increasing, and because their competitors were not themselves undergoing transformation at a quicker pace, each of these three organizations has been able to take advantage of continual, incremental improvement in its products, processes, and organizational structure. Bally and Toyota had the advantage of full support from the top echelon of their companies, but IBM Rochester demonstrates that significant progress can be made by separate groups doing what they can to improve themselves and push or pull the rest of the organization in the right direction.

These examples, plus others that will be discussed in the following chapters, indicate that when proceeding incrementally it is important not to try to do everything at once. Focus on one or at most a few things at a time, creating a progression of activities that can be linked together to form the nucleus of the new organization and a new way of doing business. Small successes should be made visible to the rest of the organization and, when necessary, integrated to demonstrate to top management the direction in which to go.

As Bally illustrates, even when top management fully supports it from the beginning, the change process need not provide an overriding vision to govern that process from the start. The vision can develop over time, even unfold "just in time" to light the way to new areas for incremental improvements as progress is completed in old areas. Vision is important, but it is more important at the beginning to instill the desire to change. If the people in a firm have not been made uncomfortable enough that they are willing to change, it doesn't matter what direction the vision points them to.

Transform the Business

There are many companies for which incremental change would clearly be too little too late. Firms facing greatly increased turbulence or competitors well on their way to Mass Customization cannot wait for incremental improvement to take hold. They must move quickly to get rid of the old ways, increase flexibility and responsiveness throughout the entire organization, and figure out how their products and services can be mass-customized. They must transform the business.

Motorola Pager Division. One organization that has successfully transformed itself is Motorola's Pager Division in Boynton Beach, Florida. In the 1980s, the U.S. pager industry was hit by a high degree of market turbulence: Japanese companies entered the market with high-quality pagers selling for under $100 at a time when the products of the half dozen American producers were about $200. By 1985, most of its domestic competitors were out of the business, and Motorola knew that drastic transformation would be necessary to save it from the same fate. "You can streamline the traditional system to get maybe a 20% improvement," declared Christopher B. Galvin, senior vice president and chief corporate staff officer, "but to get orders of magnitude of change you have to rethink the whole system."[8] Incremental improvement would not be enough for Motorola; orders of magnitude improvement were needed in costs and quality to meet and then beat the competition. And customization would provide Motorola with an advantage over its mass-producing competitors.

To make this transformation, Motorola put together a twenty-four-member cross-functional team to design a new manufacturing process and assembly line to produce its Bravo line of pagers. This team was charged with creating a completely automated, computer-integrated assembly line yielding tremendous economies of scale—but with *lot sizes of one*. Although the task was estimated to need three to five years to complete, the team was given only eighteen months. To make that schedule, it scoured the world for the best ways of doing every little thing in the factory and vowed to avoid reinventing anything. All the technology would be purchased off the shelf, earning the project the code-name Bandit. As T. Scott Shamlin, director of manufacturing at the pager facility, explained, "We had no time for an evolutionary approach. We had to abolish the Not Invented Here syndrome that's a part of American culture. Bandit became an antonym for NIH."[9]

The team completely re-engineered the Bravo pager, cutting to 134 the number of parts designed for robotic assembly. Of these, 109 were electronic devices placed on a circuit board that provide much of the pager's customization capability. Between various hardware and mostly software features, the new pager had 29 million possible variations, any one of which could be produced immediately with zero setup time and a true lot size of one. Plus, total manufacturing time was cut from over five hours to under two.

Motorola's transformation was not confined to the manufacturing line. Len deBarros, director of manufacturing for the pager division, recalled: "We didn't want to look at just the manufacturing process. We wanted to revamp the entire business cycle, from the time a salesperson takes an order until the time the pager is packed and shipped."[10] This total cycle time for an order used to take a month or two. By completely redesigning the order process and incorporating the right information technology for each step in the process, the company cut order time to an hour and a half. Today, a Motorola salesperson can sit down with a customer and design the set of pagers that exactly meets that customer's desires. The specifications are entered into a portable Apple Macintosh and electronically sent to the company's headquarters in Schaumburg, Illinois. From there, orders flow automatically to IBM mainframes in the Boynton Beach factory and then to a set of fault-tolerant Stratus computers that determine the exact production schedule. This information is then passed on to Hewlett-Packard computers on the factory floor that control twenty-seven Seiko robots, and the customer's first pager begins its trip down the line. Elapsed time: fifteen to twenty minutes. A little over an hour later, that first pager is inspected, labeled, and boxed.

Part of the Bandit project's mission from the beginning was to be a showcase for computer-integrated manufacturing within Motorola. As Shamlin has said, "It's a zero setup time, hands off, true lot size of one, asynchronous pull, build-to-order manufacturing operation. It's a perfect environment for an advanced CIM system."[11] *Everything* was automated, whether it made sense or not. Interestingly, after completing the project the team found that some things on the line, such as first placing the unit on the housing to go down the line, are better done by people.

That first Bandit line, up and running in December 1987, exactly eighteen months after the team started, has since been dismantled, with the pieces being used in various other pager lines in the factory (a testament to the flexibility of the technology they chose). But Bandit transformed the way pagers were made, and all of the lines in that factory are now models of mass customization. Capitalizing on its newfound flexibility, Motorola has introduced new lines of pagers that have become fashion items for business and home use, available in many colors and different styles. By moving into the fashion business, Motorola is increasing turbulence for its competitors.

As Bandit became a model for the pager division, that division has become a model for Motorola to transform itself into a mass customization firm. Thanks in part to Bandit, Motorola won the Malcolm Baldrige National Quality Award in 1988. In an interview the year after winning the award, George M. C. Fisher, president and CEO, stated that being receptive to change is "becoming an increasingly important factor for competitive success: to be able to change designs quickly, to be able to customize products for specific markets."[12] Once you have that capability—the ability to mass-customize—Fisher advocates using it to its fullest: "You go to every customer and say, What do you want? Whatever it is, we can do it. If you drive that capability as a distinctive competence, while your competitor is building a million of the same gadgets at a very low cost, I'll bet the company that does something different for every customer is going to win."[13] Fisher is transforming Motorola to win that bet.

   Société Micromécanique et Horlogère. Another company for which incremental improvement would not have been enough is SMH, the very old and very traditional (and largest) Swiss watchmaker.[14] While Motorola redesigned a current product and then focused primarily on the manufacturing and order processes that allowed a customized version of the product to reach a customer's hands as quickly as possible, SMH created a new product and then focused on regenerating new versions of that product as quickly as possible through time. It all began with a dramatic change in market turbulence.

   Watchmaking had long remained the most prototypical of Craft Production industries, with individual watchmakers applying their skills to the gears and jewels of one watch at a time. Mass production techniques were first introduced to the watch industry with the advent of digital quartz technology in 1968. Prices dropped dramatically in the 1970s and 1980s as watchmaking shifted from Craft to Mass Production. This shift devastated the Swiss watch industry, which saw its share of world production drop from its traditional level of 85 percent down to the low teens.[15] The number of Swiss firms in the industry dropped as well. SMH resulted from a 1983 merger that rescued Switzerland's top two watchmakers from bankruptcy. It was able to hang on, but not without a complete transformation.

   The plummet in watch prices during the 1970s allowed consumers to purchase many more watches than they had before. Watch buyers became increasingly fashion conscious, owning multiple watches and using them as accessories that happened also to tell time. By the mid-1980s, watch purchases were approaching 100 million units a year, a 400 percent increase in just ten years. Consumers were buying, on average, one watch every other year instead of waiting for the previous purchase to wear out or lose its status allure. By 1985, industry observers felt that the market was near saturation at an average of 3.5 watches per owner.[16]

   Increasing price and fashion consciousness, new quality standards (digital watches had reset the bar for accuracy), and high saturation levels all increased market turbulence for the industry. A mere decade after its shift from Craft to Mass Production, the industry's environment was ripe for a further shift to Mass Customization.

This reality was grasped by Dr. Ernst Thomke, president of SMH's subsidiary, ETA S.A., in the early 1980s. Thomke felt that success would come from volume sales, but only with innovative, fashionable, and prestigious products. At Thomke's behest, two micromechanical engineers designed a new kind of watch, reducing by one-half to one-third the number of parts and injecting the quartz movement directly into a one-piece plastic case. To further decrease costs, the case was not screwed shut but sealed by ultrasonic welding. Since this prevented the watch from being repaired, the watch was envisaged as a fashion accessory rather than a pure status symbol. The manufacturing process was designed for pure mass production, with heavy utilization of computers and robots.

The product was given the brand name Swatch (*Swiss* + *watch*) and launched in 1983 with twelve styles available in red, brown, and tan. Sales were dismal until Thomke and SMH discovered the formula for success: increased variety and short product life cycles while maintaining mass-production prices. SMH tweaked the prices, distribution, and advertising, but most important, it transformed the product design and manufacturing processes to increase the number of watch models, sizes, colors, and styles. It introduced spring and fall collections in 1984 and then moved to six seasons per year. Its engineers developed a system of "perpetual innovation" that allowed them to renew collections every six weeks with eighty to one hundred new watches. With so much variety turned over so frequently, each and every customer could buy a watch with the virtual certainty that the exact watch would never be worn by anyone else he or she knew.

The success of SMH and the Swatch brand continues to be dependent on the flexible technologies used in manufacturing to provide variety and low costs, on the abilities of designers to create and exploit the latest fashion trends, and on the abilities of engineers to turn design into reality in a short time. SMH transformed not only itself but the entire industry, as the rules of competition in watchmaking now require both low costs and high variety.[17]

Computer Products, Inc. While it took several years for SMH to hit upon the system of perpetual innovation and thereby shift fully to the new frontier of Mass Customization, Computer Products, Inc. (CPI), of Boca Raton, Florida, did not have even that long. When

John Lemasters took over as CEO in March 1988, the computer industry had just started to decline from its high growth rates and CPI was losing $27,000 every day.[18] Lemasters needed to transform the $120 million company, and quickly.

Just a few years earlier, CPI had been a high flyer, growing at over 35 percent a year (profits were growing even faster) and being named one of the "100 best little growth companies in America" by *Business Week* in 1985. However, some of that growth was fraudulently inflated with phony orders dating back to 1984. The discovery of these orders in 1986—along with misguided acquisitions, poor product quality, and weak customer relations—led to the loss of more than $33 million from 1986 to 1988.[19]

When CPI's board brought in Lemasters to turn the company around, he knew he didn't have any time to waste. Without quick and dramatic changes, the company would soon be out of business. After two months of study, one of them prior to joining the firm, Lemasters brought his top management team together and made it clear that pain and turmoil would be the order of the day until the company was once again on solid footing. He quickly followed this up with three dramatic actions. First, any division that was unlikely to show a profit within three years was put up for sale. Lemasters decided to focus on CPI's core businesses of power supplies and subsystems for computer manufacturers, power systems for military applications, and process automation systems. Second, Lemasters closed three plants to reduce manufacturing capacity and laid off 400 people, reducing employment 20 percent to 1,650. He also fired four of the five corporate officers because they did not meet his stringent requirements for managing the company. Third, Lemasters instituted a total quality management (TQM) program to improve product quality and reduce costs.

It was through total quality management that CPI began to discover the power of Mass Customization. TQM focused the company not only on improving quality and reducing costs, but on meeting its customers' individual wants and needs, for in the end it is the customer that determines quality. CPI found that two of the things its customers valued most were speed and customization. The company focused on delivering products faster than any of its competitors, and shortened its new product development time to bring innovations to the market quicker. It emphasized solutions instead of products, packaging customer services along with its products to tailor them to be exactly what the customer wanted.

Lemasters was able to transform Computer Products quickly. In 1989, his first full year at the helm, the company moved into the black and continued its profitable ways in the following two years. With the threat of bankruptcy diminishing in 1990, Lemasters and his new management team were able to set a "strategy for the 1990s" that firmly grounded the company in Mass Customization. As Lemasters related in the company's annual report, this instructive strategy has five principles:

The evolution of Computer Products during 1990 was driven by a unique business philosophy, a philosophy founded on a set of principles that continues to serve as the foundation of our long-term planning and marketing strategies. These principles were the underpinning of our success in 1990 and will serve as our platform for growth throughout the decade of the 1990s. . . .

- **High-growth niche markets**—We are a product-driven company that focuses on niche, high-margin industrial electronic markets. We are not a manufacturing company that searches for markets; we are a customer solutions company that searches out and supplies products for high-margin growth opportunities.
- **Global diversity**—We are a global company, with native operations in North America, Europe, and the Asia-Pacific region. We have a widespread international sales network consisting of 200 distributor locations in 26 countries. Our global diversity and many sales channels protect us from regional market fluctuations and provide barriers against competition.
- **Competitiveness via added value**—The value of our products is not in the hardware alone. We offer customers added value in the form of software, systems integration, product customization, applications development, and distributor service and support. We are successful because of who we are, not merely because of what we provide.
- **Strong cash position**—We are a financially strong company, with a cash position that gives us the resources to develop new technologies and products internally or seek out and acquire those technologies or companies that fit our long-range plans.
- **Reward for entrepreneurial innovation**—We've organized our company as individual entrepreneurial business units, managed by people who treat the business as if it were their own. We provide a system of incentives that attracts and retains quality people and rewards innovation and good management.

These beliefs are the guideposts directing our company's worldwide operations. Our ultimate goals are stability through geographical diversity; protection from competition through technological and geographical barriers to entry; increased profits through sales of niche, high-margin products, coupled with value-added services; and maximum creativity and personal output through decentralized management and incentives.[20]

Following through on this strategy in 1991, cross-functional teams (engineering, marketing, and finance) in the Government Electronics business began meeting regularly with customers to determine their needs and wants. These teams found that the requirements for fast development and individual customization were even stronger than before. They then developed a "library" of standard building-block circuits and modules that could be used to develop new products quickly. According to Richard H. Miller, president of the business, "Using these standard modules, Government Electronics[21] cut its product development time in half, from twelve months to less than six months, reducing our lead time and costs, and making us more responsive than many of our competitors."

Similarly, the Process Automation business announced in February 1992 a library of control modules and with it the completion of the first open architecture in the industry. As John Pittman, president of the division, explains,

Our open architecture design gives companies absolute control over their process control systems. A system can be customized to fit a customer's unique requirements, using a mix of standard, off-the-shelf products. As Computer Products pioneers the development of more powerful open architecture systems, we are aligning ourselves with partners—systems integrators, original equipment manufacturers, and third-party software houses—who will work with us to deliver open architecture-based solutions demanded by our customers. Our role has changed dramatically. We see ourselves as a company that enables our customers to shape precisely their process automation solutions, rather than applying a rigid pre-configured product.

Finally, the Power Conversion business also completed its shift to Mass Customization by reducing its development times, focusing on the individual wants and needs of its customers, and, in 1992, bringing to market a new line of high-density power converters that is mass-customized. The HFS 200 series is designed around a large number of pre-engineered modules that lets customers create power converters to precisely fit their systems and design engineering needs. Working with CPI sales representatives or distributors, customers use a menu of options to mix and match exactly what they want. Re-

flecting the organization's shift, Dennis L. Akers, the vice president/
general manager responsible for the project, says:

This is a customer-focused operation. Our commitment is to provide a new
level of flexibility so that we deliver to each customer modular power solutions in a single pre-engineered package that reflect their specific system and
design needs. In addition, customers have the benefit of designing their own
power supplies using pre-approved technology.

Transforming businesses. Computer Products, Inc., has successfully
completed its transformation from a company that produced standardized power supplies and, for various reasons, was losing money
at a rate that threatened its survival, to a set of related businesses,
each focused on the individual wants and needs of its customers and
on providing low-cost products and services customized to those
needs. In between was a lot of pain and upheaval, including layoffs,
firings, plant closings, selling businesses, and all of the turmoil associated with completely changing the way the businesses were run in a
few short years.

Turmoil is a necessary part of transformation, but it keeps many
companies from going down this path until a crisis develops that is
so big they have no choice. This may be human nature, and it may
be unavoidable. But business transformation is indeed the only appropriate path for companies that are undergoing a major increase in
market turbulence or whose competitors have already shifted to the
new frontier. It is clear from these and other examples that transformation can happen only when instigated or at least fully supported
by top management. Without that, those who want to resist will
always have tacit if not explicit support to do so. It will not work.

With top management support and the advent of a crisis, business transformation can proceed in earnest. (If a crisis is not yet at
hand, perhaps one can be manufactured by pointing to increased
turbulence and the transformations of competitors.) When a company
is trying to transform a business quickly, it is often appropriate to
tear down the entire system and start over from scratch, as Motorola's
Pager Division and, to a lesser extent, Computer Products did. Then,
challenge people to do the seemingly impossible, unfettered by the
old ways of doing business. Promulgate and build upon successes,
using them to drive home the need to change and the direction to go.
As SMH demonstrates, that direction may not always be visible at
the beginning, but the concepts of Mass Customization presented in

this book should provide clear reasons for why a business has to change and, as discussed later in this chapter, a clear vision and strategy to point the organization in the right direction. Chapter 9 discusses further how to transform businesses, providing a progression of activities that, taken incrementally over time or quickly over a few years, will lead organizations into the new frontier of Mass Customization.

Create New Businesses

The realities of increasing market turbulence have forced some organizations, like Motorola's Pager Division, SMH, and Computer Products, to transform themselves in a relatively short time, while giving others, like Toyota, IBM Rochester, and Bally Engineered Structures, longer time frames over which incremental improvement can be successful. A third category of firms moving to Mass Customization is new businesses created specifically to provide variety and customization at mass production prices. These businesses—in services as often as manufacturing—are generally based on the application of new information and/or telecommunications technologies to drive down costs while increasing customization.

France Télécom (Minitel). A prime illustration can be found in the telecommunications industry itself, which is probably moving to Mass Customization faster than any other industry in the United States.

While standard phone service used to be the only option, customers can now get a dozen or more optional services, and hundreds more are being developed. This variety pales in comparison, however, to the world's premier mass customizer in telecommunications, France Télécom, which created a new business in the late 1970s to provide individualized services over standard phone lines. Today, the public services available on the Télétel system number about 15,000, with the incremental cost of adding a new service so small that an average of 15 are added every day.[22] Many of these are provided by new businesses created solely because of the availability of Télétel (or Minitel, as the service is more popularly called after the name of the terminals that dot more than 6 million homes and offices in France). An additional 15,000 private services have been developed by companies for their internal use through the Minitel infrastructure.[23]

Backed by the deep pockets and long-range strategic horizon of the French government, Minitel was formed by the government and enabled by new videotex technologies that allow individualized information to be sent across the mass medium of telephone lines. In 1978, President Valéry Giscard d'Estaing formulated a vision to make France less dependent on foreign information technology and bring it out of the backwater of telecommunications (it had one of the worst phone systems in the Western Hemisphere, and only 45 percent of homes had service). D'Estaing charged his state telecommunications agency to tie together computers and communications in a way that would "informationalize" French society and economy. Minitel was born soon after, in 1981, as terminals were provided free of charge to any French home or office that wanted one.

Originally devised to provide on-line directory assistance services to a population of phone users growing so fast that hard-copy directories could not keep up, the structure of Minitel allows virtually any service that can be accessed on-line to be put in service cheaply and efficiently. Minitel itself provides central management of the system, including transmission processing and customer billing, which allows the smallest of service companies to gain economies of scope in marketing (users can explore any service at a very low cost) and distribution (the companies do not have the expense of collecting these minute sums from hundreds or thousands of users every month).[24] The plethora of services available from Minitel itself and the industry of information service providers that has grown up around it include messaging services (including adult chat lines called *messageries roses*), leisure and games, news, local municipal information, legal advice, weather information, and banking services.[25] Minitel forms the infrastructure of some entire French industries, such as shipping, for which an application called Teleroute matches the requirements of individual shipments and the capabilities of trucking companies to get them to the right place at the right time.[26] A surprisingly similar application provides a clearinghouse for organ transplants, matching the needs of each individual with a donor. Minitel is now exporting its system and many of its services to other countries.

Azimuth Corporation. Minitel has provided an infrastructure with great economies of scope for the creation of a myriad of new businesses that provide customized information services. The capabilities of modern technologies (particularly, but not limited to information and telecommunications technologies) allow companies to produce and deliver many other customized goods and services at mass production prices, even without Minitel's infrastructure.

One such company is Azimuth Corporation of St. Paul, Minnesota. In 1985, Azimuth's founders, James Kubiak and Dan Gilroy, obtained a consulting contract with 3M to develop an application for Scotchcal™, a new type of film. Kubiak and Gilroy discovered that the film was ideal for the instant production of signs, posters, banners, and other large printed materials, so much so that they created a new business to market instant signs.[27] Backed by a loan from 3M, seven Sign-tific® stores were soon operating in the Twin Cities.

Azimuth soon discovered the power of Mass Customization. As Kubiak recalls, "We could provide small businesses with high-quality, one-of-a-kind signs at a similar price to GM buying 50,000 of the same signs. We found a number of other graphics products not available to small businesses at low prices and went into the custom graphics business." Through personal computers, laser printers, and unique materials such as Scotchcal, Sign-tific stores now mass-customize name tags, desk plates, plaques, stationery, business forms, and many other products. Customers can choose from a wide variety of colors, textures, surfaces, sizes, and shapes. Sign-tific will incorporate any logo or special graphic into any of its products. Its artists sit down with a customer and together they design the one product that meets that customer's requirements. They'll even develop a logo for the customer gratis—advertising agencies charge $500 for just the first hour of such a consultation.

Azimuth also illustrates an important reality of off-the-shelf customizing technologies: alone they do not provide a sustainable competitive advantage. They are easily copied; anyone with the appropriate graphics and business experience can purchase computers and materials to do the same thing as Azimuth. Off-the-shelf technology may get you into the game, but you have to build on it for sustained performance. Kubiak realizes that while his company was built on customizing technologies, "our competitive advantage is not through technology. It's based on distribution leverage and quality of service." To that end, Kubiak now works with Bizmart Inc.—a chain of office superstores owned by Intelligent Electronics of Exton, Pennsylvania, that provides discounted products to small businesses—to operate "stores within a store," providing business services to the same customers. By the end of 1991, fifteen stores were in place within Bizmarts with more in the works. A similar arrangement with Deluxe Corporation has resulted in test stores, called Deluxe Forms Centers, that mass-customize business forms for small businesses.

Personics Corporation. Many new businesses are also being created with unique technologies, or off-the-shelf technologies with proprietary twists. One prime example is the mass customization of music on cassette tapes by Personics Corporation of San Carlos, California.

A tremendous amount of variety exists in music stores today; customers can choose from thousands of selections in numerous genres on records, cassette tapes, and compact disks. Personics, however, took consumer choice orders of magnitude farther by creating a system that produces individualized cassettes right in the store. A customer chooses his own selections from four to five thousand individual songs. A salesclerk enters the songs, and a customized cassette pops out within five to ten minutes, complete with a laser-printed label with the customer's name, title, list of the selections, and copyright information.[28] Each selection costs $1.10, for an average price of $11 per tape, and usually results in 3 to 5 percent of the store's sales.

All of this is accomplished with a personal computer specialized by Personics to attach to two compact disk jukeboxes that contain sixty CDs each. Personics uses proprietary technology to compress that data onto the CDs, storing three times as many songs as standard CDs and yielding a music database of more than ninety gigabytes available for mass customization.

While a terrific example of using technology to give customers a one-of-a-kind product that is *exactly* what they want, on demand, and at close to mass production prices, Personics also illustrates that it is not always enough. The company went into Chapter 11 in 1991, when copyright hassles with music companies made it nearly impossible to obtain current hits. The founder of Personics, Charles Garvin, relates:

We underestimated the music industry's extreme conservatism and ran into their great fear that someone will come along and cannibalize their hits—despite loads of evidence that the system actually increased net music sales. For every piece of music we wanted to put on the system, we would have to prove it was a terrific idea to six or seven different people, and even then they would want huge advances.

Consumers loved it; retailers loved it. But the music sources dried up.

Garvin likens the situation to the early days of both the cable and the videocassette industries. Movie companies were deathly afraid of the competition that the new television options posed to theaters and tried to prevent their releases from being shown. It took a decade or more for them to realize the tremendous potential in the new forms of distribution that cable and VCRs provided. Today, the movie studios make more money from *each* of these avenues than they do from their first-run theatrical releases.

Personics still exists, customizing tapes for promotional offerings and via direct mail to consumers likely to be interested in the predominantly older hits still available to the company. While in Chapter 11 it was purchased by two major entertainment companies, Time Warner and Thorn EMI. Its current president, Greg Ballard, hopes that one day the music industry will recognize the great promise of mass-customized music.[29]

Creating new businesses. New businesses are at an advantage in applying the concepts of Mass Customization because they do not have the baggage of a history steeped in Mass Production, nor the old system's vestiges of hierarchical organizations, functional barriers, lack of customer focus, and so on. New businesses can start fresh and immediately strive to fulfill the individual wants and needs of customers through mass-customized products and services. While any new business can do this, even those created by existing companies, the opportunities provided by information and telecommunications technologies have allowed hundreds and probably thousands of technology-based businesses to spring up, firmly planted in the new frontier of Mass Customization. Minitel, Azimuth, and Personics are but three examples; many more will discussed in Chapter 8 to illustrate specific methods of mass customization.

It is important that new businesses focus from the beginning on providing products or services tailored to individuals. A clear vision of this can energize a new organization and ensure that the focus remains right in front of everyone over time. But it is crucial that any strategy that ensues from the vision be adaptable to changing circumstances and market conditions, as Azimuth illustrates. That adaptability should extend to the realization that an initial competitive advantage based on technology is rarely enough; you must ensure that your advantage is sustainable. Never rest on past or current successes, but constantly stay ahead of the competition through continuous innovation and ceaseless searching for new ways to develop, produce, market, and deliver mass-customized products and services.

In today's turbulent environment, it is rare that any new business can go it alone without help from partners, usually larger, more established companies. Minitel can draw on skills, experiences, and support from France Télécom; Azimuth gains crucial distribution leverage from Bizmart and Deluxe; and Personics may soon get back into retail outlets with the assistance of Time Warner and Thorn EMI. Understand where your core competencies lie, and seek out partners that will complement those competencies with their own that together can yield an unbeatable combination.[30] Then you will be prepared to succeed in the new frontier of Mass Customization.

The Journey to Mass Customization

The shift to Mass Customization is indeed a journey. Some companies can make the transformation quickly, in a matter of a few years, mostly because if they don't they will be out of business. Other companies can afford to proceed incrementally, taking many years and even a decade or more to fully enter the new frontier, usually still ahead of their competitors. Still others sprout up firmly planted in Mass Customization. But no matter how you get there, as Tom Pietrocini of Bally Engineered Structures likes to say, the journey never ends. You can enter this frontier, but you cannot settle in it. A large part of it involves searching for the requirements of individual customers: current customers whose requirements will change over time as well as new customers whose needs have yet to be met or even ascertained. Further, meeting those needs quickly, and exactly, encourages customers to want even more exact fulfillment of their desires, even more quickly.

Entering the new frontier is no guarantee of success, as Personics demonstrates. The requirements necessary for success in a turbulent marketplace go up with the turbulence, maybe exponentially. Success requires more than knowing that Mass Customization is the direction to take or having the technology to begin the journey. Sustained success—whether proceeding incrementally, through business transformation, or creating a new business—is best achieved by four steps:

- Gain knowledge of the shift and the desire to change.
- Create a vision that excites and energizes.

- Develop a strategy on how to proceed.
- Execute well.

The journey starts with knowledge and desire, without which no significant progress can be made. It advances through a vision that excites and energizes all concerned to reach the destination and through a strategy that tells them how to proceed, yet remains adaptable to changing circumstances. But the journey's success is determined by how well people execute.

Knowledge and Desire

The first step is to change your mental model of how the world of business operates and its formula for success. The old ways of Mass Production no longer work in an increasingly turbulent world. Table 7-2 contrasts many of these with the new ways of Mass Customization. A number of people find it difficult to accept the new principles, but it is critical, first, to gain the knowledge and understanding of the new competitive realities and, second, to possess the desire to change.

The entire organization needs to make the shift. The feedback loops pictured in Chapters 2 and 3 can be used to demonstrate how the world has changed, and the Market Turbulence Map presented in Chapter 4 can be used at all levels of an organization as a tool for verifying how those changes have affected a business. Formal use of the map with the most appropriate people in an organization is best, and can be made easy to do with PEC Corporation's **Q&View for Mass Customization** software. But even informal use can provide the impetus to change. At several IBM classes on this topic, following an introduction to market turbulence and a brief discussion of the seventeen market environment factors that comprise it, participants were asked if their market environments were (1) less turbulent than a decade ago, (2) about the same, (3) more turbulent, or (4) much more turbulent than a decade ago. Out of more than 125 participants across various organizations in IBM, no one answered (1) or (2); one-quarter said their market environment was more turbulent and three-quarters said it was much more turbulent. Results like these, "quick and dirty" though they may be, can demonstrate that a shift to the system of Mass Customization is essential.

Hand in hand with the *knowledge* that the shift is necessary must come the *desire* to change. In every company example given, the desire

Table 7-2   The Old Ways Contrasted with the New

The Old Ways of Mass Production	The New Ways of Mass Customization
• Low-cost, consistent quality, standardized products	• Affordable, high-quality, customized products
• Homogeneous markets	• Heterogeneous markets and segments of one
• Stable demand	• Demand fragmentation
• Long product life cycles	• Short product life cycles
• Long product development cycles	• Short product development cycles
• Operational efficiency premier	• Total process efficiency premier
• Economies of scale	• Economies of scale and economies of scope
• Long runs	• Lot sizes of one
• Inflexible production	• Flexible production
• High overhead necessary	• Low overhead
• High inventories: build to plan	• No inventories: make to order
• High cost of variety	• Low cost of variety
• Separation of thinking and doing	• Integration of thinking and doing
• Lack of investment in worker skills	• High utilization of and investment in worker skills
• Poor management/employee relations	• Sense of community
• Breakthrough innovations	• Breakthrough and incremental innovations
• Separation of innovation and production	• Integration of innovation and production
• Poor supplier relations	• Supplier interdependence
• Disregard for many customer needs and wants	• Quick response to changing customer desires
• Short-term managerial decisions	• Sound long- and short-term decisions by managers and workers

to change was present; it is a necessary, although not sufficient, condition. But as discussed earlier, all too often it takes a crisis to instill the desire within an organization; the well-known boiling frog phenomenon is prevalent in companies today. It is sometimes appropriate for management to turn up the heat itself to get the organizational frog to jump. Other times it is the employees who know that drastic changes are needed, but they cannot institute the change themselves through the hierarchical morass of management. Either way, without the strong desire to change permeated throughout the organization, little significant change will occur. You have to instill that desire, even if it requires manufacturing a crisis to do so.

Vision

The second step in beginning the shift to Mass Customization is to determine and communicate where you want to go, which needs to be done at two levels. First, the vision of top management must make it clear to all that momentous change is necessary; second, it must point out the direction and magnitude of the required change. On the first level, the firm's vision statement should get across points like the following:

- The primary stakeholder of the firm is the *individual customer*— not an amorphous market out there somewhere, but the individual living, breathing customer whose unique needs and desires have to be understood, met, and exceeded at every opportunity.
- The imperative of ensuring that each customer's individual needs are met does not dismiss the co-equal imperative for low cost and efficiency throughout the firm.
- Fulfilling these two imperatives together requires that each business and function be strategically flexible and quick to respond to changing conditions—whether in products, markets, or technologies.
- Each business and function must therefore be challenged to figure out how its part fits into the value chain of the entire company in order to move closer to the mass production of individually customized goods.

The second level of the vision should be to point the firm specifically in the right direction. There are many ways to mass-customize, some more appropriate to particular firms than others, some easier to start with than others. The best way to indicate the right direction is to describe a point on the horizon that all can see: the goals of what mass customization should achieve.

Often, goals are developed that lack structure and completeness; they become "just a list of stuff." One technique that has proven useful to a number of firms for providing structure is to divide the "space" of possibilities into six dimensions familiar to all: who, what, where, when, why, and how. Each dimension individually can provide a context for increasing variety and customization; and together they can provide a structure for how the firm embraces the wants and needs of each customer.

IBM Rochester used this technique to develop its vision for the AS/400. Another example is Ted Turner's Cable News Network (CNN). Turner's vision, implicitly, if not explicitly, checks off each of the six dimensions, one by one. Turner's original conception of CNN, launched in 1980, was as a cable news service that would be available twenty-four hours a day—*whenever* people wanted news, they could simply turn on CNN. It was "news on demand," news that fit viewers' individual schedules, rather than the station's. Turner also focused early on providing familiar news *wherever* people want it by securing the placement of his service on cable networks across the country, and then across the world through satellite links. As of the end of 1991, CNN International could be seen in more than 150 countries—and counting.

From these two initial dimensions Turner has branched out to provide further layers of variety and customization. To achieve mass customization through economies of scope, Turner's organization uses the raw material of gathered news stories in as many venues as possible. The cost structure is much lower than that of the three TV networks, not only because Turner pays less: "Unlike the networks, where correspondents have to fight for airtime, CNN uses practically everything its reporters file."[31] Not only has Turner eliminated waste, but he practices just-in-time production (breaking news is aired instantly—another aspect of the *when* dimension) via flexible technologies that reduce labor and setup times (portable satellite links that can be carried, set up, and operated by two-person crews instead of the usual four).

All of this allows Turner to reach the individuals in his audience *whoever* they are, with *whatever* news they want, and to a lesser degree, *however* they want it. Customers can choose from the straight CNN service or they can watch its sister-service *Headline News*, which cycles through news, weather, business, sports, and entertainment every half hour. *CNN Headline News* was launched in 1981, going from concept to market in just ninety days. Each segment comes on at the same time after each half-hour mark so that viewers know when to see what they want; these reports are constantly updated to provide the very latest news, or to provide variety in the less immediate news. If viewers want more in-depth news, CNN provides shows tailored to each subject, except for the weather (found on the Weather Channel, which, surprisingly, Turner does not own). The raw news material is further tailored for different audiences in a number of ways, including direct feeds to more than 250 broadcast stations. CNN International uses the same news as CNN in the United States, but then provides more than three hours each day (and growing) of programming specially edited for international audiences. In January 1992, CNN began the "checkout channel" to provide its service to customers waiting in line at supermarkets, airports, fast-food restaurants, and potentially anywhere else viewers have a few moments to catch up on the news (and, of course, see the occasional commercial).

CNN also addresses the last dimension, *why*, to some degree by realizing that the reason most people watch the news is to be informed about things that affect their lives, not to be told what to think. As G. Cleveland Wright, professor of journalism at Indiana University, points out,

Ideological critics of the media, left and right, agree on one thing—that the press is too arrogant, too ready to tell people what to think. By its very structure, CNN is populist. It provides the raw materials of the story and lets the viewers form their own opinions.[32]

Of course, not wanting to miss any niche, CNN provides a few programs of commentary for whoever wants them.

In recognition of the large impact of his vision on his audience and competitors, Ted Turner was named *Time*'s Man of the Year for 1991. As the magazine noted:

Only a glint of thought to its founder, Ted Turner, a dozen years ago, CNN is now the world's most widely heeded news organization. . . . As a source of knowledge in turbulent times, CNN may be without a peer.[33]

In these turbulent times, Turner has found ways to mass-customize television news by focusing on who, what, where, when, why, and how. He is following the same sort of progression with movies through his WTBS superstation and TNT network.

Certainly much more could be done and probably will be done, over time. As telecommunications and cable technologies advance, more opportunities to serve individual programming interests will be developed. For example, one day you will be able to provide a profile of exactly what news topics you are interested in, and CNN (or a value-added service provider) will constantly search the raw material of news stories for those that exactly fit your needs and "download" them right to your television set or VCR. You will be able to search through old stories by fast-forwarding, as in newspaper microfiche at a local public library. Similarly, you'll pick any movie in Turner's vast library and it will be downloaded to you immediately—in black-and-white or colorized versions, whichever you prefer. This type of service is available from customized newspapers and on-line databases, and the technology is already available for television. It is "simply" a matter of lowering the cost of the technology, spreading it across the entire country and globe (which telecommunications and cable companies are working on), and applying the concept of fully mass-customized TV news. Indeed, Ted Turner and CNN are working with multimedia providers to supply such customized news.[34]

Whenever a company starts using words like *whatever*, *wherever*, and *whenever*, or *anything*, *anywhere*, and *anytime*, it is a sure sign that it has begun the shift to Mass Customization. Each of the six dimensions, individually or together, can be used by any company to help analyze how its goods and services can be customized. Table 7-3 provides a list of sample questions for each dimension with which to begin the search. Of course, other techniques can be used. Further, a vision can be built around specific methods for mass-customizing products or services, which are discussed in Chapter 8. The most important thing to do in this step is provide a clear direction for the organization so it can begin to coalesce and move in that direction, away from Mass Production and toward Mass Customization.

Strategy

Next, the firm must incorporate Mass Customization into its strategy. This strategy should connect where the firm currently stands and its desire to change with where it wants to go by laying out the first stepping-stones along the journey.[35] It is unnecessary and likely impossible to know where all the stones should be placed. As B. Charles Ames, a partner in the investment firm Clayton & Dubilier and formerly chairman and CEO of Uniroyal Goodrich Tire Company, points out:

Change has always been an issue in business, but what is new is that its velocity, magnitude, and impact add up to a new factor—turbulence. And there are powerful forces feeding the storms of turbulence in the 90s: Political change, accelerating technology, environmental initiatives, increasing globalization, the information explosion, and demographic shifts.[36]

Table 7-3   Six Dimensions for Customizing Products and Services

Dimension	Sample Questions to Ask
Who	• Who needs my product/service? • What about it is inherently personal so that it can differ for each individual? • How do my customers differ? • How can I satisfy whoever wants my product/service?
What	• What do customers do differently with my product/service? • What different forms can it take? • How can I satisfy whatever customers want from my product/service?
Where	• Where do customers need my product/service? • How do customers differ in where they buy, receive, and use it? • How can I provide my product/service wherever customers want it?
When	• When do customers need my product/service? • How do customers differ in when they buy, receive, and use it? • How can I provide my product/service twenty-four hours a day? • How can I provide my product/service the instant customers want it? • How can I provide my product/service whenever customers want it?
Why	• Why do customers need my product/service? • How do customers differ in why they buy, receive, and use it? • Is my product/service a means or an end, or something in between? • How can I add more value to help my customers completely meet their true desired end?
How	• How do customers need my product/service delivered to them? • How do customers differ in how they buy and use it? • What can I do to provide my product/service however my customers want it?

In the face of these new forces, detailing the position of all the stepping-stones may be impossible, and is not even desirable. In an increasingly turbulent world, maintaining strategic flexibility is of the utmost importance.[37] That is, strategies should be robust and capable of addressing rapid environmental changes without waiting for a new strategy cycle. Just as product development and the production floor should be flexible and able to respond instantly to changes in customer needs, so too should strategic initiatives be flexible and able to respond to changes in the firm's total business environment: products, markets, technologies, life cycles, competition, financials, economic conditions, and so on. When flexibility in strategic planning is combined with responsiveness in a company's processes, the result is a new level in competitive advantage, one that could perhaps best be described as *agility and anticipation.*

Shell Oil pioneered the technique of scenario planning to achieve a high level of strategic flexibility in anticipating changes in an uncertain and increasingly turbulent environment.[38] With this technique, alternative futures are envisioned and the firm's best responses to each alternative are sought out and determined. Scenario planning allowed Shell to anticipate and respond quickly to the 1973 oil shock as well as the oil glut of the early 1980s. It came out of these experiences in far better shape than any of its major competitors, and by 1989 had become the largest and most profitable oil company in the world.[39]

In an increasingly turbulent world, the time frame of strategy cycles has to decrease along with product life cycles and development cycles. It is not the time horizon that decreases; rather, it is how often, how fast, and how incrementally responses must be made to changes in the firm's environment. At the same time, it is crucial to maintain constancy of purpose and clarity of vision: the tension between the vision on the horizon and the strategy responsive to the turbulent storms here and now must be maintained to ensure that frequent strategic initiatives do not degenerate into Brownian motion. Each new strategic thrust, therefore, must be tested against the current business environment, potential future scenarios, and the firm's vision for Mass Customization.

Bally Engineered Structures maintains strategic flexibility through its ninety-day plans. Each is a stepping-stone based on the most current conditions facing the firm, but each also moves the firm along a path that connects past progress with future goals along the most expedient route. Predicting that route more than ninety days in advance would be too inflexible and unresponsive to the firm's changing market environment. Just as Bally and many other companies have integrated thinking and doing on the factory floor, they are integrating thinking and doing in the strategy process. Top management defines the broad strategic intent, while the doers at all levels determine the most appropriate strategic actions—and then execute them.

Execution

When executing the strategy a key consideration is how to treat this "thing" called Mass Customization. Is it a paradigm for management? For workers? Is it an all-encompassing system? A process for change? Should it be treated as a program? Should it become part of the culture of the organization?

Mass Customization can be any of these, and the answer depends on the circumstances of the particular organization. It is a *paradigm* for viewing the firm and the business world that provides rules to the game and a formula for success. For organizations deeply mired in Mass Production and/or facing crisis, this can be the best approach: people may need to be hit over the head to knock the old ways out and prepare them for the new.

In other organizations, treating Mass Customization as a well-defined *system* for developing, producing, marketing, and delivering goods and services that are individually customized might yield the most favorable results. This may work best in organizations that are more regimented and not yet in crisis.

Mass Customization can also be used as a *program* for achieving these same results. This may be most appropriate for companies that have already embraced total quality management as its system, as Toyota, IBM, Bally, Motorola, and Computer Products have all done. As these companies illustrate, there is a tremendous synergy between TQM and Mass Customization. One of the keys to what these and many other companies have done is redefining quality as "satisfying and exceeding the current and future wants and needs of individual customers." Quality is no longer "adhering to specifications" or "elimination of variation." Quality is achieved in the mind of every satisfied—and delighted—customer.

While a particular company's approach to Mass Customization depends on its individual circumstances, two things are clear. First, if it is treated as a program, great care must be taken that it does not come across as a fad, as the latest "program of the month." It may be appropriate to institute specific programs to attack particular aspects of the equation. Reducing cycle times, instituting database marketing techniques, educating workers for multiple skills, cutting setup times, creating new services, and so on, can all be done on a program or project basis. Second, over time Mass Customization must become part of the culture of the organization to be truly successful. This is no easy task. Mass Production has been a big part of the culture of so many organizations for so long that the new frontier of Mass Customization may seem to be totally alien territory. But that frontier must be crossed not only by top management or isolated functions but by the entire organization, which can then create a new culture better suited to a turbulent environment.

CHAPTER 8

Mass-Customizing Products
and Services

ONCE a vision and strategy are in place, the specific task of deciding how to undertake the low-cost production of individually customized products and services remains. There are five fundamental methods for achieving this goal:

- Customize services around standardized products and services.
- Create customizable products and services.
- Provide point-of-delivery customization.
- Provide quick response throughout the value chain.
- Modularize components to customize end products and services.

None of these methods are mutually exclusive and in practice they often overlap; many companies use a combination of several and, occasionally, all of them. Together they provide a progression of ways that a firm immersed in Mass Production can move to Mass Customization in each key link in its organizational value chain, as shown in Figure 8-1. The order of the list goes from the easiest place to start—customizing services around existing standardized products or services within the marketing and delivery links—and progresses through more pervasive and fundamental techniques that require more drastic change and improvement throughout a firm's organization, including development and production.

171

As outlined in Chapter 7, the use of flexible information, tele-communications, manufacturing, and other technologies can also be an excellent place to start, particularly for new businesses. Many examples in this chapter will show how these technologies can provide the flexibility and responsiveness required in today's turbulent world. A great deal has already been written on the importance of these technologies and how to utilize them,[1] but flexible technologies are not by themselves a method of mass customization. Rather, in concert with investment in people, technology is the tool by which each method discussed in this chapter can achieve the required flexibility and responsiveness for a business to develop, produce, market, and deliver low-cost yet individually customized products and services. But flexible technology will not by itself turn mass producers into mass customizers.[2] To be effective, the tool of flexible technology must be wielded within an organization that knows that flexibility and quick responsiveness are crucial imperatives and has the desire to change whatever is necessary to implement them; that has a vision of the ultimate foreseeable goal and a flexible strategy for reaching it; and that is focused on using technology to meet and exceed the desires of individual customers through one of the methods of mass customization.

Customize Services Around Standardized Products and Services

Completely standardized products can still be customized, before being sent to customers, by people in marketing and delivery. Because this method can be implemented in these last two links of an organization's value chain without affecting development and production (see Figure 8-2), it is the easiest and most popular place to start.[3] Marketing and distribution can change the product, add features, combine it with other products (including those from other companies), and provide a host of services that allows each customer to receive the individual attention he or she wants and deserves.

The IBM System/360, announced in 1964, provides a classic example. The System/360 revolutionized the computer industry by providing an extremely broad range of computing power under one common architecture. From the user's standpoint, each System/360 was a standardized product, in fact the first computer to be mass-produced.[4] However, each System/360 was also a completely cus-

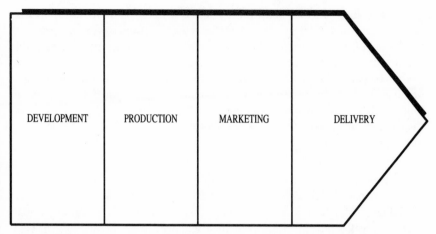

Figure 8-1 Key Links in an Organization's Value Chain

tomized product, as David Mercer described it from his own experience as an IBM marketing executive:

After spending some time in IBM it eventually dawned on me that in fact IBM had developed a near perfect marketing operation. The unit of this ideal marketing, however, was not the anonymous "average" consumer that I was used to in the consumer goods companies where I had previously worked. It was instead the very specific, identified, individual customer.

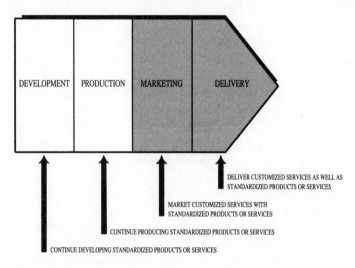

Figure 8-2 Changes in Value Chain to Customize Services Around Standardized Products and Services

Thus there was no significant market research commissioned to discover general needs, because the needs of *each* customer were investigated by the field force . . . in great depth—far more so than any market research could address, and of course quite specific to each unique customer. The overall IBM product strategy could be almost entirely technically based. . . because its job was only to provide a series of very generally applicable building blocks, from which the *field force* built ("configured" in the jargon) the unique end product that *exactly* matched the needs they had identified in the customer's business.[5]

Mass customization of the IBM System/360 was thus accomplished through IBM's field force. Obviously, it was very expensive for IBM to lavish such extensive resources on every customer, a cost that was reflected in the price of the computer. However, it was generally *cheaper* for the customers to have IBM provide their customization than to do it themselves, as IBM's field force was much more experienced and could reuse at least some software created for previous customers.

In an effort to save costs in its marketing and service operations, IBM eventually developed standard application software. Over time, it gave up Mass Customization—investigating the needs of each customer and fulfilling them—for Mass Production—trying to sell what development determined the large homogeneous market for mainframe computers needed. IBM's new market-driven quality thrust to provide total solutions for individual customers, initiated in 1987, has moved IBM back in the direction of Mass Customization. IBM Rochester has been at the forefront of this activity and, as described in Chapter 7, began by providing customized services.

While this method is resource-intensive and therefore costly, the value-added is usually high enough that a premium price can be charged (unless, of course, a competitor is already mass-customizing in development and/or manufacturing). Most important, beginning here can give development and manufacturing operations the time they need to develop their own techniques of mass customization, as is occurring at IBM Rochester.

Many service companies are using this method, customizing services around standardized offerings. For example, travel services are all standardized, allowing a customer to reserve and use the identical mass-produced commodity service, be it an airplane seat, a hotel room, or a rental car. However, leaders in these industries are finding ways to provide additional services that customize the experience.

In airlines, the availability of first- and business-class seats provides one rather small level of variety. The choices available in such traditional in-flight services as meals, drinks, radio headphones, movies, magazines, newspapers, duty-free catalogues, and, more recently, telephones and modems allow customers to enjoy a variety of experiences. Northwest Airlines announced that it will take all of this an order of magnitude further by allowing first- and business-class passengers to access an interactive passenger entertainment center built into the armrest or seat in front of them.

This new service, Worldlink, is primarily intended for long flights over the Pacific Ocean. Using headphones, a touch-sensitive screen, and sometimes a joystick, passengers can choose not only their own movies but news, entertainment, and sporting events as well. They can make telephone calls from their seat, shop interactively, access connecting gate information, process passports, and of course play video games. Some of these services are free, and some are for a fee. Payment can be made through a built-in credit-card reader. Through Worldlink, Northwest Airlines has figured out how to mass-customize the airplane experience.

Hotel chains such as Marriott Corporation are also busy customizing the hotel experience. There are a number of options available in hotels: non-smoking versus smoking rooms, corner versus side rooms, king-size versus double beds, different floors, closeness to fire exits, and amenities such as pools and exercise equipment, concierge service availability, and so on. But more often than not customers take potluck and accept whatever room the front desk assigns when they check in. Marriott is first of all creating different hotel chains for different guests: *Marriott* for upscale business and leisure customers, *Courtyard by Marriott* for business travelers on a budget, and *Residence Inn by Marriott* for patrons on extended stays. This is not unlike the "focused factory" approach in manufacturing, in which specific machines and workers are dedicated to a specific product line, allowing them to excel at producing it. Marriott dedicates specific staff to these different types of hotels, and allows them to excel at meeting specific customer service requirements.

Within each hotel, Marriott is then mass-customizing its standard hotel rooms through its Guest Recognition System. By "remembering" the preferences of their hotel guests (i.e., storing them in a central database that can be accessed locally), Marriott can provide customers with the room, services, and amenities of their choice. It does not limit access to this information to management or even the front desk, but all staff members who interact with guests can become familiar with guest preferences through the system.[6]

In the rental car industry, the Hertz Corporation has also added customized services around its standard commodity service. It has long had an "express" service to decrease the time-to-rent for its best customers. In 1990, it added the Hertz #1 Club Gold® service to completely individualize the car rental experience.

With Gold service, the company records the types of cars customers prefer and tracks incoming flights to ensure that it has the right mix of vehicles on hand. Whenever a customer arrives, Hertz pulls his or her car up to a special weather-protected stall, opens the trunk, places the keys in the ignition, turns on the motor to warm the car when it is cold (local law permitting), displays the customer's name and stall number on a computer-controlled directory board, and, finally, places the completed rental agreement on the rearview mirror along with a customer satisfaction survey. The Gold customer, who pays an annual premium for the service, simply boards the Hertz bus, takes it directly to the special Gold area, places any luggage in the trunk, and checks in at the exit gate. At many locations, when the customer returns, a Hertz service representative comes to the car and handles the return on the spot through a hand-held computer, rather than making the customer wait in the standard checkout queue.[7]

Travel companies have a natural advantage in customizing standard services: frequent usage programs have forced them to develop databases that track the purchases of most of their customers. While not originally intended for mass customization, these databases allow the companies to track the preferences and experiences of each customer, and then apply that knowledge to customize future experiences. The simple storing and tracking of sales information can provide many avenues for present and future customization.

In fact, information itself is one of the most easily customized of standard products. Once collected in a database, information can be accessed by anyone with the proper security or authority. It is a completely standardized, mass-produced commodity, but one with tremendous potential for economies of scope: everyone who accesses it can do something at least a little bit different with it. The capabilities of computers and telecommunications have created an entirely new "information industry" to provide customized services in accessing and making useful the tremendous volume of standard information available. H. Skip Weitzen, adjunct professor of management studies at the University of Maryland, coined the term "infopreneurs" to describe the profusion of companies that are now practicing this form of mass customization:

The Information Revolution has created an "information overload" that blocks effective communication. Infopreneurs help separate irrelevant information (that which will not be useful in making decisions) from relevant information (that which is vital in making well-informed decisions). However, even useful information must be systematically arranged and presented to facilitate decision making. The problem of information overload and the need to repackage useful data have ushered in new opportunities for infopreneurs to customize information.[8]

Customized services that can be performed on standard information include personalizing, categorizing, generalizing, analyzing, integrating, repackaging, facilitating, monitoring, filtering, locating, and matching, not to mention making the information convenient and readily accessible whenever and wherever a customer wants. Companies that are mass-customizing information include:

- Dow Jones News/Retrieval®, which provides on-line access to news wires, business journal articles, *The Wall Street Journal* and other newspaper articles, financial reports, stock quotes, book and movie reviews, an encyclopedia, sports and weather reports, and so on. Using a profile of key categories and topics, Dow Jones continually and automatically searches all incoming news and provides its customers with only the information they want to see. Peter Kahn, CEO of Dow Jones & Co. (parent of Dow Jones News/Retrieval, *The Wall Street Journal*, and a number of other business information services) proclaims: "The strategy that has existed here for some years is to provide business and financial news and information however, wherever, and whenever customers want to receive it."[9]
- Mead Data Central, which provides comprehensive electronic databases specifically for the legal (the Lexis® service) and medical (Medis® service) communities, as well as one for business and government information (Nexis®). In addition to providing an electronic clipping service for any of its customers, Mead creates and maintains private databases for legal firms, including the text and images of all internal documents.

- Dialog Information Services, Inc., which makes literally hundreds of electronic business databases available for on-line retrieval.
- FIND/SVP, which specializes in finding specific information its customers require but do not know how to obtain. This company uses all of the electronic databases mentioned above, as well as maintaining its own company, subject, and report files.
- DataFAX Communications Corp., which provides customized wire service reports and instant individual investor portfolio tracking via Touch-Tone telephone requests and interactive fax responses. Norberto Blumencweig, DataFAX president, plans on providing his company's proprietary technology as the backbone for other companies to provide their own customized services:

  The potential of interactive fax is limited only by a marketer's imagination. Any kind of information from up-to-the-minute stock quotes, bank statements, breaking news, to airline schedules, movie reviews, recipes, coupons, catalogues, instructional guides, sports statistics, etc., can, with our technology, be made available to anyone with access to a fax machine.

- INDIVIDUAL, Inc., which provides what is essentially a customized daily newspaper, *First!*[10] INDIVIDUAL uses sophisticated expert system technology to search news wires for pertinent stories based on subscriber profiles, formats the stories together much like a newspaper, and either faxes or electronically mails the customized newspaper to its subscribers daily.[11] Customers can rate each article's usefulness to refine the expert system technology and ensure high relevance of the selected stories.

Whether providing customized services around standardized services like airline seats, hotel rooms, rental cars, and information, or providing customized services around standardized products like computers, several key guidelines can be used when following this method of mass customization:

- Customers do not buy technology; they buy service. Find the aspects of the standardized product or service that are inherently personal—areas in which each customer would most like to make a personal choice. The six dimensions discussed in Chapter 7—who, what, where, when, why, and how—can be particularly useful for finding these characteristics. The questions provided in Table 7-3 can be used for this search process.

- Customers do not purchase customization per se; they purchase service value. The customized aspect of a service can be a great marketing angle; however, if customization does not add value, customers will not pay for it. If it does add value, they will generally pay a premium.
- If what you sell is part of a system or network of other products or services, one of the first places to look at for a customizing service is integrating the entire package. Be willing to do anything that your customers want done to their system—including purchasing, subcontracting, and using competitive products and services.
- If your business depends on repeat sales, start keeping track of all your customers and all their purchases. Make every customer encounter a learning experience. This has long been a staple of grocers, butchers, and other local businesses that depended on personal relationships to anticipate and encourage future business. Today, information technology makes it possible for organizations of all sizes to keep track of a virtually limitless number of locations, customers, purchases, and choices, and then place this information in the hands of everyone who comes in contact with customers. This information can also be used in development and production to create new products or services that better meet customer needs.

These guidelines are useful for starting a firm on the path of Mass Customization by customizing services around standardized products or services. Success with this method can show the entire organization the tremendous potential inherent in customization, making it easier to progress through the other techniques. While most customizing services can be done in the delivery link of the value chain, application-specific customization—changing the product to match the exact application for which the customer uses it—can be a source not only of service revenue, but of ideas for extending the product and embedding customization further back into the organization. Involving the development and production links can be a great way to begin focusing them on figuring out how to mass-customize the products directly, thereby increasing the value to customers while reducing the costs necessary to provide services in the delivery function.

Create Customizable Products
and Services

The opposite tactic of customizing services in the delivery function is to create in the development function products and services that are essentially mass-produced—each is no different from the next as far as the production and delivery processes are concerned—but that are *customizable* to, and often by, each customer. The effects of this technique on the organization's value chain are shown in Figure 8-3.

In 1991, Gillette introduced the Sensor razor, which "automatically adjusts to the contours of your face," as its ads proclaim. It could have segmented the "face" market and tried to develop a variety of products to fit each segment. Instead, Gillette created *one* product that automatically personalized itself. Shick soon followed the same tactic with its own Tracer brand, and Braun (a subsidiary of Gillette) introduced the Flex Control electric razor that always keeps the razor head at a ninety-degree angle to the user's face. All of these products are standardized and mass-produced, yet all, by their very nature, are customized to the individual user.

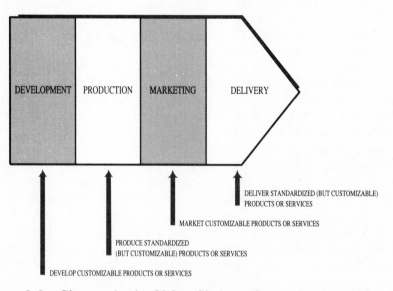

Figure 8-3   Changes in the Value Chain to Create Customizable Products or Services

Feet are as different as faces; proliferating variety has long been the case in the shoe industry, not only in sizes, styles, and colors, but in microtargeting shoes for how they are to be used. (Remember when you went to the store and asked for a "pair of sneakers"?) So shoes are also becoming a popular target of customizable products. The most successful has been Reebok's Pump, which contains a pocket of air that the wearer can pump up to provide the exact cushion desired. Gamefeet of Boca Raton, Florida, markets in sports specialty stores cushion foam insoles that mold to each foot, providing an exact fit. Numerous varieties of insoles match the differing requirements of the wearers of the numerous varieties of athletic shoes now available. Finally, Belgian Shoes of New York City sells primarily one style of slipperlike shoe in numerous colors, materials, and trims. Temporary soft soles mold to each foot, and after a week, customers return for permanent, custom-fit rubber soles made from the soft-sole molds.[12] As opposed to Gamefeet, Belgian Shoes, by moving that final manufacturing step out to the customer (the third method of mass customization discussed), provides the custom fit in the shoe itself.

Office furniture is another industry in which many companies are focusing on customizability, as the differing personal characteristics of individuals influence comfort, alertness, and over the long term, health. Herman Miller Inc., Haworth, and a number of other manufacturers have created automatically adjustable office desks, not just for different users but for a single user who wants to switch positions for comfort during the day. Haworth's has nineteen different positions. Steelcase Inc. created a line of office chairs, the Criterion™ series, that are continuously customizable across six dimensions: back height, arm height, foot ring height, back angle, seat angle, arm width. Purchasers can also customize the chairs with a number of options (mechanical or pneumatic height adjustment; upholstered, plastic, or soft armcaps; armless; foot ring, foot plates, hard casters, soft casters, or glides; and so on).

Because they are designed to be put to so many different uses by so many different companies and people, computers and their applications have long had to have high degrees of customizability to even play in the market. Users can customize their own "system environments," often making an application look and feel completely different by the differing options chosen. Customizable products are playing an increasing role in the design of computers as well. While standard memory chips have become pure commodities, the fastest-growing segment of the semiconductor industry has been ASICs, or application-specific integrated circuits. These provide engineers with a wealth of options that they can program to perform almost any function. In 1992, one of the best manufacturers, LSI Logic Corp. of Milpitas, California, announced new CoreWare technology, which combines a suite of standard but selectable microprocessors with customizable circuitry. Its chairman and chief executive officer, Wilfred J. Corrigan, likens this to the interchangeable parts innovation of the American System of Manufactures:

Before the standardization of the rifle's component parts, every rifle in the world was a "custom firearm." In today's electronic systems, the emergence and dominance of a variety of standards requires best of both worlds custom logic and standard cores. Our CoreWare technology brings this essential synthesis to the systems designer.

Producing customizable services can be just as effective as customizable products. Here, "customizable" really equates to the concept of "self-service," allowing a standard service available to anyone to be different and customized by everyone. ATMs, pioneered by Citicorp, allow customers to choose where, when, and what banking services they want. Minitel and other videotex providers like Prodigy (a joint venture of IBM and Sears) have created "service environments" through information and telecommunications technology in which the customer has a wealth of services that can be personally selected. Electronic databases and other forms of mass-customized information are similarly customizable by their users.

Customizable products and services are most useful when the needs of customers change over time (or similarly when a used product is resold to someone else). Matsushita's washing machine with 600 distinct cycles, for example, may never repeat the same cycle in consecutive washings as each load changes in its characteristics. Similarly, users of the service examples given above may request different services with every use. Flexible manufacturing systems, like computers, are customizable products that can be re-programmed and reconfigured over time to yield very diverse capabilities for the same, or different, customers.

A company embarking on creating customizable products or services must be aware of a number of important considerations:

- As with providing customized services around standardized products, the six dimensions mentioned in Chapter 7 can be useful for determining how to make a product or service customizable. Again, Table 7-3 provides questions pertinent to this task.

- Finding the most personal, most individual characteristics of the product or service is key. Then, expend the research and development effort required to embed the personal aspects of those characteristics within the product or service.

- Product customizability is fundamentally based on embedded technology. Consequently, initial customizability alone can rarely provide a long-sustainable competitive advantage. That is good news if your competitor was the first to market. Gillette was the first to come out with a customizable razor, but within months similar products were produced by both Shick and Braun. It is important, therefore, not to rest after adding a customizable feature. Sustained advantage can only come from continued enhancement and development of new features and, most important, by combining it with other techniques of mass customization.

- Customizable service concepts are not easily copied because high fixed costs of the service-creation environment can yield high barriers to entry. Still, constant innovation and evolution are required to keep the barriers high. When it is done well—as by Prodigy and especially Minitel with videotex, Dialog Information Services with electronic databases, and American Airlines with reservation systems—more profits can be made by selling access to the infrastructure to other service providers than by trying to do everything yourself.

- Self-service providers usually meet with initial resistance from customers, who are used to having someone else perform the service for them. First, ensure that the self-service mechanism really provides customizable convenience. Second, devote significant marketing effort to overcome initial resistance. Automatic teller machines (ATMs) were once suspected by customers of reducing service levels as well as bank costs; today, 63 percent of ATM users would use them even if there were no waiting for a teller.[13]

Creating customizable products and services can be a good way to start because it does not generally require drastic changes in a firm's value chain, but does begin to change people's thinking about the concept of customization. The relative inability to sustain competitive advantage without continued development combined with changing mind-sets help push the organization further into Mass Customization as a way of doing business.

Provide Point-of-Delivery Customization

There is only one way to know *exactly* what customers want: be at the point of sale to let them tell you or to draw it out of them. And there is only one way to instantly provide exactly what they want: produce it right there, at the point of sale and delivery. Or at least perform the final, customizing production step right there, right then, as depicted in Figure 8-4.

While Personics's in-store system for mass customization provides a wonderful high-tech example, this technique has been used for decades for numerous low-tech products that have one inherently personal characteristic—a characteristic that could be produced or serviced locally. Men's suits, for example, have long been purchased off the rack and then tailored to the individual within a few days.

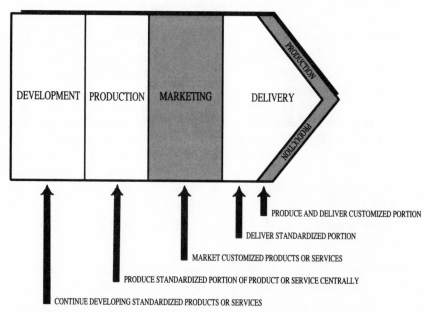

Figure 8-4 Changes in the Value Chain to Provide Point-of-Delivery Customization

T-shirts are standard, untailored products, but you can go into almost any shopping mall and purchase one that can be instantly customized with a choice of hundreds (if not thousands) of heat-applied transfer designs. T-Shirts Plus of Waco, Texas, is one of the best at this; its methods of instant point-of-sale customization include not only heat-applied transfers but lettering, customer photo transfers, airbrushing, and computerized embroidery.[14]

Point-of-sale customization is a particular favorite of sporting goods manufacturers: bowling balls, tennis rackets, ice skates, ski boots, and other items are all mass-produced at centralized factories, with an "appropriate" selection shipped to retail outlets. When a customer decides which of these selections meets his or her basic needs, a trained expert in the outlet performs the final manufacturing step that customizes the product for that customer: drilling holes in the bowling ball to match the customer's hand, stringing the customer's personal choice of material on a tennis racket to exact tension specifications, adding the choice of blade to ice skates and sharpening them according to the customer's wishes, and (more recently) forming the inside of ski boots to the customer's feet.[15]

In the past decade or so, a number of companies have adopted this technique for the complete manufacture of customized products, shifting from centralized batch production to localized, one-at-a-time, point-of-sale production. Eyeglasses, which *have* to be customized, used to be produced in central factories that batched orders from hundreds of optometrists. Today, Lenscrafters, Eyelab, Eyeworks, and a host of other operations mass-customize eyeglasses in an hour.

This same principle has been applied to a number of service industries. Photograph developing, shoe repair, printing and copying, dry cleaning—all used to provide centralized, standardized, mass-produced services that took a few days to a few weeks or more. Today, by moving the entire process to retail outlets, these inherently individualized services can be accomplished in a few minutes to an hour or two at locations convenient to most consumers.

When the delivery time of the product or service extends much beyond an hour, during which customers can shop or run other errands, it can no longer be classified as point-of-sale customization, since sale and delivery generally become two transactions. While it is no longer instant in nature, point-of-delivery customization has the advantage of moving production even closer to the customer—right to the home. For example, Englert, Inc., of Wallingford, Connecticut, markets a machine that mass-customizes gutters as they are about to be put on a house. In the back of a van, a coil of flat aluminum is run through the machine, which forms a continuous, seamless gutter and then cuts it to exact specifications. This process is actually cheaper than the mass production of gutters and results in a higher-quality product, as gutters cut to the required length have no seams to leak. Englert sells a similar machine for custom-fit, commercial metal roofs.

One tire "retailer" (the word is in quotes because the operation has no storefront, only a toll-free number) will match the price of any other retailer, then bring its truck and installation service right to your car. OnSite AutoCare of Fairfield, Connecticut, changes oil, performs lube jobs, and provides other automobile services at your office with its "garage on wheels." Pizzas are no longer just delivered to your home; Domino's is experimenting with producing them *on the way* to your home. And it will soon gain economies of scale in order processing through a national toll-free number that automatically routes the order to the closest location, anywhere in the United States.[16] Kentucky Fried Chicken, Taco Bell, Dairy Queen, and a number of other fast-food organizations have created mobile outlets to service customers wherever they may be.[17]

Mobile production can apply to strictly service firms as well. One company particularly adept at this activity is Progressive Corporation of Cleveland, Ohio.[18] Progressive Insurance practices pinpoint marketing, focusing on individuals in what the industry calls its "nonstandard pool"—people whose policies were canceled or rejected, generally because of prior accidents combined with "poor" demographics. By keeping exhaustive records on customers and studying their demographics in great detail, Progressive is able to locate those individuals in the nonstandard pool who do not in fact have much higher risks of accidents than the standard pool.[19] For example, while owning a motorcycle is by itself almost enough to place someone in the nonstandard pool, Progressive knows that middle-aged motorcyclists with young children do not have worse-than-average accident records.

For all its customers, Progressive mass-customizes more than fourteen thousand separately priced policies to meet most insurance needs. But more than that, it has transformed the nature of claims processing by moving it to the site of accidents. Traditionally, processing an insurance claim has been a back-office, batch-oriented service that can take weeks. Realizing that customers were dissatisfied with the length of time it took and that settlement costs went down with the time, Progressive, in 1988, began operating twenty-four hours a day, seven days a week.[20] In 1989, it implemented a new claims system, dubbed Pacman for Progressive Automated Claims Management, which relied on a work station–based expert system. By 1990, 90 percent of all customers were contacted within twenty-four hours, and 31 percent of the claims were settled in seven days or less.

In 1991, Progressive completed its progression by taking claims settlement to the customer:

Adjusters are issued vans with PCs and modems, fax machines, and cellular telephones, all linked to a central dispatch unit and the Pacman system. When an accident occurs, the policyholder calls a 24-hour claims number and is connected with an operator who attempts to establish an appointment within the next two hours with one of the roving adjuster vans. The adjuster drives to the location most convenient to the customer (accident site, repair garage, office, home, etc.) and processes the paperwork which has been faxed or modemed to the van. In addition to taking claims information and issuing payment, adjusters also make tow truck, hotel, or other arrangements for stranded policyholders. The claim is processed in the field, and in most cases, the policyholder has a check within three hours.[21]

Providing on-the-spot, customized claims settlement has proved even cheaper for Progressive than the old centralized batch method. That is part of the power of Mass Customization.

As these examples show, moving production, or at least the final step of it, to the customer is a fast-growing technique for mass customization. These guidelines will help in pursuing this course:

- This method is most appropriate for products and services that have one inherently individual characteristic on an otherwise relatively standard commodity. Then, the standard portion can be produced centrally and the customized characteristic can be produced at the point of delivery (and if it is quick, at the point of sale).
- Generally, it is easier to move the production of process- or service-oriented characteristics to the customer than to move discrete manufacturing steps.
- Moving the entire production process to the point of delivery can transform a business and its profit potential, but, as seen in Fig-

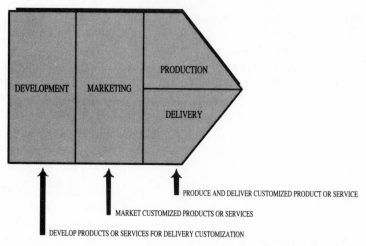

Figure 8-5 Changes in the Value Chain to Move All Production to the Customer

ure 8-5, it affects the entire organization. Production and delivery have to be integrated, and development must consider that its new products or services will be customized at the point of delivery. This requires significant innovation and often some invention. Focus on miniaturizing, processing lot sizes of one, eliminating all non-value-added time, and applying information technology to speed the response and make individualization economical.

- Almost universally, companies that practice point-of-delivery product customization maintain high inventories of raw materials and/or the standardized portion of their products. (Services have an inherent advantage here: customers usually supply the raw materials themselves.) There are still gains to be made in lowering costs and improving quality by having the inputs to the localized production process delivered just-in-time.

- Another way to gain economies of scale is to centralize an aspect of the product or service where that makes sense, such as the toll-free national order processing of Domino's and the mobile tire installer. This is the flip side of customizing around standard services—standardizing around custom services—and it can be very effective.

Provide Quick Response Throughout the Value Chain

Providing quick, even instant, response to customer desires is an even better way to push an entire organization onto the path of Mass Customization. Committing the delivery function to rapidly meeting customer requests starts a chain reaction that flows from the point of delivery back through the distribution and marketing processes, the production process, and finally to the development process. As illustrated in Figure 8-6, each point along the flow must drastically alter itself, reducing cycle times and increasing variety, to provide whatever customers want when they want it. Each process must eventually come to embrace Mass Customization.

Greatly reducing time throughout a firm's value chain has become known as time-based competition. Its power and benefits have been expounded over the past few years by consultants, academics, and practitioners, most notably and most well by Tom Peters, George Stalk, and Philip Thomas.[22] What is now clear is that time-based strategy does not stand alone, but rather merges into the new frontier

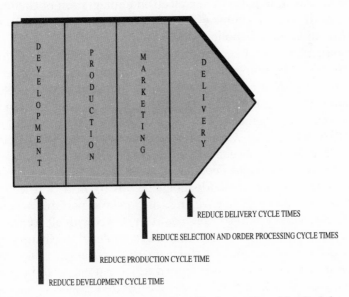

Figure 8-6   Changes in the Value Chain to Provide Quick Response

of Mass Customization. Reducing time throughout the value chain goes hand in hand with market fragmentation, proliferating variety, and individual customization. To some degree, it does not matter where in the value chain time reduction begins. If success in one part of the process is supported and followed through by the rest, it will begin to move the organization away from the Mass Production mode of operation and toward Mass Customization.

There is one exception. Providing instant response is one of the primary motivations behind Personics's in-store cassette system, Minitel, ATMs, and many of the other technology-based products and services discussed so far. However, it is the technology or infrastructure that provides the response. Once developed and installed, it does not drive other functions. When real people and a variety of products are involved in the delivery, instant response forces the rest of the organization to support that delivery by changing the nature of what everyone does. Hertz's #1 Club Gold service cannot be accomplished if the many people responsible for delivering customers to the Gold area, readying cars for service, and providing service contracts are not integrated into a single customer-focused value chain of processes. Similarly, Progressive's mobile claims-processing service would be impossible without the electronic integration of the on-site field agent, the central claims office, and the independent sales agents who write and hold the policies.

The Peerless Saw Company provides a good example of a time-based strategy beginning in manufacturing and development.[23] To reduce the time from customer order to delivery, Peerless developed a computer-driven laser system for cutting saws. In combination with other process improvements, this led to delivery time dropping from fourteen weeks to three. Once this improvement was made, Peerless found that customers began experimenting with the design of the blades because they could get them developed and manufactured so quickly. The company took advantage of this by next drastically reducing the order cycle. It gave the sales people portable terminals tied in to its main system so they could sit down with customers and together design a new saw. Once that was completed, the manufacturing process was initiated directly from the customer's shop. What began in Peerless's factory soon spread to its marketing and distribution processes. The end result: mass-customized saws.

It seems as if the entire apparel industry in the United States is moving to provide quick response to customers through the multicompany value chain of retailers, apparel manufacturers, textile mills, and fiber producers. In fact, in 1985, the Crafted with Pride in the U.S.A. Council proposed tying all the various operations together to provide the flexibility to respond quickly to changing customer wants and needs. The proposal was named Quick Response.

The vision of Quick Response is to have "the right product at the right place at the right time at the right price"—yet another variation on the dimensions of who, what, where, when, why, and how. Before Quick Response began to take hold, new styles took from fifty-six to sixty-six weeks to reach retail customers through the traditional value chain network, with value-added time a mere 6 to 17 percent.[24] In an industry more fashion conscious than any other, producers could not respond to changing markets in less than a year. Replenishment of existing designs took twenty-five weeks, so responding to unexpectedly "hot" items was also difficult. The industry's lack of response resulted in an estimated $25 billion loss every year in forced markdowns and lost sales.[25] But that is not what drove the industry to change: it was low-priced foreign competition that created market turbulence, especially for the textile manufacturers. The industry clamored for the usual protection measures from Congress, but did not rest with that. Through the Crafted with Pride in the U.S.A. Council, it did something about the situation itself. The industry began taking time out of the value chain and putting variety into it.

Led by The Limited and Levi Strauss at the retail and apparel manufacturing levels, and Milliken and Du Pont at the textile and fiber manufacturing levels, firms throughout the industry are reengineering their processes and applying information and telecommunications technologies to accelerate time. Each organization along the value chain is linking together through these technologies so that the entire chain knows what is selling at the retail level, and therefore what to produce and distribute at each preceding level in the chain.

Major progress has already been accomplished in the replenishment cycle: reordering, producing, distributing, and restocking of existing styles. The industry has reduced the time from twenty-five weeks toward six weeks, with a stated "ideal" of two weeks.[26] (The true ideal should, of course, be the just-in-time, instantaneous delivery of apparel goods.) At twenty-five weeks, retailers can do nothing but purchase what they believe will sell for the season and hope for the best. What does not sell at normal prices must be heavily discounted; what sells out signifies the lost opportunity of additional sales. At six weeks, and especially at two, retailers can order much smaller amounts of many more styles, then reorder what customers really want most. The gains of Quick Response can be seen in the following implementation for women's slacks that Milliken participated in:

In this program we were tracking 18,000 pairs of slacks in 225 stores. We looked at the sales after the first four weeks of sales. It is very important to look at sales early because if you wait until the end of the program, what happens? Everything you bought was sold, perhaps as a markdown, but sold nevertheless. You've got to look at the data, for both color and size, while there is a full offering in the store. In the slacks program, we saw early on that size 10 had far too much inventory and was headed for serious markdowns. On the other hand, a lot of sales were going to be lost in size 16. In the same program, a color analysis revealed problems with charcoal. Before the program started buyers wanted to drop the color because sales were forecasted very low, at only 4 to 5 percent of sales. In addition, charcoal was the most expensive color, and the retailers wanted to have fewer colors in the line. After the first four weeks, we found to our surprise that charcoal was the third highest selling color. With quick response we were able to get the goods dyed and back on the selling floor quicker in the right colors and sizes. These are not difficult analyses. But few people have the short-cycle manufacturing and information interchange to do it.[27]

Fast replenishment of this sort leads to better fulfillment of customers' desires, as retailers need stock fewer items of each type, and therefore can stock more variety in the same shelf space. Italian producer Benetton is probably the consistent world leader in this area. Through an information linkage to independent retail shops, its sales agents, its supplier network, and international customs, through short-cycle, networked production techniques that the company calls "supplier symbiosis," and through the ability to dye products after their manufacture,[28] Benetton is consistently able to replenish stock in any country—centrally from Italy—in less than one week.

Many American companies are also world leaders in Quick Response. Levi Strauss has lowered its replenishment cycle to four days for the KG menswear chain through its LeviLink system, providing both companies with a significant competitive advantage.[29] Haggar Apparel Co. has increased its overall sales 25 to 30 percent through quick replenishment of only half the volume it ships.[30] And Chalk Line Inc. allows its retailers to market its entire selection of athletic jackets without having to carry much inventory by replenishing any item in four days. During championship playoffs, Chalk Line also uses "blank stock," jackets in generic team colors—comparable to Benetton's gray sweater stock—to allow stores to order jackets of "whatever team wins the title"; these are completed, shipped, and delivered within twelve to twenty-four hours of a game's end.[31]

Beyond the replenishment cycle, gains are also being made in the cycle from design to initial delivery. Here, The Limited and its manufacturing arm, Mast Industries, lead the way. According to Tom Peters, by re-engineering its processes and using advanced technologies like high-resolution computer-aided design systems and satellite links between all of the players, "Mast Industries shoots for a turnaround time of 1,000 hours [42 days] between recognizing a new style and delivering the merchandise to the stores."[32] The competitive advantage of providing new designs that satisfy customers' wants and needs is far greater than that of replenishing existing stock. But by decreasing time first in the replenishment cycle, the additional advantages of paring time from the design cycle become clearer, more desirable, and more doable. With these improvements, proliferating the variety available to customers becomes easier, more effective, and even cheaper than the old ways of mass production. Fast development, manufacturing, and distribution cycles allow companies like Benetton and The Limited to refresh their styles constantly to match their consumers' wants at any given time.

The next step is full mass customization, the low-cost production of individually customized apparel. With the exception of mass-customized T-shirts, few companies are able to do this today. One that can is Custom Cut Technologies of Cleveland, Ohio, which mass-customizes men's suits. Retailers tied into CCT's systems can use proprietary potentiometer technology to measure each individual. The measurements are sent electronically to the operation in Cleveland, where CAD software pulls up the pattern from a database and dynamically changes it to fit the individual. A laser system cuts the pattern, and a traditional sewing shop produces the final garment. Elapsed time: three to four weeks. One competitor, Custom Vêtement Associates, the U.S. subsidiary of French apparel manufacturer Vestra, depends on traditional measurements with all their subjectivity, but has taken further time from the manufacturing process. Saks Fifth Avenue and other retailers are linked with Vestra's manufacturing operation in Strasbourg through the Minitel system. As *Business Week* describes the process:

Tailors take key measurements from customers and plug them into a terminal. Every night the data are sent to a central computer in New York and beamed via satellite to France. In the morning, after nine inspectors look at different pieces of data, a computer-controlled laser cutter selects the appropriate material and cuts the garment. A staff of tailors does the finishing touches, and the suit is shipped within four days.[33]

Because of the popularity of time-based competition and its obvious strategic advantages, much has been written about it and many more examples could be cited. It is a great way to begin the shift to Mass Customization, for it focuses an organization on meeting the needs of customers as quickly as possible, which allows for more variety to be produced at lower costs. And it can begin anywhere in the value chain, pulling or pushing the rest of the chain as need be to go along with it.

The absolute key to success with this method is the personal and electronic integration of the value chain through instant communication linkages, common databases, and multifunctional and cross-organizational teams. Whether across many companies or across different functions of the same company, each link in the chain must know not only what is desired by the next link but what the real demand, the real wants and needs of real customers, are at the end of the chain. Without timely data that accurately reflect exactly what is happening at the final (retail) link, organizations at the beginning of the chain will get "whipsawed" by the changes, amplifications, detractions, and other miscommunications that can result as link after link interprets what the previous link says about what it thinks it knows.[34]

Note that in the system of Mass Production, customers are at the *end* of the value chain. They are sold whatever the production function produces. In the system of Mass Customization, customers are also at the *beginning* of the value chain, which exists to produce what customers want and value more highly than the money they are asked to give in exchange. In effect, the chain really bends around to become a loop, with customers an integral part of it, creating what futurist Alvin Toffler has labeled the rebirth of the "prosumer," producer and consumer in concert defining and producing the product, a common occurrence with Craft Production prior to the Industrial Revolution.[35] This specific feedback loop within a value chain, like the general feedback loop of Mass Customization described in Chapter 3, encourages more customer interaction and information, faster cycle

times, and greater variety and customization. The primary engine of
the customer-integrated value chain is faster cycle times. Further, as
cycle times decrease, the number of opportunities everyone has for
learning how to work better and how to serve the customer better
increases. This results in much greater organizational learning and in
the continual improvement so necessary in today's turbulent world.[36]

The following tactics have proven useful to a variety of organizations in implementing a strategy of providing quick response throughout the value chain:

- Companies can start by simply doing more faster with fewer
  people. However, care must be taken to not introduce mistakes
  and lower quality while reducing time. For true transformation,
  work processes must be redesigned from scratch, eliminating all
  waste and all non-value-added time to concentrate on the value-
  added activities required to satisfy individual customers.
- In redesigning processes from scratch, do not start with a blank
  slate. Like Motorola with its Bandit pager line, benchmark within
  your organization and against other companies exceptionally
  good at the processes you want to improve. Use available tools
  and techniques; the objective is to *redesign*, not *reinvent*.
- Provide those performing the value-added work—especially
  those closest to the customers—with all of the information and
  authority necessary to make decisions. Eliminate the succession
  of approvals and the constant communication up and down the
  layers of management that slow organizations. While you're at
  it, eliminate the layers.
- Create within and outside your organization partnerships focused
  on fulfilling the requirements of individual customers. Eliminate
  both the "functional silos" within your organization and the
  "company silos" between suppliers and distributors. Providing
  quick response is not a zero sum game, with some companies in
  a value chain winners and others losers; the entire chain should
  profit from the gains of each link.
- You get more of what you measure. So measure time: development cycle time, production cycle time, distribution cycle time,
  percentage of time spent in value-added activities, customer response time, percentage of sales from products and services less
  than a year old, and so on. However, always ensure that any
  new measurement does not have negative consequences. Before
  implementing it, carefully think through all the ways that people

could improve it, for some of them may be detrimental to the organization in the long term.

These actions will not only create a time-based competitive advantage, but will help create an organization that gains even greater advantage through Mass Customization.

Modularize Components to Customize End Products and Services

The best method for achieving mass customization—minimizing costs while maximizing individual customization—is by creating modular components that can be configured into a wide variety of end products and services. Economies of scale are gained through the components rather than the products; economies of scope are gained by using the modular components over and over in different products; and customization is gained by the myriad of products that can be configured. Essentially, this is taking the interchangeable parts innovation of the American System of Manufacturing to a new level: modular, interchangeable parts *across* products and services. As depicted in Figure 8-7, this involves the entire organization in meeting customers' individual wants and needs.

Bally Engineered Structures provides one of the best examples. Bally can *create* an almost infinite variety of structures—walk-in coolers, refrigerated warehouses, environmental rooms, and so forth—but the company *produces* only one basic modular component, the pre-engineered panel. Economies of scale are achieved by the single process that creates a panel by foaming urethane between two metal skins. That same process easily produces seven kinds of panels (side, corner, ceiling, and so forth) in a number of different lengths and widths that can then be customized by options, attachments, finishes, and most important, by how they are designed to be configured into the end structure.

Less than thirty miles from Bally, in Coopersburg, Pennsylvania, Lutron Electronics Company designs and manufactures lighting controls (switches, dimmers, and systems to control sets of lights) for residential and office environments through modularity. Far and away the market share leader in lighting controls, Lutron provides over eleven thousand different controls across more than a dozen different

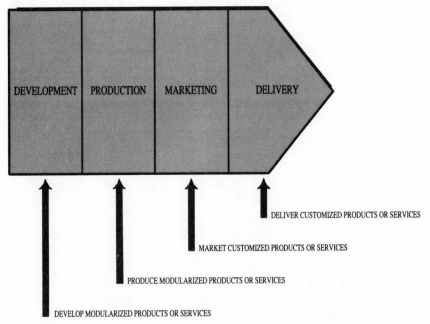

Figure 8-7   Changes in the Value Chain to Modularize
Components

product lines. Over 95 percent of its products have annual shipments
of fewer than one hundred units. In its electronic lighting systems
line, Lutron has never shipped the same system twice. Each and every
system is customized to individual specifications, but mass-produced
on a single assembly line from standard components. Through "specials" that can range from custom-matching a paint sample (should a
customer want something other than the fourteen colors Lutron provides) to integrating a lighting system with a separate security system,
Lutron provides further customizing services that tailor its products.

Lutron hires only top-notch engineers and gives them extensive
training. They spend a great amount of time with individual customers, making sure the customers get exactly the product that suits
them. Lutron personnel have been known to spend so much application engineering time with a customer that they virtually eliminate
all their profit on one sale. But from that they gain not only a de-

lighted customer but also new ideas on how to extend their products with new variety.

Lutron engineers typically design a new product line that, at first, offers only a few options. Then, by working with individual customers to discover their needs, they extend the line with product after product. Eventually, Lutron may have, say, a hundred models available for purchase. Then engineering and production together "rationalize" the product line down to fifteen to twenty standardized modular components that can be configured into the same one hundred models that customers can purchase. As Joel Spira, Lutron's chairman, describes this cyclical process, "Chaos increases new business. Order increases profits."

Although it never customizes to individuals, Black & Decker provides an excellent example of how component standardization can yield lower costs and greater variety. In the early 1970s, the company decided to redesign its line of power tools to incorporate a key safety feature. According to Alvin P. Lehnerd, former vice president for advanced technology, new business, and new ventures at Black & Decker, the company's goals were ambitious:

Develop a "family" look, simplify the product offering, reduce manufacturing costs, automate manufacturing, standardize components, incorporate new materials, improve performance, incorporate new product features, and provide for worldwide product specifications.[37]

As a direct result of simplifying, automating, and especially standardizing, Black & Decker found that it could produce an entire line of 122 basic tools—jigsaws, trimmers, circular saws, grinders, polishers, sanders, and so forth—with hundreds of variations from a relatively small set of standardized components. For example, every power tool used the same line of motors, which varied only in their wattage (from 60 to 650) and corresponding length (from 0.8" to 1.75"). Black & Decker's costs plummeted while its variety increased, creating enough turbulence for the rest of the consumer market that a number of manufacturers soon left the business.

The power of this technique of mass customization is not limited to manufacturing processes, as Lehnerd relates:

As new product concepts emerged, much of the work in design and tooling was eliminated because of the standardization of motors, bearings, switches, gears, cord sets, and fasteners. Design and tooling engineers working on a new product had only to concern themselves with the "business end" of the product and to perfect its intended function. New designs could be developed using components already standardized for manufacturability. The product did not have to start with a blank sheet of paper and be designed from scratch.[38]

Customization through the standardization of components not only increases variety while reducing costs in manufacturing, it also allows product development to produce new designs and proliferate even greater variety much more quickly. Unfortunately for Black & Decker, it lost its focus on each aspect during the 1980s. Its worldwide component variety skyrocketed—the number of motors, the highest-cost component, hit 100—without a concurrent increase in power tool variety. Finally, in the late 1980s, new CEO Nolan Archibald laid out a clear vision for the corporation and oversaw another complete redesign that, among other things, regained the focus on product variety through component modularity.[39] Black & Decker would be wise not to lose this focus and to push on toward individual customization, as its competitors are doing. Cooper Industries redesigned its own power drills to provide modular handles in different sizes to fit different-size hands, and Ingersoll-Rand has brought out a new line of tools whose handle angle automatically adjusts to fit not only each user's hand but how he uses the tool in practice.[40]

Bally, Lutron, and Black & Decker all represent discrete manufacturing, in which the concept of "component" is strongest. However, this method applies as well to process industries. Paints, for example, were historically mass-produced through batch process operations in centralized factories. However, paint stores have been providing mass-customized paints for many years by simply mixing standardized paints according to a formula provided by the manufacturer. Note that this combines the method of component modularity with moving the final production step out to the customer. Benjamin Moore, Sherwin-Williams, Home Depot, and a host of other retailers also provide the service of mixing exactly the right paint to match any customer sample by using a computer that measures the light frequencies of the sample.

Toyo Engineering Corp. created the MILOX pipeless plant system to enable companies to mass-customize specialty chemicals.[41] Toyo modularized the process into a few components: two mobile, robotic reactor units that move between charging stations, reaction

agitation stations, discharge stations, and cleaning stations that can
be arranged in any combination. A computer is given the chemical
recipe for a specific batch, then controls the movement of the robotic
reactors to the appropriate stations to create that batch. The modules
can be reused for a virtually limitless number of low-volume and
low-cost specialty chemicals.[42]

The modular component method also applies to service industries. Vacation tours are standardized: you can select from among
several predefined packages for your location of choice, and that's it.
However, TWA Getaway Vacations, Inc., of Mount Kisco, New
York, provides customized tours at the prices of standard vacation
packages (and sometimes better). According to David Thomas, vice
president, "There are very few niches left in this business. Mass-
customizing the tours is one of the few places left to build competitive
advantage." To accomplish it, Getaway Vacations purchases the various components of tours—airline seats, hotel rooms, buses, and entertainment options—in bulk, which provides economies of scale. Then
customers and agents personally design the tour package that meets
their needs. Getaway Vacations' information system mixes and
matches components and provides prices within six minutes.[43]

As these examples spanning discrete manufacturing, process, and
service industries show, there are many ways to take advantage of
modularized components that can be mixed and matched into customizable end products. The work of Karl Ulrich, professor of management at MIT, on discrete product modularity provides the basis
for a typology that can be extended to provide suggestions for mass-
customizing your own products and services.[44] Figure 8-8 provides
iconic illustrations of each of the six different kinds of modularity,
which are all discussed below with concrete examples of firms using
them to mass-customize products and services. The typology progresses from simple forms of modularity that allow great variety without really changing the nature of what is being sold, to those which
allow individual customization and fundamentally change the structure of the product or service for each customer.

Component-Sharing Modularity

In component-sharing modularity, the same component is used across
multiple products to provide economies of scope. This form of modularity is most important in putting the "mass" back into a proliferating

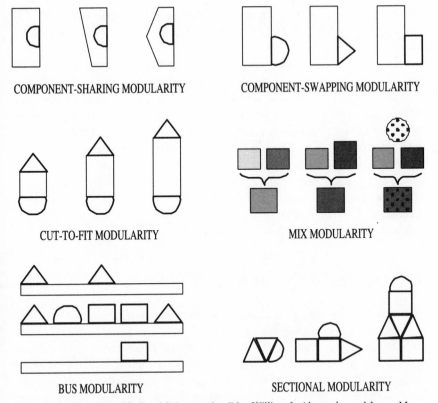

COMPONENT-SHARING MODULARITY

COMPONENT-SWAPPING MODULARITY

CUT-TO-FIT MODULARITY

MIX MODULARITY

BUS MODULARITY

SECTIONAL MODULARITY

Source: From "Patterns of Industrial Automation," by William J. Abernathy and James M. Utterback. Reprinted with permission from Technology Review, copyright 1978.

Figure 8-8   Six Types of Modularity for the Mass Customization of Products and Services

product line whose costs are rising as fast as, if not faster than, the number of products. Black & Decker illustrates this well. It completely redesigned its power tool product lines—twice—to take advantage of component-sharing modularity to greatly reduce costs while providing *more* variety and *speedier* product development.

This kind of modularity never results in true individual customization (except in combination with other types), but allows the low-cost production of a great variety of products and services. Component-sharing modularity is best used to reduce the number of parts and thereby the costs of an existing product line that already has high variety.[45] General Electric drastically reduced costs and time-to-delivery by redesigning its circuit breaker boxes to replace 28,000 unique parts with 1,275 components shared across 40,000 different box designs.[46]

Once a product line has been redesigned, even greater variety can be created without any corresponding increase in costs. Heavy equipment maker Komatsu found its costs increasing with its product variety throughout the 1970s as it began exporting to different markets around the world. To lower its costs while remaining responsive to the varied wants and needs of local markets, Komatsu standardized a core module that could be shared across all of its major products and created a number of components that could be shared across the different product models created for different local markets. This then allowed the company to move easily into new markets and provide further local customization.[47]

Component-Swapping Modularity

This method is the complement of component-sharing modularity. Here, different components are paired with the same basic product, creating as many products as there are components to swap. In many cases, the distinction between component sharing and component swapping is a matter of degree. Consider Swatch watches: Are the basic watch elements a component shared across all the fashion products (component sharing)? Or are the watch parts the basic product and the incredible variety of face styles the components (component swapping)?

A trivial case of component swapping is the form letter. Hyatt Legal Services performs sophisticated component swapping with standardized legal documents as the basic product and customizing services as the components. Create-A-Book®, a line of children's books personalized to individual boys and girls, provides another, not dissimilar example. Over a dozen professionally written and illustrated generic titles provide the basic products for this company. The buyer of a particular book, usually a relative, is asked personal questions about the recipient (such as name, mother's name, place of birth, and so on), which provide the components to swap into the basic product. A personal computer sprinkles the information appropriately throughout the text, and within fifteen minutes the pages of the book are printed on a laser printer and bound into a normal book cover. For $13.95, a price similar to that for quality titles available in retail stores, children receive their own customized book.

Customizing services around standardized products (or services), visited earlier, can also be thought of as component-swapping modularity. The standard set provides the basic product, and the customizing services are the components swapped in and attached to it. Most point-of-delivery customization is also component swapping. The basic product—for example, bowling ball, T-shirt, eyeglass frame—is produced centrally, while the customizing component—drilled holes, heat-applied transfer, lenses—is added locally. With photograph developing, shoe repair, dry cleaning, and other point-of-sale service examples, the standard service itself is the basic product, and customers supply their own components to be placed into that service.

For a company providing a standardized product or service today, the key to taking advantage of component-swapping modularity is to find the most customizable part of the product or service and separate it into a component that can easily be reintegrated. For greatest effectiveness, the separated component should have three characteristics: (1) it should provide high value to the customer; (2) once separated, it should be easily and seamlessly reintegrated; and (3) it should have great variety to meet differing customer needs and wants. True individual customization comes when there are an infinite number of components to be swapped, or as with Create-a-Book, at least as many as there are people to buy the product or service. Variety so great that customers are unlikely to run across anyone else with exactly the same product, like Swatch watches, is pretty good, too.

Cut-to-Fit Modularity

This technique is similar to the previous two types, except that in cut-to-fit modularity one or more of the components is continually variable within preset or practical limits. Custom Cut Technologies' process for mass-customizing suits clearly cuts to fit each of its components (jacket body, sleeves, lapels, and so forth). Englert's gutter and metal-roofing machines cut the raw materials to the precise measure of a house. Peerless Saw can easily laser-cut to vary the dimensions of any saw. At self-service salad bars, customers can choose the portion they desire of each ingredient.

The National Bicycle Industrial Co., a subsidiary of Matsushita in Japan, provides individually customized bicycles through cut-to-fit and component-sharing modularity combined. Its factory, as *Fortune* relates, "is ready to produce any of 11,231,862 variations on 18 models of racing, road, and mountain bikes in 199 color patterns and about as many sizes as there are people."[48] The process starts with a shopkeeper who determines a customer's model, color, and design preferences, which define the sharable components to use, then precisely measures him or her on a special frame for the cut-to-fit components. All the specifications are faxed to the factory, where a computer creates custom blueprints for both craftsmen and robots. The latter measure and cut each piece of the frame to fit the individual's measurements, weld the pieces together, and apply the base coat of paint. The skilled workers perform most of the assembly work and all of the final touches, including silk-screening the customer's name on the frame.

Cut-to-fit modularity is most useful for products whose customer value rests greatly on a component that can be continually varied to match individual wants and needs. If the current product line has components that step up discontinuously in size—such as off-the-rack suits and standard bicycles in two of the examples above—then competitive advantage can be gained by mass customizing the products to fit individuals, eliminating the compromises customers must otherwise make. This is the case with a large number of products, including beds, office chairs, and automobile seats, in which particular advantage can be gained by an organization's ability to cater economically to hard-to-fit individuals at the extremes who generally must not only compromise but sacrifice comfort and/or style to accept standard sizes.

All clothing meets the above description; cut-to-fit modularity should be the next big program in the apparel industry once Quick Response is firmly rooted. Companies like Custom Cut Technologies that are already practicing it should gain a distinct competitive advantage if they execute it well.

Mix Modularity

This type of modularity can use any of the above types, with the clear distinction that the components are so mixed together that they themselves become something different. When particular colors of paint are mixed together, for example, those components are no longer visible in the end product. Fertilizer is another commodity that has moved to mass customization. Today, fertilizer can be custom-blended for each hectare of a farm according to the type of soil, slope, amount of sun, and so forth. At least one manager in the business believes that companies will someday "customize the blend for each square meter, right as it is mixed into the earth."[49]

Mexican restaurants create an incredible variety of meals by mixing relatively few components: tortillas, beans, various meats, and various sauces. Cereal companies are mixing the same basic components to proliferate the number of breakfast cereals. Campbell's Soup varies the recipes of their soups by region of the country to cater to local tastes.

In fact, the key factor in determining if you can take advantage of mix modularity is *recipe*. Anything with a recipe can be varied for different markets, different locales, and indeed for different individuals. To reach perfect customization requires that you move from processing your recipe according to a predetermined plan to a process-to-order operation, and then economically reduce the batch size to one. Toyo Engineering's MILOX plant system comes close to this for specialty chemicals. Ideally, create a process that moves the last step out to the customer for instant, point-of-delivery customization.

Actually, that last step has already been substantially invented for many consumer products: it's called the vending machine. People can already choose various options for a cup of coffee, which the vending machine mixes. Why can't customers choose how spicy they want their instant soup, how much cinnamon to put in their cereal, how much syrup they want in their Pepsi? If Pepsi were to create a vending machine that allowed customers to vary the amount of syrup, additional flavorings (e.g., cherry, lemon, chocolate), sweetener, and caffeine according to their individual tastes, likes, and dislikes—and then charge according to the amounts of each—it not only would achieve full mass customization but would probably have a big winner on its hands. It might even be possible to add bottling capability along with personal laser-printed labels in about the same space as all of Pepsi's varieties take up in a supermarket!

Bus Modularity

This type of modularity uses a standard structure that can attach a number of different kinds of components. The term comes from computers and other electronic equipment that use a bus, or back-plane, that forms the primary pathway of information transfer between processing units, memory, disk drives, and other components that can plug into the bus. Track lighting, with different kinds of lights inserted anywhere in a track and automatically connected to an electrical circuit, is another common example.

Once you get much beyond these obvious examples, bus modularity is the most difficult type to comprehend because the bus is usually hidden and often somewhat abstract. Personics uses bus modularity: the standardized length of tape is the bus, onto which are placed any number of different kinds of songs. In services, ATMs, Minitel, TWA Getaway Vacations, and CNN all use this type of modularity: the infrastructure of each service is the bus, defining what services can and cannot plug into each one, but allowing a broad number of individually customized transactions (at least potentially, in the case of CNN). The key distinction of bus modularity is that a standardized structure allows variation in the type, number, and location of modules that can plug into it.[50]

The magazine *Farm Journal*, founded in 1877 to service farmers in the Philadelphia area, provides an interesting illustration. It went national in the early 1900s, but farming became more specialized over the years, and the magazine began producing regional versions in 1952. Beginning around 1980, it went further by customizing its fourteen issues a year. Each subscriber is asked to fill out a questionnaire about his or her particular farm (including questions about the crops or livestock raised, number of acres devoted to each crop and size of herd, and so forth), which is entered into an on-line database. Each subscriber then receives an editorial core of about fifty pages along with individualized articles—and advertising—based on the information in the database. Each month hundreds of different *Farm Journals* are sent to 800,000 subscribers, and sometimes the number of customized versions runs well into the thousands.[51]

The structure of the magazine and the process by which it is created provides the bus to which differing numbers of editorial pages, advertisements, and articles are attached for individual subscribers. The technology behind this capability is Selectronic Binding, a process developed by R. R. Donnelley & Sons of Chicago. Donnelley works with other magazines and catalogue makers, and has created similar technology for books, called Books on Demand[SM]. McGraw-Hill uses this technology—along with software jointly written with Eastman Kodak Co. that uses bus modularity in electronically building and sequencing books chapter by chapter—to mass-customize textbooks for individual college classes.[52]

The key to using bus modularity is of course the existence of a bus. If your product or service has a definite standard but changeable structure, think about breaking it up by, first, defining the product architecture or service infrastructure that is *really* required for each customer, and second, modularizing everything else into the components that can be plugged into that standard structure.

The automobile could take advantage of bus modularity. The basic platform chassis and wiring harness that connects all of the electronics can provide the bus structure; *everything else* can plug into it. GM's Pontiac Fiero, with a modularized body and other components, has come closest to this concept in actual production, and Chrysler has proposed a production concept consisting of twenty-eight modules.[53] Ford has also done work in this area. Nissan, however, appears to be the company that wants to first mass-customize individual automobiles. Its vision for car manufacture is "the five A's"—Any volume, Any time, Any body, Anywhere, and Anything.[54]

Nissan is working toward this vision through a joint university-industry research program in Japan known as Manufacturing 21. Participants in this program foresee full mass customization of automobiles in the first year of the twenty-first century utilizing not only all the different types of modularity discussed so far (bus, cut-to-fit, component-swapping, and component-sharing), but also time-compression, point-of-sale manufacturing, customizability, and every other technique discussed. An extended quote from a translation of the research report illuminates the breadth of Nissan's vision:

The most important objective is to create a system to produce low-volume, special-niche vehicles at reasonable cost. The great numbers of such models make it obvious that very fast, inexpensive new model development is necessary. . . . Reducing the time and cost of new model development and start-up is the number one priority of the Japanese auto industry heading into the 1990s. . . .

Many assembly ideas have been considered. All of the most promising ones assume final assembly of cars from large modules with each module being subassembled on a short line. . . .

Cars would have to be designed with structural modules that can be subassembled in different locations, then brought together for final assembly of the structure, followed by attachment of the body panels. The external shape of the completed body is thereby partly independent of the form of the structural framework. . . . If the design could ingeniously allow for dimensional variations, final assembly might even be done at the dealership. . . .

The success of the concept depends on cultivating the *automotive prosumer*. The prosumer participates in the design of his vehicle at a work station in the dealership. Using the car company's CAD/CAM software, the prosumer can first select a combination of body structures, drive train components, and suspension components that have been tested for safety and performance. The car company's system will permit selection of only safe, durable combinations of these modules. . . .

Many features of the car can be custom-designed, depending on how much the customer wants to pay, of course. The seat contour can be fitted to the customer, the car's lighting system designed as the customer likes, the instrument panel layout modified to suit personal preferences—again with safety checks. Within limits, prosumers can create the shape of body panels, design their own trim, and "imagineer" sound systems to their own tastes. The electronic possibilities may be particularly bountiful.

In ten years, some of the features may be commonly modified on the run. For example, the stiffness of suspension can be adjusted while the car is in operation.

The prosumer design system will check whether final designs are feasible. The production system is triggered as soon as the feasible order, with all the CAD/CAM data generated, is entered at the dealership. *The leadtime to delivery: Three days.*

To prosumers, the car company will sell the service of creating and maintaining modular-structure cars.[55]

There are few products more complex than automobiles, and few processes more complex than automobile manufacture. If automobiles can be mass-customized using bus modularity and all the other techniques—and there is little doubt they will be—most any product or service can also be mass-customized.

Sectional Modularity

The final type of modularity provides the greatest degree of variety and customization. Sectional modularity allows the configuration of any number of different types of components in arbitrary ways—as long as each component is connected to another at standard interfaces. The classic example is Lego building blocks with their locking-cylinder interfaces. The number of objects that can be built with Legos is limited only by the imagination.

With sectional modularity, the structure or architecture of the product itself can change, providing tremendous possibilities for variety and customization. Bally Engineered Structures once again provides a robust example; its modular panels are essentially highly sophisticated Lego blocks that can be interlocked to produce anything from a flower cooler to an eight-story refrigerated warehouse. Dow Jones News/Retrieval and most of the other customized information providers use sectional modularity. The individual information elements are components that can be organized in any order to create mass-customized newspapers, research reports, and so on.

Agfa Corporation of Wilmington, Massachusetts, has taken the mass customization of books, magazines, and other documents a step further with its Shared Document Management System (SDMS). This product goes far beyond the ability to select and organize articles or chapters into predefined formats. With SDMS, "document objects" can be any size and any type of information (text, tables, formulas, graphics, images, and eventually multimedia audio and video) that can be put together in any way desired by the user.

Agfa uses a relatively new technology in the computer industry known as object-oriented architecture.[56] This technology has the potential for revolutionizing software development—moving it from its traditional Craft Production orientation directly into the new frontier of Mass Customization—through the concept of reuse. In object-oriented systems, a piece of program code is a highly modular object, with the interfaces between modules simply and completely defined by the object type. Objects can be reused any number of times in any number of different programs, creating sectional modularity that allows the quick development of radically different applications. In practice, object-oriented technology has not progressed to the point where full applications can be developed completely from modules without creating any new code from scratch.

Many Japanese software organizations have taken a different route, following the trail of Japanese automakers by moving from Craft to Mass Production in the 1970s and 1980s and more recently to Mass Customization. Hitachi, Toshiba, NEC, Fujitsu, and other Japanese companies have created flexible production systems, known as software factories, where programmers focus on a particular kind of product and are provided with a strong tool structure to, among other things, reuse significant portions of program code through sectional modularity. According to Michael Cusumano of MIT, the Japanese are at the stage in software where they were in automobiles in the 1960s: their quality and productivity are much higher than that of the United States, their basic flexible production system is in place, but they have yet to generate the level of innovation and creativity to compete effectively with American companies.[57]

Sectional modularity is the most robust of the six types, but it is also the most difficult to achieve. The key is to develop an interface that allows sections or objects of different types to interlock. Few products can have mechanisms as simple as Legos, but the interfaces can be developed over time, usually by building upon those defined for component sharing and component swapping while modularizing more function into smaller components.

It may be much easier to provide sectional modularity in services. James Brian Quinn and Penny Paquette of Dartmouth, who have studied the use of technology in service industries extensively, have come to the following conclusion:

Contrary to much popular dogma, well-managed service technologies can simultaneously deliver both *lowest cost outputs* and *maximum personalization and customization* for customers. In accomplishing this, enterprises generally obtain strategic advantage not through traditional economies of scale, but through *focusing on the smallest activity or cost units* that can be efficiently measured and replicated—and then *cloning and mixing these units* across as wide a geographical and applications range as possible.[58]

In other words, many service companies achieve mass customization through the creation of low-level sectional modules—the authors call these components micro-units—that can be mixed "in a variety of combinations to match localized or individual customer needs." For example, American Express captures as micro-units each and every transaction—whether retail, lodging, entertainment, transportation, and so on—that its customers make with both its credit card and travel agency businesses, and then mixes and matches the customer patterns and company capabilities to add value for them. According to Quinn and Paquette:

[American Express] can identify lifestyle changes (like marriage or moving) or match forthcoming travel plans with its customers' specific buying habits to notify them of special promotions, product offerings, or services AmEx's retailers may be presenting in their local or planned travel areas. From its larger information base AmEx can also provide more detailed information services to its two million retailer customers—like demographic and comparative analyses of their customer bases or individual customers' needs for wheelchair, pickup, or other convenience services. These can provide unique value for both consumer and retailer customers.

The key to micro-management is breaking down both operations and markets into such detail that—by properly cross-matrixing the data—one can discern how a very slight change in one arena may affect some aspect of the other. The ability to micro-manage, target, and customize operations in this fashion, because of the knowledge base that size permits, is becoming one of the most important uses of scale in services.[59]

One of the interesting but little-used facets of sectional and, to a lesser extent, bus modularity is that products can become reconfigurable. Legos, of course, can be rapidly reconfigured into something completely different. Agfa's Shared Document Management System allows any document to be reconfigured by "sliding" in and out different modules, from whole chapters to sentence fragments (although at least an entire page would have to be reproduced). Upgradability and reconfigurability have long been provided by mainframe and minicomputer providers through bus modularity; it is now becoming important to personal computer owners, and in 1991, manufacturers began responding with bus modularity that makes it unnecessary for owners to throw away a model to gain significant enhancements. And Nissan has explored the concept of "the evolving car" that owners could bring in for the latest innovations or styling every few years.[60]

In both products and services, the ability to mass-customize through sectional modularity provides the most robust capabilities for Mass Customization.

Cautions in Implementing Mass Customization through Modularity

While the opportunities for using all six types of modularity are tremendous, as with any method there are potential drawbacks that may cause particular problems in some organizations. These need to be understood and effectively managed.

First, the performance of a product can always be optimized and its manufacturing costs lowered by reducing or eliminating modularity. This fact may be bothersome to many engineers. However, it is true only for a single product (or a close-knit product family), or for a standard service experience process. Mass customization through modularity, with its dual focus on low costs and variety/customization, will yield better performance and lower costs whenever the task is to create a number of similar but clearly differentiated products or services. The greater the number of products, and particularly as that number approaches the number of individual customers, the greater the cost and performance advantage of modularity.

Second, customers may perceive some sets of modularized products as being overly similar. In the 1970s, General Motors was heavily criticized for sharing too many components among models, making them look too much alike. It is important that design take into account what customers find most personal about a product or service—like body styling in a car—and ensure that those areas retain the most variability, preferably obtaining individual customization. Today, American automakers provide many more "peripheral" options than their Japanese competitors, but still share basic styling across makes of cars, something that Toyota, Nissan, Honda, and the other Japanese producers almost never do. The latter concentrate their variety on what is most individual about the car, and therefore proliferate body styles and models.[61] While they share fewer components than their American counterparts, Japanese automakers are moving toward completely modular and mass-customized cars through activities like Manufacturing 21.

Third, competitors can reverse-engineer modular designs more easily than unique designs. As Ulrich notes, "The same properties that make a design easy to reuse by the original manufacturer make the design easy to copy by competitors."[62] Anyone can copy the design of Legos and make Lego-compatible building blocks (Tyco Toys Inc. did that). Further, and finally, while the availability of "off-the-shelf" solutions can hasten product and service development, it can also lead to less innovative solutions over time than if the development process had encompassed greater scope.[63]

The answer to both of these is that sustained competitive advantage comes not from the creation of a mass-customized product or service; it comes from providing the most value for each individual customer throughout the value chain and continually through time. In a turbulent world, one can never rest on present, much less past, achievements. No matter what technique of mass customization is used, sustained advantage comes through constant innovation and increasing value creation, and from investment in not just technology but in the people in development, production, marketing, and delivery whose experience and flexibility cannot so easily be copied, and who can continue to innovate mass-customized products and services over time.

CHAPTER 9

Transforming the Organization
for Mass Customization

ORGANIZATIONAL forms suitable for Mass Production are decidedly unsuitable for Mass Customization. When a company enters the new frontier and begins mass-customizing its products and services, its organization begins to change. When a company gains experience and success, particularly as it progresses through the methods of mass customization—each involving another functional unit until the entire company is doing its part—then the organization begins to transform itself into something potentially very different.

Organizations suited to Mass Production are characterized by stilted hierarchies with deep functional separations, rigidly specialized resources (both workers and technology), and the separation of thinking and doing. On the other hand, organizations suited to Mass Customization, depicted in Figure 9-1 as the culmination of all the organizational effects discussed in Chapter 8,[1] are characterized by integrated functions with dynamic boundaries (in practice if not on paper), flexibly specialized resources (both workers and technology), and the integration of thinking and doing. To be successful at Mass Customization requires an integrated organization in which every function, unit, and person is focused on the individual customer, all have eliminated waste and in particular reduced cycle times, and each does whatever is necessary to develop, produce, market, and deliver low-cost, customized products or services. All functions reach out to

213

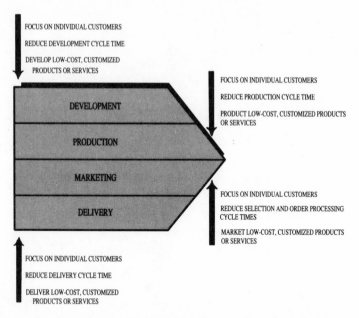

Figure 9-1   Culmination of Changes in an Organization to Mass-Customize Products and Services

customers, with different levels of interaction with each customer and with each other depending on the needs of the particular market opportunity.

Transforming an organization in such a way requires the focus of top management above and beyond what is placed on the task of figuring out how to mass-customize products and services. To be successful in an increasingly turbulent world, management must concentrate not only on *what* the organization must do but even more important on *how* the organization can accomplish its goals. Transformation begins with the outputs of the organization, but advances through the processes by which it accomplishes its work.

The Increasing Importance of Process Capabilities

In the system of Mass Customization, product life cycles diminish, new products and services are quickly developed, variety is constantly proliferated, and customization occurs with each sale. In this environment, the very notion of "product" becomes increasingly vague. Is "the product" the flow of invention and innovations that together make up a life cycle? Is "the product" the standardized set of functions leaving the plant floor, with anything that happens in marketing or distribution just variations on a theme? Is "the product" the functional components that can be proliferated or individually customized? Or is "the product" the bundle of products and services purchased by any particular customer at any particular time?

Within the system of Mass Production, a basic tenet has long been the simultaneous development of product and process. Processes suitable for products in one stage of the life cycle do not apply to products in another stage.[2] Further, the focus on operational efficiency in production demands that a new process be created—or an old one heavily modified—for each new product, so that its variable costs are as low as absolutely possible.

In Mass Customization, all of this changes. The importance of any individual product decreases because there are so many of them.[3] Processes become decoupled from products and now outlast individual products—some of which are developed and sold only once—and can outlast entire product life cycles.[4] Indeed, it is the *process life cycle* that has become more important, reflected in the tremendous movement in American businesses to redesign or re-engineer processes and benchmark them against the best practices in the world. Process capabilities cut across not only products but organizations and companies as well.

Therefore, the way to transform organizations and the products and services they produce is to acknowledge the increasing importance of process capabilities and transform those processes for today's turbulent environment.

Dynamic Stability

Market turbulence demands that organizations have what professors Andrew Boynton and Bart Victor call *dynamic stability:*

Firms faced with rapid, unpredictable market change are creating stable, long-term, yet flexible process capabilities that both decrease product time to market and increase product customization in a cost-efficient manner. These firms . . . are managing these contradictory requirements by becoming "dynamically stable" organizations—firms designed to serve the widest range of customers and changing product demands ("dynamic") while building on existing process capabilities, experience, and knowledge ("stability").[5]

To develop, produce, market, and deliver mass-customized products and services with decreasing product life cycles and diminishing sales per individual product, Boynton and Victor's research has found, companies are investing in general-purpose processes that are more flexible, more responsive, and more easily reused across products and product families. These have longer process life cycles relative to the products and services they create than with Mass Production, and can therefore provide a stable base for the dynamic flow of products and services.[6] This is not to say that these processes never change, but that once developed, process change is evolutionary and often developed for its *potential* applicability to a broad range of future products, rather than necessarily the result of producing any particular product (although of course that happens, too).

The typical Japanese company, like Toyota, has long invested in its process capabilities and incrementally developed them over time to eliminate waste, inventory, and time. It is then able to apply those stable processes over an increasing variety of new products, handling more products at *any one time* as well as more products *through* time than its typical American competitor. CNN's basic processes for gathering, analyzing, and disseminating news have changed little since its inception in 1980, yet the number of news stories processed and the number of outlets for those stories grow every year. Bally Engineered Structures' basic manufacturing processes have changed little since 1983, yet through incremental improvement in its administrative processes and investment in information technology Bally now delivers one-of-a-kind structures in less time and at lower costs. Boynton and Victor provide the example of Corning's fiber optics organization:

Corning, one of the world's largest manufacturers of fiber optics, continually faces demands for increased product customization and faster delivery. At the same time, competitive pressures demand that Corning produce an extremely cost-competitive product. To meet this dual challenge of matching increased customization with rapid product delivery and low-cost production, Corning is converting and expanding its process manufacturing capabilities from single-product capacity ("black Fords only") to a long-term, stable, flexible manufacturing platform capable of building customized fiber products to order. Initially, Corning designed the fiber optic sector (including the factory) to be the most efficient producer of standard fiber optics. Corning's objective was to be the best "mass producer" in the industry. However, given the revolutionary change in fiber optic product market—hundreds of fiber optic products now exist—and given the changing capabilities in process technologies towards increased flexibility at low cost, Corning had decided to move away from being a mass producer. Instead, Corning is concentrating on achieving dynamic stability, thus giving the firm the power to simultaneously compete on low-cost, rapid product delivery, and increased product customization.[7]

Unlike most companies today, Corning does not define itself as a business by the set of products or services it delivers, but by its ability to apply its glass and ceramic knowledge—what its management refers to as its "treasury of process knowledge."[8] Similarly, Tom Pietrocini, president of Bally Engineered Structures, is looking toward expanding into what the business press would call "unrelated businesses," but for him are simply new areas in which to apply the process capabilities learned in Bally's incremental transformation. What may look like conglomeration in the old paradigm can in fact be "sticking to the knitting" in the new paradigm, precisely because individual products and services are now less important than the processes that produce them. Therefore, businesses no longer need to be defined by their products, but can be defined by their processes.[9]

To illustrate dynamic stability, Boynton and Victor use a product-process change matrix, shown in Figure 9-2. The horizontal axis is a continuum of process change, from stable, evolutionary changes that build upon an organization's capabilities to develop, produce, market, and deliver products or services, to rapid, dynamic change that requires new capabilities and makes obsolete old know-how and experiences. Similarly, the vertical axis shows a continuum of product change, from stable products or services that are very standardized over time to dynamic products that incorporate great variety and individual customization.

Firms grounded in Mass Production like to stay in the lower-left quadrant with its evolutionary product and process change. These firms require the stability that rests in this quadrant. Every once in a while, their research and development groups develop a new winner that can be mass-produced, forcing these firms to undergo brief periods of dynamic product and process change as they retool for new product lines. After brief periods in the Invention quadrant in the upper right of Figure 9-2, these firms move back into the Mass Production quadrant. Further, mass producers are also dependent on the

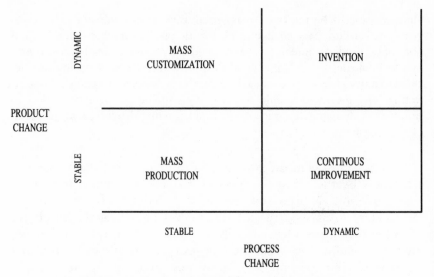

Figure 9-2   Product-Process Change Matrix

craft producers in the Invention quadrant that create the specialized machines necessary for process advances.[10] Thus, the typical Mass Production firm operates on an axis that goes from the lower-left to the upper-right quadrant, as shown in Figure 9-3.

However, when market turbulence increases, the demands on firms' products and services move from stable to dynamic, toward more variety and customization developed more rapidly. Firms must move from the lower-left, Mass Production, quadrant to the upper-left, Mass Customization, quadrant. However, Boynton and Victor make it clear that the right path is not the direct path from lower left to upper left; firms' existing mass production processes can in no way produce the dynamic flow of products required under greatly increased market turbulence. Rather, these firms must spend time in the right half of Figure 9-2, undergoing often revolutionary process change while they transform their processes for the new market environment. Generally, companies first re-engineer their processes without greatly increasing their variety and customization, moving them from the Mass Production quadrant to the Continuous Improvement quadrant.[11] Once this period of revolutionary process change has occurred, firms are prepared to use these re-engineered processes to increase the dynamic flow of goods and services, moving them diagonally to Mass Customization.

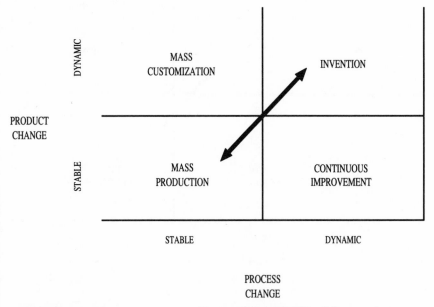

Figure 9-3   Product-Process Change Matrix: The Mass
Production Axis

Of course, as market demands continue to increase, so does the
need for continued dynamic product change. Just as Mass Production
firms occasionally needed to retool completely new processes for completely new products, Mass Customization firms will need to improve
their processes incrementally and occasionally completely re-engineer
those processes for new demands, creating a new level of dynamic
stability. As shown in Figure 9-4, this creates a Mass Customization
axis opposite to that given in Figure 9-3 for Mass Production firms.[12]
It is also possible that dynamically stable firms will choose to undergo
revolutionary product change concurrently with their process re-
engineering, creating an axis from Mass Customization to Invention
along the top half of the figure.

This is a much different environment from that encountered
during the many decades that Mass Production has been effective.
Dynamic stability provides the structural means by which businesses
can shift from Mass Production to enter and expand the new frontier
of Mass Customization. It provides a path by which unknown and
dynamic product demands can be managed and ordered through process stability.

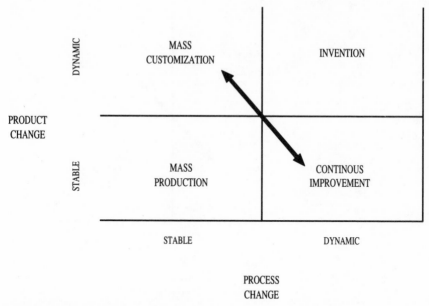

Figure 9-4   Product-Process Change Matrix: The Mass Customization Axis

While the thrust of this book concerns the shift from the Mass Production to Mass Customization quadrants, it should be noted that for companies making the same shift from the Invention quadrant there are particular issues quite distinct from those faced by mass producers. For the craft producers that are the primary members of Invention the most important of these is not losing the quality and personalization associated with craft products and services. Many companies in craft-based industries have been able to use the techniques given in Chapter 8—primarily modularity—to lower their costs dramatically, but have concurrently lowered their quality and personalization. These include companies in industries like pre-fabricated houses, specialized machinery, retail legal and tax preparation, and Saturday-morning cartoon production. In essence, many of these companies have gone too far in the direction of "mass," overshooting Mass Customization and landing in Mass Production. This is not true of all firms undergoing this shift. For example, modular housing companies in Japan and Scandinavia truly mass-customize high-quality, individualized houses that show no resemblance to pre-fab houses in the United States. Many specialized machine makers, such as Ingersoll Milling Machine in the United States, Yamazaki Mazak in Japan, and Valmet Paper Machinery in Finland, similarly achieve both low costs and high-quality, craft-produced specialized machines.

Interestingly, another issue particular to the dynamics of craft-based industries is that, while companies can shift to Mass Customization, they may not be able to say so. As Håkan West, vice president of Systems and Procedures for Valmet, relates:

Paper machines are among the largest in the world, generally from 100 to 130 meters in length in a production line of 200 to 300 meters. They create paper that begins as pulp made of 99 percent water through rolls and equipment running up to 100 kilometers per hour. Our customers demand quality, and they demand that we meet their exacting, individual specifications. While we are continually reducing our costs through investment in a computer-aided design system and increasing functional modularity, we could never associate the word "mass" with anything we do. While we are trying to use mass customization techniques, we prefer the term "systematic customization."

This is similar to the situation that Matsushita ran into with its National Bicycle Industrial Company. When it began providing individually customized bicycles in just a few days, many customers reacted negatively—delivery was just too quick for them to believe the product was really custom made. To completely satisfy its customers, the company had to *delay* the delivery of its bicycles up to two weeks!

While craft producers and others in the Invention quadrant can take advantage of many of the techniques given in the previous chapter and create the dynamic stability necessary for Mass Customization as discussed in this chapter, they must take into account the full effect of this shift on the quality and personalization of their products and on the perceptions of their customers.

Structural Innovations

Creating a dynamically stable organization, as Bally, Corning, CNN, and Toyota have all done, does not happen easily, and except for the rare new business built from the beginning on a vision of Mass Customization (like CNN), it does not happen overnight. This transformation requires innovation in the structure of the business: in the processes by which it develops, produces, markets, and delivers mass-customized products and services as well as throughout

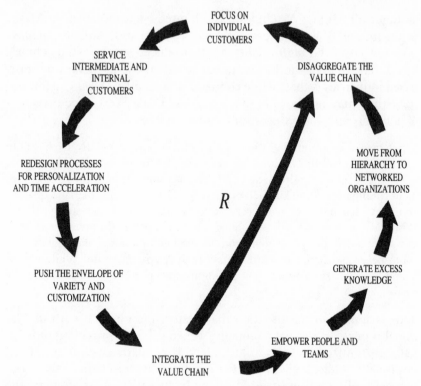

Figure 9-5 Structural Innovations to Transform Organizations for Mass Customization

the value chain of organizations that execute these processes. Each of the structural innovations discussed below can be a powerful force for change within a business. Together their effects can compound exponentially, for as seen in Figure 9-5, each flows from and reinforces the others.

Focus on Individual Customers

Most firms that believe in the paradigm of Mass Production focus much more on the products they have to make and sell than on the customers they have to cultivate and retain. They produce for inventory, and that inventory has to be sold. Recently, many of the best of these companies have changed their focus from products to markets; becoming market-driven is an excellent first step away from Mass Production.[13]

The basics of market-driven management are to segment, target, position, and create. *Segment* your customers and potential customers into meaningful groups that have homogeneous needs within each group. *Target* those market segments that (1) match the capabilities of the firm and (2) have the highest business potential (generally done in terms of revenue, profit, or return on assets). *Position* your firm and its existing and potential products and services in each of the target segments; positioning provides the reason for being, the unique differentiating characteristics that would cause targeted customers to purchase from you. Finally, *create* the products and services that meet the requirements of your target market segments. Of course, this should be a continual process through which customer satisfaction and feedback are actively sought and incorporated in each phase of these activities. It is crucial not only to ascertain what the customers in your target markets need at the moment, but to figure out their latent desires and lead them to new products and services they never knew they were missing.

The next organizational step on the path to Mass Customization is to search for ever-finer granularities of markets within the fringes of each target market segment; in other words, to move the focus from products to markets to niches. Generally, each market can explode by an order of magnitude into niches that have their own identifiable, quantifiable, and profitable characteristics. Using the methods discussed in Chapter 8, customers in each of these niches can be satisfied with a variety of products and services.

Finally, focus on the individual customer. This is important not only for those in sales and marketing who deal with customers every day; it should be drilled into everyone throughout the entire organization that the primary stakeholder of the firm is the *customer*, whose individual needs and desires have to be understood, met, and exceeded at every possible opportunity.[14] Further, every business, organization, and function throughout the entire value chain must be challenged to determine how its link can push and pull that value chain closer to the low-cost production of individually customized goods and services.

Service Intermediate and Internal Customers
As Well

Few companies that are encountering market turbulence can succeed without satisfying their customers' expectations. But the required task is not so simple, for there are really three distinct kinds of customers that need to be taken into account: *final* customers, the ones that purchase and use your products or services; *intermediate* customers, such as retailers, franchisers, dealers, and distributors, that may take temporary title to your products but sell them to the final customers; and *internal* customers, those in your company that take your work output, add value to it, and move it along the value chain toward servicing intermediate and final customers.[15] In a number of industries the situation is even more complex. In computer systems, for example, final customers can be further segmented into those that make the purchase decision (who may or may not be users of the system), those that support the system with operations or programming once it is installed, and those that use the system in carrying out their day-to-day activities. That is why hardware and software vendors expend so much energy on ensuring that their products are customizable by each constituency.

The needs and wants of each *kind* of customer as well as those of each *individual* customer must be serviced. Because of the increasing importance of processes, the notion of internal customers has gained prominence in recent years. It can be crucial to improving quality, reducing cycle time, and satisfying final customers.[16] Nevertheless, it is important to ensure that internal customer/supplier relationships do not gain pre-eminence. Internal customer needs should always be linked to external customer needs or strategic initiatives. Many companies, including Bally and IBM, have found it useful to refer to them as little "c" customers to recognize their importance while differentiating them from those that actually purchase and use products and services, the Big "C" Customers.

There's still more. For companies selling to other manufacturers and service providers as part of *their* value chain, an outstanding differentiator is to help *your* customers service *their* customers. Working together as a partnership, you can increase quality, enhance flexibility, reduce cycle time, lower costs, provide innovations, and in general make your customers more effective in their pursuit of fulfilling their own customers' individual requirements. Every single company in the world is part of one or more value chains that lead inexorably to consumers, even those that view themselves as pure "industrial" or "business services" enterprises. By helping your customers service their customers, and their customers service the next set of customers, and so on across the chain until the consumer is reached, you can become invaluable to the entire chain and thereby gain a distinct competitive advantage.

Redesign Processes for Personalization and Time Acceleration

A change of mind-set that can jump-start the organizational transformation to Mass Customization naturally flows from shifting the focus from products to markets to niches to individual customers. To keep that engine running and make a business effective requires redesigning business processes, particularly to personalize the flow of products and services and accelerate the cycle time of each process.

A process can be thought of as a black box that takes an input, adds value to it, and provides an output, cutting across organizational boundaries as necessary. In many companies, processes are ad hoc activities that occur with little repeatability or dependability. In others, processes are well defined, but everything inside the black box is organized for the sole efficiency of that process, causing ineffective linkages, large batches, and long cycle times. In both cases, organizational structure can be so compartmentalized that people rarely talk to those in other areas, even when servicing the final customer demands that they do.

Redesigning processes can break down the vertical compartments and organizational barriers by examining the value chain of the company in a horizontal, logical, customer-focused manner.[17] Processes as they currently exist should first be analyzed to determine who the customers are, what inputs are provided, what value-added occurs, and what the outputs are. This alone can crystalize what needs to be done in the minds of the employees and ensure that organizational boundaries do not hamper performance. The revolutionary change required in the right half of Figure 9-4 to provide dynamic stability comes when everyone steps back to see what processes *ought* to be performed and *how* they should be redesigned.

The revolution necessary in processes throughout the business is the same as the revolution that has been occurring on the plant floor of companies moving from Mass Production to Mass Customization: companies must eliminate waste, eliminate inventory, improve quality, decrease cycle times, drastically reduce or eliminate setup time, and reduce lot sizes to one.

Eliminating waste in process redesign means this: if the process neither adds value to the final customer nor helps the chain of internal customers add value to the final customer, eliminate it. If a step within the process does not add value, eliminate the step. Processes have to be streamlined to the point that work activity equals value-added activity.

Eliminating inventory involves removing all the crutches that prop up an inefficient or ineffective process. These include having more people than necessary, taking or demanding more time than necessary, requesting more information and retaining more data than necessary, and batching both the inputs and the outputs to achieve operational efficiency. Once these crutches are removed, all the aspects of the process that cause quality defects will become readily apparent and can be redesigned for high-quality output and total process efficiency.

It will then be possible to drastically reduce cycle times. Just as work activity should equal value-added activity, process cycle time should equal value-added time. This requires that the setup time—the time to change over from one set of inputs being processed into one set of outputs to a new set of inputs—be drastically reduced or eliminated. Whether on the plant floor, in the back office, or on the front line, reducing setup times involves three things: eliminating tasks that do not need to be done, streamlining all remaining tasks so that cycle time equals value-add time, and performing as many of those tasks in parallel with the preceding process operation as possible.[18]

All of this will allow you to reduce the process lot size to one. No batches, no inventory, no waste, no non-value-added time: just the process implementers humming along servicing the one customer who at that moment in time is the most important individual on earth.

One company that has done all of this is the United Services Automobile Association (USAA), which provides insurance for military and ex-military personnel. It completely redesigned its policy services processes through information technology, replacing the paper files that made their way through the back office in batches with computer images accessible individually by any service representative. USAA accomplished virtually everything discussed above: it eliminated its paper inventory, eliminated waste in the process, brought its cycle time down to its value-added time, and now works in lot sizes of one customer who gets personalized service. In the words of Robert F. McDermott, CEO of USAA,

It changed the way we think. Now when you want to buy a new car, get it insured, add a driver, and change your coverage and address, you can make one phone call—average time, five minutes—and nothing else is necessary. One-stop, on-line, the policy goes out the door the next morning about 4 a.m. In one five-minute phone call, you and our service representative have done all the work that used to take 55 steps, umpteen people, two weeks, and a lot of money. . . . It's a revolution in the relationship between the company and the customers, who now have instantaneous access to and control over their own financial transactions, no matter whom they're talking to. We've got 14,000 employees, but every time you call, you're talking to someone who's got your file in front of them. Someday, we won't even mail the policies out. You'll trust us to make the changes and keep the policy here.[19]

Of course, you cannot transform your processes once and rest. After they have been redesigned for personalization and time acceleration, focus on continual improvement. What seems like a side benefit is really one of the primary reasons to reduce cycle time: every cycle provides an opportunity to learn and improve. The faster your cycle time, the more cycles you go through; the more cycles you go through, the greater the opportunity to learn how to improve your processes, and thereby your products and services.

Push the Envelope of Variety and Customization

For a company armed with redesigned processes and greatly reduced cycle times, the moment has come to go forth and multiply: push the envelope of variety and customization by constantly producing new products and services and continually updating processes for greater possibilities. USAA, for example, has so successfully developed a stable base of process capabilities that the same processes used to sell and service insurance policies are now being used to market consumer goods to the very same customers.

When processes are capable of a dynamic outflow of products you can practice "expeditionary marketing," rapidly developing and marketing a great number of products or services with numerous variations to test the markets and discover which ones will find a home.[20] Each success can be followed by another series of variations for rapid proliferation of variety and to move far ahead of the competition in more closely satisfying individual customers. Rapid development, flexible production, individualized marketing, and instant delivery can each provide a sustained competitive advantage; together they can leave the competition in the dust.

Customized services or "specials" provide another powerful source of ideas. Working with individual customers to tailor your products or services to be *exactly* what they want can focus the organization on what Mass Customization is all about, but just as important, your customers can be the best source of innovative ideas.[21] Lutron Electronics often spends most of its profits on a sale in custom applications engineering, but then uses those experiences to design its new products. At Bally Engineered Structures, president Tom Pietrocini attests that "specials turn into micromarketing segments and within them are the new markets of tomorrow."

Integrate the Value Chain

There is an old adage in the computer industry: "You always ship your organization." In complex products and systems, like computers, customers can easily see the structure of the organization that designed and built them; the organizational boundaries are clearly marked in what doesn't work quite right and in the cumbersome and difficult interfaces. The same is true of any product or service whose appropriate process management does not cut through organizational boundaries. At many insurance companies, you would have to talk to three different people if you wanted to do something as simple as change your address on home, auto, and life policies. You know exactly how they are organized. At USAA, you would talk to one person and that would be it.

Organizational boundaries exist not only internally within companies, but are even more apparent between companies. Whether internal or external, every boundary provides an opportunity for miscommunication, turf battles, parochial conduct, and all manners of quality defects at the expense of satisfying the wants and needs of the final customer—as well as the wants and needs of the *next* customer in the chain of customers leading to that final one that pays everybody else's expenses.

The answer is not vertical integration, creating internal boundaries in place of external ones. And that is not what most companies are doing. A study by the U.S. Office of Technology Assessment found that the value chains of entire sectors of the economy—the study calls them economic networks—are very interdependent, and became even more so during the 1970s and 1980s.[22] The demand for flexibility in today's turbulent world requires not vertical integration but *value chain integration:* open communication lines that allow everyone in the entire chain to focus on the next customer, and most of all on the end customer, combined with activities that proceed concurrently rather than sequentially. Vertical integration focuses on product competencies; value chain integration focuses on process capabilities.

When a company is integrated, all the personnel in that company know the vision of the organization and how they contribute to it. Similarly, when a value chain is integrated, all those in every link know the vision of the chain—which should be some variation on the theme of satisfying the individual consumers who create the need for the chain—and further know how their activities, no matter how small, contribute to that vision. Information flows seamlessly and immediately throughout the chain, through each link internal to a company as well as each link across companies. Every process knows everything necessary to accomplish its specialized task, and is kept up to date with the changing end-market environment through its links. Therefore, the work of each process can occur in parallel to an extent unimaginable without the constant personal communications and the instantaneous electronic communications that must occur for a value chain to be integrated.

Value chain integration turns a stand-alone company into the dynamic extended-enterprise form of the New Competition discussed in Chapter 6. It means becoming partners with your suppliers and your downstream links to the end customer, with each link committed to each other and to shared visions, goals, and strategies. It means complete and open information exchange about current and future wants and needs, end-customer demands, development and production needs, and so on, without dictating how something should be accomplished. It means sharing profits in good times and sharing costs in bad times. If it sounds like a marriage, it is supposed to. When a couple has difficulties in a marriage, their friends can tell. When there are difficulties in the integration of your value chain, your customers can tell.

Empower People and Teams

Top management can instigate and even institute each of the structural changes discussed so far: focusing on the individual customer, servicing intermediate and internal customers as well, redesigning processes for personalization and time acceleration, and integrating the value chain. However, these initiatives often come from below. Further, no matter where they start, it is the employees of a firm who must make the real changes, and who have the knowledge to do so. Chances are that the average person, when asked how to improve the process he implements, will have a wealth of ideas for doing just that.

"Empowerment" is one of those concepts which are becoming buzzwords, but that does not mitigate its usefulness or its essential nature in today's environment. The person who is responsible for and actually performs a task is in a better position than anyone else to determine how that task can best be done, and how it can best be improved. Get out of the way and let him do it: that is empowerment.

Of course, many employees may be out of practice or reticent to speak out. The separation of thinking and doing that became inherent in the system of Mass Production is still a major force in many companies. Working beyond that will require time, patience, trial and error, and tolerating the many failures along with rewarding the many successes.

It will also require creating and empowering cross-functional teams that can quickly bring together the diverse skills, knowledge, and experiences necessary to accomplish internal change amid a rapidly changing external world. Teams should be focused on a particular horizontal task—a project focus, not a functional perspective—and given the power, authority, and tools to accomplish it. Empowerment to teams means that they become self-directed or self-managed; they have all of the requisite knowledge, experiences, and skills to accomplish their task—or know where to get them. And they have the authority to do whatever it takes to see that the customer is satisfied, eliminating the organizational handoffs that stand in the way of value chain integration and customer satisfaction. Self-directed teams can effectively destroy the functional and organizational boundaries built up over the years, and may represent the only effective way of doing it.[23] They can become the entrepreneurial lifeblood that transforms calcified corporations.

Generate Excess Knowledge

A corollary to the separation of thinking and doing is the belief that excess knowledge is inefficient: workers need to know only how to do the task they are assigned and nothing else. Similarly, functional organizations need only know about their function; let the other organizations worry about what they have to do, you worry about what you have to do. Mass Production delineates tasks, functions, and knowledge and doles each out up and down the management hierarchy.

While one could argue over whether that ever was the best policy, even in the heyday of Mass Production, it is clear that in today's environment this attitude will no longer work. When uncertainty and instability are the rule, and flexibility and responsiveness essential requirements, then "excess" and redundant knowledge becomes crucial to survival.[24] When customer desires are constantly changing and technological change is accelerating, there has to be some base of knowledge that can be drawn upon, for the first time perhaps, to lead a firm to the right responses.

The move to cross-functional, self-directed teams is one way companies have been applying excess knowledge in parallel to formerly serial, one-function-at-a-time tasks. Overlapping responsibilities at the boundaries of processes (and organizations) creates open and frequent communication, and in turn develops redundant knowledge that can be applied and transferred through each process linkage. Rotation of people through different experiences brings excess knowledge to those experiences and creates new knowledge that can be brought to bear on the next occurrence.

Innovative companies like Bally Engineered Structures are creating databases of their people's skills and experiences that can be accessed across the company, allowing anyone to instantly find the person with the right knowledge to apply to a new situation. Victor Basili of the University of Maryland advocates going a step further: building an "experience base" or "warehouse" that packages experiences in the form of knowledge, processes, tools, techniques, and products in a database for reuse throughout a corporation.[25] An experience warehouse *mass-customizes knowledge and experiences* by allowing people to easily and quickly select those available in the database and dynamically tailor them for the current task at hand.[26] IBM in Toronto is developing such an experience warehouse to be used for software development.

Move from Hierarchy to Networked Organizations

Yet another vestige of Mass Production is the steep hierarchies still prevalent throughout corporate America. Hierarchy was probably a necessary development to handle the growth and size of corporations over the past hundred years. Its "command and control" structure and vertical communications were suited to the relatively stable and controllable environments that allowed Mass Production to flourish. It is particularly unsuited to turbulent environments that reward fleetness, agility, and responsiveness. Traditional hierarchies are not yet being eliminated in many organizations, but they are being assuaged and slowly transformed into networks, self-managed teams, or "clusters," which Quinn Mills describes as

a new way of organization that changes the behavior of those in it to meet the demands of the business environment. Clusters succeed because they make it possible for a firm to hire the best people, develop an ongoing commitment to quality, be quickly responsive to shifts in the marketplace, and provide a process of rapid revitalization when performance declines.

A cluster is a group of people drawn from different disciplines who work together on a semipermanent basis. The cluster itself handles many administrative functions, thereby divorcing itself from an extensive managerial hierarchy. A cluster develops its own expertise, expresses a strong customer or client orientation, pushes decision making toward the point of action, shares information broadly, and accepts accountability for its business results.[27]

There are as many forms of clusters and networks as there are organizations creating them, and none are without problems. Further, it is premature to envision a day when hierarchies will completely disappear. But flattening hierarchies, giving autonomy to groups, and facilitating horizontal and networked communications are necessary steps to long-term success in a rapidly changing business environment.

Disaggregate the Value Chain

The most radical structural innovation that can be used to transform an organization, but one that more and more companies are turning to, is to break it up. More specifically, it is to *disaggregate* the internal value chain, to separate the appropriate pieces into not only their own organizations but their own companies. This is the logical culmination of the movement toward networked organizations and the significant and broad-based trends of decentralization, process redesign, and outsourcing (as well as the latter's governmental cousin, privatization).[28]

The purpose of decentralization is to push decision-making authority down in the organization, closer to where the action is and to where the people are who have the knowledge to apply to the decision. Greater flexibility and responsiveness ensue through not having to gain approvals up and down the organizational hierarchy. But all too often people are uncomfortable with newfound autonomy and the responsibility that goes with it. If they can still pass the buck back upstairs, too many will. And top managers are often reluctant to give up their power, despite their rhetoric to the contrary. Why not turn a decentralized unit into its own company? It increases flexibility and responsiveness, crystalizes everyone's focus on the task at hand—to run a business that results in the satisfaction of individual customers—while eliminating all excuses and temptations to revert back to the old ways of doing things.

Many companies today are outsourcing various functions and activities: cafeteria management, building maintenance, data center management, information systems development, and transportation logistics seem to be the most popular functions, but the list includes health services, product design, secretarial support, manufacturing, sales, and almost any other function you can name. While many of these can be viewed as "noncore" activities, and a firm should rarely (if ever) outsource its own source of sustainable advantage, it is not that any one of the above functions is unimportant. Companies are outsourcing because of one simple fact: they can get better service, at lower costs, from other companies that specialize in one activity, do it well, and learn by doing it for many others. Why not turn your specialized functions into their own companies? Let them service other companies' needs and thereby gain economies of scope (as well as scale as they grow), new experiences and skills, and last but not least, profit.

Process redesign reorganizes the activity of a company, if not the organizational structure, into a horizontal chain of suppliers, processes, and customers. Each process views the next link as its customer—simultaneously keeping in mind the final customer that pays for the whole chain—and services its needs. But these internal processes are really monopolies, and the next customer is really a captive market. While focused individuals committed to customer service can counteract natural monopolistic behavior (i.e., arrogant attitudes, poor customer service, slow innovation, inflexible processes), and are doing so in many companies, it is not easy to do and even more difficult to sustain. Why not let appropriate processes become their own companies? Create innovation-spurring competition by forcing processes to go after new business while allowing their customers to choose among suppliers. If your internal processes can't cut it in open competition, don't their customers—your company—deserve better? And if their internal customers do not gain enough value to pay for the services provided, shouldn't that expense be eliminated?

One of the premier companies at managing a disaggregated value chain is Asea Brown Boveri (ABB). The Swedish company Asea and the Swiss company Brown Boveri merged in 1987 to form the largest electrical systems and equipment company in the world, with 240,000 employees and annual revenues of more than $25 billion. ABB is a global company that realizes that every single product must be adapted to local markets. To do that, it uses many of the methods of mass customization discussed in the last chapter to gain global economies of scale and local tailoring.[29] When asked how such a large organization can be both global and local, Percy Barnevik, ABB's president and CEO, replied:

ABB *is* a huge enterprise. But the work of most of our people is organized in small units with P&L responsibility and meaningful autonomy. Our operations are divided into nearly 1,200 companies with an average of 200 employees. These companies are divided into 4,500 profit centers with an average of 50 employees.

We are fervent believers in decentralization. When we structure local operations, we always push to create separate legal entities. Separate companies allow you to create *real* balance sheets with *real* responsibility for cash flow and dividends. With real balance sheets, managers inherit results from year to year through changes in equity. Separate companies also create more effective tools to recruit and motivate managers. People can aspire to meaningful career ladders in companies small enough to understand and be committed to.[30]

ABB has disaggregated its value chain into twelve hundred companies along both country and functional boundaries, hundreds of them through acquisitions, yet runs its Zurich headquarters with only one hundred people. How does Barnevik do it?

I believe you can go into any traditionally centralized corporation and cut its headquarters staff by 90% in one year. You spin off 30% of the staff into free-standing service centers that perform real work—treasury functions, legal services—and charge for it. You decentralize 30% of the staff—human resources, for example—by pushing them into the line organization. Then 30% disappears through head count reductions.

These are not hypothetical calculations. We bought Combustion Engineering in late 1989. I told the Americans that they had to go from 600 people to 100 in their Stamford, Connecticut headquarters. They didn't believe it was possible. So I told them to go to Finland and take a look. When we bought Strömberg, there were 880 people in headquarters. Today there are 25. I told them to go to Mannheim and take a look at the German operation. In 1988, right after the creation of ABB, there were 1,600 people in headquarters. Today there are 100.[31]

Companies that are creating "free-standing service centers" and other forms of disaggregation exist the world over. Along with many other Japanese firms, Kuniyasu Sakai, cofounder and former chairman of Taiyo Kogyo K.K., practices the philosophy of *bunsha* or "company division." Sakai has constantly divided his company into smaller ones over the past forty years "because he thinks it makes sense for a very fundamental reason: If an individual is closer to his work, is more responsible for what happens as a result of his or her actions, that person is likely to do a good job. And if a good job isn't done, then failure is right there, with no place to hide from it."[32]

In Italy, Massimo Menichetti took over his family's textile mill and found that the large, integrated mill had become too bureaucratic to adapt to the fast-changing textile industry. He broke it up into eight independent companies, and sold 30 to 50 percent of the stock to key employees. The value chain of the organization remained the same, but now each company was forced to service the next link in the chain, and Menichetti demanded that they build up sales to outside companies to 50 percent of the total within three years. Once he proved successful, other integrated mills in Italy followed suit.

Formerly, in each large mill, one group of managers oversaw the entire process, from assessing the market to designing fabric to supervising every detail of production. Now, small groups—sometimes a family—take total responsibility for their part in the process. Each shop has certain special skills. One may be particularly good at producing high-quality knits for dresses; another may be expert at mixing colors. Work is contracted out to whichever shop can meet the market's needs at the time. Each, therefore, has great incentive to stay in touch with fashion trends and environmental changes and to be ready to react quickly. Otherwise, it would lose business to other producers and might even go out of business.[33]

Not every business can or needs to disaggregate down to the family level, but the principle applies to all sizes of companies. The largest example is certainly IBM, which announced in December 1991 that it "would move from being a single, integrated company to become a spectrum of increasingly autonomous businesses and independent companies."[34] In explaining this new direction for IBM, Chairman John Akers related it directly to increasing turbulence in the information technology industry, saying,

I think we've come to a fundamental question: Given the velocity of change in our industry, should we continue with the same fully integrated business model for our company? I believe we have to conclude the answer is "No."[35]

IBM is disaggregating its value chain along two dimensions. First, it is segmenting its manufacturing and development lines of business and its marketing and services organizations into their own companies. Each company will become autonomous, responsible for its own financial success, and will report to corporate IBM as it would to a holding company. The manufacturing and development companies will be free to market their products through other companies; the marketing and services companies will be responsible for developing total solutions that meet each customer's individual needs, no matter where they get the product and services that comprise each solution. Eventually, IBM intends to report the results of each company separately, and may offer shares in them.

Second, IBM is spinning off many support functions outside the core value chain that are primarily service related. According to former IBM Senior Vice President David E. McKinney, who was responsible for accelerating the creation of these IBM Affiliates, as the company calls them: "They will have to be profitable on their own. They will compete in the marketplace in which they specialize. They will serve IBM and other customers."[36] By the end of 1991, IBM had already created more than one hundred affiliates, most of them in individual countries, much like ABB. They include the Integrated Systems Solutions Corp. (ISSC), which provides "avowedly customer-tailored, highly flexible"[37] data center (outsourcing) management and other information system services in the United States and served as a model for other IBM Affiliates; the Employment Solutions Corp., which provides recruiting services, also in the United States; and Information Systems Management Ltd., a facilities management firm in Canada, jointly owned with two Canadian firms. Other companies provide property management services in the United Kingdom and translation, maintenance, and manufacturing engineering services in Japan.[38]

Despite its apparent advantages, this is indeed a radical prescription for IBM and for the many other companies that are following the same path. Will it work? In particular, what will prevent a disaggregated company from disintegrating? As that last word implies, it is vital that a company first have an *integrated* value chain before it *disaggregates* that chain, as Figure 9-5 depicts with the arrow leading directly from the former to the latter. There will be a natural tendency for disaggregation to build barriers between the separated companies, to develop the same self-focused functional orientation that exists in bureaucratic organizations. This is counteracted by the fact that now each organization has a real customer-supplier relationship or, better, a partner-partner relationship in seeing to it that the final customer in the value chain is delighted with the results of the entire chain. It is counteracted by the removal of the monopoly/captive market relationship that formerly existed. And it is counteracted by the open communications and information-sharing characteristic of integrated value chains.

Johnson & Johnson illustrates this by coming at it from the other direction. J&J has long relied on small, autonomous companies to be flexible and responsive to the special needs of different health care markets. By the 1980s, it had more than 150 different companies, most of which had their own specialized sales forces, often selling to the same customers. As competition intensified and its market turbulence increased in the 1970s and 1980s, J&J found that it had to integrate its companies to achieve a competitive advantage.[39] It did not change the decentralized organizational structure that was ingrained into its culture and at which it excelled, but rather turned to information technology. Each sales rep was provided with a laptop computer to access a centralized database of *all* Johnson & Johnson customers and their history. While maintaining their separate specialties, sales reps can now work together on accounts instead of at cross-purposes. In manufacturing, Johnson & Johnson expects computer-integrated manufacturing to provide the architectural "glue" linking workers and sites and supporting companywide strategic thrusts like just-in-time manufacturing and total quality management.[40]

Another clear and present danger in disaggregated value chains is their openness to technological shocks coming from outside the community.[41] The Swiss watch industry, for example, was a disaggregated community that became highly efficient and flexible in making all manner of mechanical watches. In the 1970s, the industry was almost wiped out because of the shift in technological paradigms to quartz watch movements that was precipitated from outside the community (even though the technology was in fact invented inside the community). The key reason for this was that the Swiss watch industry was not *integrated*, for as one study makes clear,

the network structure of production, while efficient and flexible, was also fragmented. Faced with the need to shift from a technology based on mechanics to one based on electronics, a time-lag built into the fragmented system inhibited rapid information flow. . . . [and] organizations could not form a single voice to respond. The watch industry's collective research efforts to pioneer new technology could not overcome organizational inertia and infighting that arose with the need to commercialize the new technology.[42]

While even disaggregated value chains that are also integrated are not immune to responding poorly to technological shocks, the glue of integration can provide the rapid information flows, single voice, and focus on the end customer that can mean the difference between three potential futures: prosperity, mere survival, and going out of business.

If done properly, and done well, the *simultaneously integrated and disaggregated value chain* results in a community of affiliated firms, each specialized in its link of the value chain, open to technological innovation, and flexible in its ability to respond to the requirements of the community while focused on meeting the needs and wants of the final customer. In other words, the company and its value chain have moved beyond the dynamic extended enterprise and been transformed into a *flexible specialization* community, which, as discussed in Chapter 6, Michael Piore and Charles Sabel have identified as an alternative to Mass Production. It is the integration focused on the end customer that can provide the sense of community so important to flexible specialization.

In an old story about two stoneworkers, each is chiseling a large square stone, but one is dour and working halfheartedly while the other is happy and working away feverishly. When the first fellow is asked what he is doing, he replies, "Making a stone." When the second fellow is asked what he is doing, he replies, "Helping to build a great cathedral!" Both workers are part of a disaggregated value chain, but only the second is *integrated* into that chain as part of a community focused on the end customer.

When achieved, the advantages of a simultaneously integrated and disaggregated community are many.

- Individual performance is improved. Simultaneous integration and disaggregation pushes decision making out closer to the customer. It crystallizes everyone's focus on the business. Individuals are closer to the work and more responsible for their actions, and it eliminates excuses; people can no longer hide within the bureaucracy.
- Functional and process performance is improved. Simultaneous integration and disaggregation opens internal monopolies to innovation-spurring competition. Each link in the value chain becomes a real customer-supplier partnership, and the entire chain gains better service, at lower costs, from flexibly specialized companies. The true costs of processes and their value-added contributions are better determined through open market pricing than through arbitrary, overhead-laden transfer prices or no prices at all. Further, internal processes that do not in fact add value worth their expenses can more easily be eliminated.
- Company performance is improved. With simultaneous integration and disaggregation, niches once thought too small for the aggregated firm become attractive markets for the disaggregated companies. In response to the needs of multiple customers, companies must constantly innovate and gain new skills and process capabilities. Excess process capacity can be applied and profited from, and economies of scope are gained by applying skills across multiple customers.
- Community performance is improved. With simultaneous integration and disaggregation, the community as a whole grows and gains economies of scale. Flexibility and responsiveness are enhanced by reducing the size of firms and by the ability to take advantage of the differing skills of every company in the community.

In addition to these advantages, the value delivered to the final link in the chain, the end customer, can be greatly enhanced and personalized. That is what an organization can deliver when it has incorporated not only this innovation, but each structural innovation discussed above to transform itself for the new frontier of Mass Customization.

CHAPTER 10

Exploring the New Frontier

MASS Customization is indeed a new frontier. The principle of variety and customization through flexibility and responsiveness requires new ways of managing and new uses of technology. It shares elements from previous approaches to management, but requires new visions and strategies, new methods of developing, producing, marketing, and delivering products and services, and new forms of organization better suited to turbulent times.

The Limits of the Frontier

Like any system of management, this one has its limits. It was the limits of Mass Production that brought that system to a halt in many industries; had those limits been known to its practitioners, the shift to Mass Customization could have been quicker, smoother, and less painful. It is important, therefore, to enter this new frontier with full knowledge of *its* limitations and dangers. Understanding what they may be ahead of time, you can scout for them, find paths to maneuver around them, and maybe even discover what the nature of business competition will become should your competitors join you in crossing into the new frontier.

It will take many years to fully scout the new territory of Mass

Customization; we cannot know the entire lay of the land until it is more populated. But Figure 10-1 shows the limitations to the feedback loop of Mass Customization that can be foreseen. Some of these are the same or analogous to the limitations of Mass Production depicted in Figure 2-5. As described then, the loops marked by a "B" are balancing loops that limit the degree to which the primary feedback loop can reinforce itself. All three of these loops in Figure 10-1 balance the degree to which companies that follow the Mass Customization paradigm can increase their variety and customization as they decrease their development and life cycles. The other two arrows are shocks to the system that can arrive, with or without warning, to bring down the reinforcing mechanism.

Product and Process Technology Shocks

First, product and process technology shocks can happen in any industry, at any time, no matter what system of management the companies in that industry subscribe to. New technologies and innovations may be absorbed more readily in the new system of Mass Customization, with its shorter cycles and penchant for new products, than in the old. However, radical innovations—often by firms outside the industry—can create a new dominant design with so many compelling properties that it can consolidate demand and wipe out previous designs, no matter how much variety and individual customization were present.[1] With Mass Customization, new products and processes that *reverse* demand fragmentation by creating new dominant designs should be feared most.

There are few examples of this phenomenon, but some can be cited. The McDonnell Douglas DC-3, which combined in one aircraft the ability to handle efficiently both short and long flights, consolidated airplane demand around its design, thereby eliminating many competing aircraft. The Boeing 727 had a similar effect decades later. The UNIX operating system is threatening to do the same for minicomputers. Because it is cheap, widely available, and almost ubiquitous across the college campuses where most programmers learn their trade, many in the industry believe it will eventually eliminate all but perhaps one or two proprietary minicomputer operating systems.

An earlier example in the computer industry illustrates a joint product and process innovation that consolidated demand. As detailed in Chapter 8, the IBM System/360 wiped out a tremendous amount

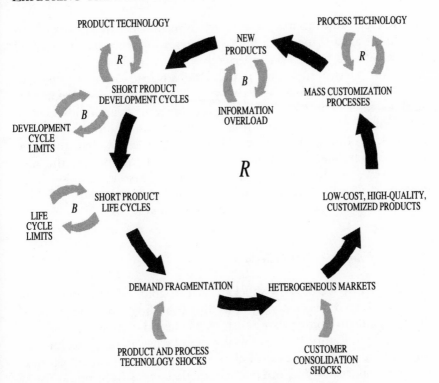

Figure 10-1   The Limitations to the Feedback Loop of Mass Customization

of variety in the then-nascent computer industry. It combined functions that were previously available only separately on scientific and business computers, supplanted all of IBM's product lines, and was so successful that many competitors exited the business. At the same time, it provided a basis for even greater variety and customization through its modular architecture and ability to be customized by IBM's field force. This customization process was just as important to the S/360's success as its architectural innovations.

The government also can easily wipe out variety and customization by fiat, as it did in the "medigap" segment of the insurance industry in 1991. Federal law mandated ten standard insurance policies that could be sold to senior citizens who want to supplement Medicare coverage. This eliminated thousands of individualized medigap policies in an attempt to make product comparisons easier.

Radical innovations often come from outside an industry, and are almost always met by a flurry of innovation from the entrenched and threatened firms.[2] As a perfectly rational and often appropriate response, it has been known to delay the advance of a new dominant design. However, it is almost always only a matter of time before this strategy fails. The fast cycle time capability of firms following the paradigm of Mass Customization positions them to innovate quickly features, products, and services that may hold a new technology at bay—for a while. This time should be used to embrace the new technology, not to build barriers against it. Mass Production firms have traditionally found it difficult to accept that philosophy; the same should not be so for Mass Customization firms.

Customer Consolidation Shocks

In addition to technology shocks that can consolidate demand, the wants and needs of customers can also consolidate to homogeneity. It is difficult to point to any customer consolidation shocks, as they are labeled in Figure 10-1, in the absence of a precipitating technology shock. One possibility could be customer reaction against "baroque" changes: flourishes and ornamentation that serve little or no useful purpose. Some trivial differentiation *can* provide customer value: witness Cabbage Patch dolls, particularly popular in the late 1980s. Each doll was unique, thanks to production techniques that made trivial variations in each doll. But if a company or industry were to run out of steam in innovations that provided real customer value, or simply spent too much time and energy on nonvalued flourishes, the risk exists for customers to reconsolidate around old or new designs that provide real, differentiated value. Be sure that the dimensions along which you customize are most valuable to your customers, and that customization does not become baroque.

To customize goods and services individually often means that companies must know and keep track of a great deal of information about individuals. This has already raised a number of privacy issues with particular products and could result in customer consolidation shocks. Consumer databases that track the purchases and shopping habits of individuals, such as Lotus Development Corp.'s Market-Place, have come under fire for compiling too much information about individuals. The Caller ID service from telephone companies that displays the telephone number of incoming callers has also been labeled an invasion of privacy. Worries exist over the ability of AT&T and other telephone companies to find out too much about their customers by analyzing their calling patterns. This has spawned at least one new mass-customizing service: Private Lines Inc. of Beverly Hills, California, provides a service that allows a subscriber to call one number and reconnect to any other; only Private Lines' 900 number appears on the telephone bill.[3] Similar fears are arising with respect to credit card companies.[4]

As companies increasingly collect and apply information about their current and potential customers, the privacy issue is not likely to go away. First, companies have to be absolutely certain that they do not abuse information they collect; that can only lead to consumer antagonism and government regulation. Second, consumers must realize the value in such information, not only to companies, but to themselves. With database marketing techniques, consumers are more likely to be given the opportunity to try products and services they want and, more important, are probably *less likely* to be bothered—by mail, by phone, and eventually by TV—by offers, ads, and gimmicks for unwanted products and services. Unsolicited offers may never disappear, but if done well, individualized marketing should eventually eliminate the pejorative "junk mail."

Similar to this issue is consumer antagonism and threatened regulation toward companies that sell "sin" products and services such as alcohol and cigarettes. For example, in 1991, the G. Heileman Brewing Co. launched a malt brew called PowerMaster, with 31 percent more alcohol than its top-selling Colt 45 brand, targeting it directly at low-income, inner-city blacks. Heileman eventually ceased selling PowerMaster after the Bureau of Alcohol Tobacco and Firearms withdrew its approval to use the name. Similarly, R. J. Reynolds dropped plans for marketing Uptown, a cigarette aimed at blacks, because it encountered consumer and government pressure. Companies that sell a product or service with one or more detrimental characteristics need to be careful about targeting a particular group of consumer. It is likely that individualized direct marketing would cause less rancor than public segment marketing.

One other way customer consolidations may occur is by mass reactions against accelerating obsolescence. With decreasing product life cycles and increasing rates of continuous innovation, consumers sometimes find that a product they *just* purchased has been rendered obsolete by a newer and even more whiz-bang product. This leaves them feeling frustrated and irritated. It is rarely a problem with services, since they are generally consumed as they are purchased. It is also less of a problem with individually customized goods than with proliferating variety.

Customer rebellion against technological obsolescence is especially troublesome when ongoing purchases of associated products are involved, as with music. Less than a decade after compact disks arrived, the technology is being threatened by digital audio tape. Consumers are already reacting against the new format because they do not want all their expensive compact disks to become obsolete so quickly. The same thing can happen in industrial markets.

This kind of rebellion can be tempered to some degree by activities like the following:

- Maintain the sale, and particularly the servicing, of old models as new ones are introduced.
- Promote the continued viability, or at least do not attack the respectability, of older models through advertising, user groups, support magazines, and other means.
- Design upgradability into each product, so the latest features can be retrofitted onto older models. These can generally be offered at a higher per unit price than the same features bundled into a new model.
- Failing that, guarantee your customers' technological satisfaction via, for example, an automatic trade-in provision at a preset price.

This list is only a beginning. As they move into the new frontier of Mass Customization, companies will figure out new and innovative ways to handle fears of technological obsolescence and other customer consolidation shocks.

Information Overload

In addition to the two kinds of shocks that can limit the feedback loop of Mass Customization, there are three balancing feedback loops shown in Figure 10-1. The first involves the amount of information that customers can effectively absorb. As new products and services are developed, customers may become overwhelmed with proliferating variety and with the information they require to decide which product is right for them. This is especially true for high-impact products and services like mutual funds and life insurance policies—and is why the federal government regulated medigap insurance policies. It is also true for more mundane personal care products like cough syrup and shampoo, as customers are not exactly sure that there is *really* a difference in the great variety of choices. Some customers do not want to have to figure out what type of cough they have; they just want to run into a drugstore and get cough syrup. Period.

This limit can interact with nostalgic feelings for "a time when life was simpler," as was evident in an entertainment piece in *The Wall Street Journal*, which surveyed the fascination in the Seattle area with the enormous variety of coffee-related products available in espresso bars. After humorously discussing this at length, the author closes with the related topic of brewpubs:

An overcrowded espresso bar seems like the ultimate experience in beverage intimidation—until you find yourself in a brewpub, one of the dozens of Northwest establishments serving beers and ales brewed on the premises. A solid grounding in Budweiser or even Heineken is inadequate preparation. (A chemistry degree, however, is a plus.) . . .

My standard pub procedure is to get someone who knows his hops from his barley to order for me, then I sip quietly and murmur comments like "Hmm. Good one."

Occasionally, the regional furor over liquid nourishment becomes so oppressive that it's best just to sit things out. At a restaurant one recent evening, my attempt to sidestep the inevitable beverage fuss proved a failure. "Anything to drink with that?" the waitress asked. I told her I'd just have a glass of water.

"What kind?"[5]

While entertaining, the feelings the writer describes are becoming more common with proliferating variety: intimidation, oppression, being overwhelmed by choices, and believing that a science degree is necessary to make intelligent choices.

Having to absorb more information to make an intelligent choice also means that activities like grocery shopping take longer than they used to. And as more function becomes embedded in customizable products, it can become increasingly difficult for customers to figure them out. The classic cases are the office phone with so many buttons that no one can figure out how to simply transfer a call and—ridiculed from coast to coast by late-night comedians—VCRs that people buy so they can watch any TV show they want whenever they want to, but can't figure out how to program them.[6]

Customers are not the only ones with problems in this regard.

Retailers often have trouble finding the shelf space and keeping in stock all the varieties available. Even a company's own personnel can have trouble keeping track. For example, in the early 1970s, IBM created the Application Customizing Service for manufacturing and distribution firms. Through a questionnaire administered by an IBM systems engineer and consultations with applications programmers, this service resulted in a software product individually customized to each firm. While every customer received a customized application, IBM found that when a customer called with a problem it could not tell exactly what set of programming instructions that customer had or how to fix them. Because of the information requirements, servicing applications became so difficult that IBM standardized two versions of the product, one for manufacturing firms and one for distribution firms.

Information overload is a threat to Mass Customization that balances the ability of a company to continue to develop a dynamic flow of products and services, as seen in Figure 10-1. If it is not prevented or overcome, companies will either have to reduce variety back to a level that does not induce information overload or lose out in the marketplace.[7]

There are two primary ways of preventing this problem. First, as discussed in Chapter 8, add variety and customization along those dimensions that provide the most value to customers. This will make it easier for your customers to tell the difference between your various products and services (as well as those of your competitors), to appreciate the differences, and therefore to know which are right for them.

Second, make the information necessary for selecting the right product or service as accessible, as easy to use, and as quick to assimilate as possible. The names of the products, the amount of information and the size of type on the labels, color coding, packaging, size—all of these (and more) can be used to provide information to customers. Especially as the amount of variety increases and moves into the realm of individual customization, it becomes important to provide tools that allow customers to design their own product, preferably without costly help from your sales representatives. These can be powerful marketing tools in their own right. L. S. Ayres & Co., for example, developed an "electronic dressing room" called Magic Mirror, through which a computer shapes a variety of apparel fashions around a customer's reflection in a mirror. Elizabeth Arden, Inc., uses a similar system that measures skin tones and shows customers how individual make-up treatments would look on their faces.[8] Ingersoll-Rand visits manufacturing plants with a tool called the Ergo-Analyser that simulates different tool configurations so that assembly workers can choose the one that's right for them.[9]

Tools such as these, along with menus (like those accompanying all ATMs and well-designed VCRs) and services (like those provided by IBM Rochester, Peerless Saw, and National Bicycle) will make or break many companies as they move into Mass Customization. The problem of information overload must be prevented.

Development Cycle Limits

The second balancing loop involves natural limits to decreasing product development cycles. Just as maximum saturation levels limit demand stability and the ability to produce standardized products and services in the feedback loop of Mass Production, minimum development cycles limit the ability to constantly innovate new products and services in the feedback loop of Mass Customization.

When a company has done everything it thinks it can to continually lower its development cycles and has finally hit the floor that must surely exist, there are only three ways to proceed. First, it can stay there and live with the limitation to the number of new products and services it can develop. By itself this is not likely to cause the company to slip backward in providing variety and customization. It just reaches a state of equilibrium that it hopes will remain competitive over time.

Second, it can create completely parallel development groups, each responsible for successive versions of its product. Ideally, two such groups would cut the development cycle in half, three in a third, and so on. This is, however, an expensive option. Further, the ideal will probably never be reached because of potential communication problems between groups and potential integration problems between products.

Third, a company that has hit the floor in development cycles can figure out how to cut a hole in it and drop to a new level. In other words, there is only one safe assumption when it comes to how short development cycles can get: instantaneous. Any particular method or process of developing products and services will of course have a lower limit to its cycle time. But *never* assume that no amount of innovation, no amount of process re-engineering can lower that time. Short of instantaneous development cycles, there will *always* be a way to do it. You have to find it.

Instantaneous development cycle time sounds like science fiction. It isn't the new frontier, but the "final frontier" of Gene Roddenberry, who created two future inventions for his *Star Trek* adventures that have virtually instantaneous development (and production) cycles: the "replicator," which combines molecules and atoms (through sectional modularity, of course) into almost anything, and the "holodeck," which creates a holographic "virtual reality" that people can step into and experience.

Replicators and holodecks are indeed science fiction, although the potential of custom-building molecules and the existence of methods for providing virtual realities are becoming more doable every year.[10] However, virtually instantaneous development and production cycles are not science fiction; they are becoming a reality today, although the standard conception of development cycle time may need some revision. In the new competitive frontier, the key measure is the time between the identification and fulfillment of customer requirements. And by that measure, cycle times are indeed decreasing toward zero.

Companies that have moved the final, customizing production step out to their customers develop never-before-realized products and services in almost zero time. Someone who buys a bowling ball that is almost instantly customized to his or her hand has a product that never before existed. Yes, it is only trivially different from any other bowling ball. And, yes, it took nothing to "develop" that product and next to nothing to produce it; the development process is automatically integrated into that final production step.[11] But it is still a distinct product that fulfills a unique customer need.

That is a major part of the power of Mass Customization, particularly when its techniques are put to use to create individualized products and services of much greater differences than the average bowling ball. By providing customized services, by developing customizable products and services, by moving production out to the customer, by taking time out of the value chain, and especially by using modularity, companies can develop and produce brand-new products and customers can experience brand-new services—with almost instantaneous development and production cycle times.

The Limited can conceive a new style and have it in its retail apparel stores within forty-two days through the value chain integration that comes with its Quick Response program. SMH can develop a new Swatch watch collection every six weeks through its system of "perpetual innovation." Peerless Saw can design and develop a novel industrial saw in three weeks by taking almost all of the non-value-added time out of the process. Bally Engineered Structures can create a new refrigerated warehouse in ten days through sectional modularity. Toyota can deliver a car in Japan—with a combination of options that no other customer has chosen—in five days by taking time out of the value chain. Meanwhile, Nissan envisions that in the next decade product modularity will allow it to provide the *service* of developing, producing, and delivering a completely customer-designed car in three days. Lutron Electronics can develop and produce one-of-a-kind lighting controls and systems in a day without flexible automation. Motorola can create a unique pager in an hour and a half with the utmost in flexible automation. *CNN Headline News* can develop and deliver a fresh news show not just in half an hour but *every* half hour of every day. Create-A-Book can compose unique children's books in fifteen minutes. And TWA Getaway Vacations can develop unique, customer-designed travel packages in six minutes through information technology and modularity.

Although each of these products and services is different from any other ever developed, obviously none of them is completely new. All are either pre-engineered combinations or variations of other, previously developed products and services. But probably far less than 1 percent of new mass-produced products could be considered to be entirely new—that is, not based somewhat on previous product generations—so the distinction here is really only one of degree. There are indeed mass customization processes that border on having instantaneous development and production cycle times and yield different products and services. In particular, total modularity such as Bally has and Nissan envisions can yield *very* different products with short development times, as anyone who has ever played around with Lego blocks can attest. Most companies can use the same techniques to lower their development times to the same levels—a matter of days—or less.

Of course, these techniques are not enough to keep a company successful over the long term. Every company needs four distinct and concurrent development activities:

1. *Mass customization processes*, as described above, that provide pre-engineered but virtually instantaneous fulfillment of customer wants and needs.

2. *Incremental platform innovation* that continually pushes out the envelope of variety to increase the chances that particular customers can get precisely what they want.

3. *Follow-on platform development* that incorporates continual technological improvements and increases the basic value of a product or service to a customer.

4. *Breakthrough innovation research* that anticipates latent customer needs and leads the firm into new businesses with new products or services that can be mass-customized.

Bell Atlantic, one company that has ongoing development efforts in each of these four areas, is a company focused on achieving zero development cycle time. Regis Filtz, vice president of Carrier Access Services, initiated a process re-engineering effort in 1991 to drive down the development time of custom carrier connections for businesses that want to move voice, data, and video directly from one location to another. Before these efforts began, the design, development, and implementation of a connection could take twenty business days or more. Filtz relates that "from the very beginning we established zero cycle time as the goal. Customers need instantaneous connections, and the business opportunity once we can achieve it is enormous." In less than six months he was seeing improvements of 80 percent, with custom connections down to several days and in some cases several hours. But even that is not enough for Bell Atlantic. Filtz says that the technology exists to effectively anticipate customer needs, which will soon allow the company to reduce the average time to one day, and in several years to reduce it to zero—the time it takes to punch a few buttons on a terminal, or about the same time it takes to make an ordinary phone call today.

Bell Atlantic is also driving down the development time of new phone services through the creation of an Advanced Intelligent Network (AIN). Current services, such as Call Waiting and Call Forwarding, took several years to develop and deliver to customers because they are programmed into individual phone switches. AIN technology separates the service logic into its own processors, which can be independently programmed. Mark Emery, Director of AIN Services Planning, reports that

AIN technology will make it possible to create a new telephone service in months, even minutes, rather than the years the development of a new service typically entails today. The difference works out to delivering new services potentially thousands of times faster and less expensively than under current industry practice.

The frontier of Mass Customization is wide and vast; new techniques that push down the development cycles times of ever-more innovative products will continue to be developed. As long, that is, as the pioneers and settlers of this frontier embrace the same mind-set as Bell Atlantic and assume that there are no limits to cycle times—other than zero.

Life Cycle Limits

There are two major concerns with the life cycles of classes or platforms of products and services from which individual products and services are created. These issues can limit the feedback loop of Mass Customization and stop it from reinforcing itself. The first is fear of technological obsolescence, which can cause customers to rebel against new product and service classes that too quickly make obsolete their recent purchases. This issue was addressed above with other potential customer consolidation shocks.

The second major issue concerns what happens to a firm that shortens its product life cycles and then finds itself running into a natural limit that levels off the cycles. This has been thoroughly investigated by Christoph-Friedrich von Braun, who demonstrates mathematically the following logical sequence:

- If a company shortens its product life cycles; and
- If that company benefits by gaining a percentage of sales sooner than it otherwise would because of the increased attractiveness of its new products to its customers;
- Then the company will realize a "bubble" of increased revenue (and profits) as long as the life cycles continue to decrease. However,
- If the life cycle flattens out, as at some point it inevitably will;
- Then the company will realize a "reverse bubble" or dip of swiftly decreasing revenues (and profits).[12]

As far as it goes, this is correct and may very well have caused declining revenues in a number of technology-based and innovative industries, as von Braun intimates. However, the above premises do not necessarily hold, and *should not* hold, for companies that have shifted to Mass Customization.

First, while companies certainly hope to gain purchases *sooner* by shortening product life cycles, they also hope to gain *additional* purchases that they never would have realized because of the innovation brought to the market. These additional sales would come from customers who would otherwise have bought a product from slower competitors, now or in the future. If by shortening its product life cycles companies can gain significant and sustained advantage over their competitors, then additional sales from that advantage can ameliorate the revenue dip that would still occur when product life cycles stabilize. This is particularly true if the life cycle reductions slowly flatten out rather than abruptly halt.

Second, the length of product and service life cycles flows from the length of development process cycles. As the latter decreases, the former naturally follows. When a product is one of a kind, its life cycle is virtually instantaneous. It is developed once, produced once, and delivered once. The next product will be different. So again, in this sense, there are no safe assumptions about the natural limit to product life cycles other than zero.

It is unforeseeable, however, that breakthrough innovations could be regularly developed in near-zero time. But concurrent focus on each of the four development activities outlined above can abate the effects of flattening product life cycles from any one. New systems of developing products and services must be found for each of the four to systematically reduce product life cycles. Even before a natural limit in the cycle time of a development process is found, begin the search for a new system of development. If any natural limit is viewed as *the* overall lower limit, you are all but guaranteed to encounter increased market turbulence when one or more competitors find their way around that limit to drastically reduce their product life cycles.

The landscape of the new frontier as life cycles for major product platforms approach zero is impossible to predict, but von Braun's work provides a clear lesson: the environment will be highly turbulent, with potentially destabilizing ups and downs in revenue and profits. But unlike the pioneers of old who often paved the way for settlers with their lives, the pioneers of the new frontier of business competition will be creating more turbulence for followers than they will for themselves. When your competitors cross the threshold to the new frontier of Mass Customization, it is more dangerous to stay behind in the illusory safety of Mass Production.

The Future of Business Competition

The landscape of the new frontier is marked not only by its limits, but also by its opportunities, by new ways of business competition. Some of these opportunities for competitive advantage are known today: Chapter 8 covered the different ways that both products and services can be mass-customized, and Chapter 9 analyzed how organizations can be transformed to provide customization across the value chain. Like the limits to Mass Customization mentioned above, other opportunities can be surmised and speculated about, but cannot be known for sure until the new frontier is further explored.

One thing is relatively certain: the basis for business competition never ceases to evolve. As more companies in an industry shift to Mass Customization and practice its tenets, the competitive advantage created by the pioneers will become less of an advantage.[13] These pioneers will either continue to search the landscape for new ways of creating advantages, or they will be caught and overtaken by their followers who will themselves find the future of business competition.

At the beginning of Chapter 9 the increasing importance of process was discussed. In the system of Mass Production, a key advantage creator has been the coupling of product and process life cycles. As seen in Figure 10-2, this coupling matched the process capabilities with product volume. When breakthrough product developments necessitate switching over to a new product family, the old process also gives way to a new process designed specifically to make production of the new product as efficient as possible.[14] Any significant separation of process capabilities and product volume is considered inefficient.

In the system of Mass Customization, on the other hand, a key advantage creator is the *decoupling* of product and process life cycles. As discussed in Chapter 9, the importance of individual products decreases as the same processes can be used to develop, produce, market, and deliver many products and product families. This dynamic stability is shown in Figure 10-3, where the long-term, stable processes allow the creation of a dynamic flow of products and services. As product life cycles decrease and the flow of products and

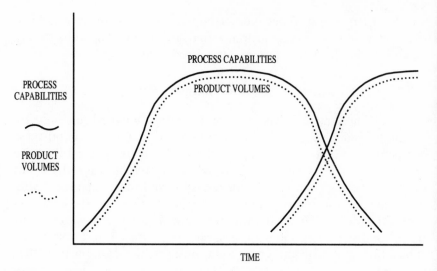

Figure 10-2   Mass-Produced Products: Coupled Product and Process Life Cycles

services increases, a company's stable process base provides a distinct net advantage over its competitors, particularly if they still have coupled product and process life cycles that require significant resources for the development of new processes for every major new product.

However, as more companies move into the new frontier, the net advantage created by dynamic stability will lessen. Competitors will eventually follow, product life cycles will eventually run into natural limits, and other limits and dangers of the feedback loop of Mass Customization may be encountered. Companies striving for new advantages will have to switch to new processes to move ahead of the competition and around the natural limits. Those companies that are able to do this faster than their competitors will once again achieve significant advantages. While their competitors are imitating their old processes, the best companies will already be moving on to their next set of processes, and the ones after that, and so on.[15]

This results in the situation seen in Figure 10-4. The logical, although by no means certain, progression of business competition will be shortening *process* life cycles. Yesterday, companies gained advantage primarily by either low costs or significant differentiation (but never both, according to the strategy pundits). Today, high quality has become a cost of doing business and companies gain advantage by shortening their product life cycles with constant product

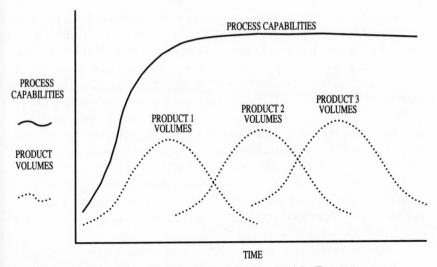

Figure 10-3   Mass-Customized Products: Stable Processes
Producing Dynamic Flow of Products

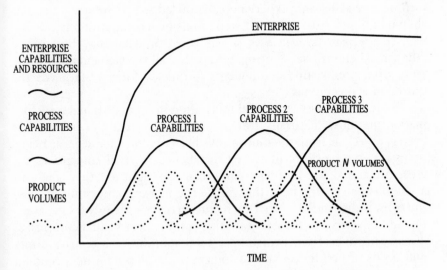

Figure 10-4   Mass-Customized Processes: Shortening Process
Life Cycles

innovations, providing both low costs *and* great product variety and customization. Tomorrow, at least in industries that continue to be marked by high turbulence, the mass customization of products and services may become the cost of doing business. This would force companies to gain advantage through shortened process life cycles with constant *process* innovations and great *process* variety and customization. As companies today are moving to the mass customization of products and services, tomorrow they will be moving to the *mass customization of processes* uniquely suited to new market opportunities. Those which both do it first and do it well will further increase the market turbulence of their competitors while increasing their own advantage. As discussed in Chapter 9, this may be beginning as companies implement concepts like experience warehouses that enable quick process development.

What is beyond tomorrow? What will happen when companies converge onto shortened product and process life cycles, constant product and process innovations? Figure 10-4 provides a clue. Once processes follow products into decreasing individual importance, it is the dynamic flow of processes and products *from the enterprise* that becomes important. The enterprise—whether a team, division, company, corporation, or disaggregated community of all of the above—is the total of the capabilities and resources it can bring to bear on the progression of market opportunities. It is a portfolio of people and technology, skills and experiences, knowledge and information. As shown in Figure 10-5, the next step in business competition may very well be the *mass customization of enterprises*, or what may be labeled "the virtual enterprise":[16] bringing together all the elements of a company from pre-existing components to quickly satisfy the needs required of a specific task.[17]

This is one more structural innovation in organizational transformation that flows naturally from decreasing product and process life cycles, as well as from the innovations presented in Chapter 9 as being necessary in a world of increased turbulence. Virtual enterprises are cross-functional and multicompany teams brought together solely to accomplish a specific task; then, once the market opportunity fades, the team is disbanded so that each enterprise can reapply its capabilities and resources to the next task through the next virtual enterprise. Tasks can range from providing a total solution to meet the wants and needs of one individual customer, to developing a new product or service that itself can be mass-customized for thousands or millions

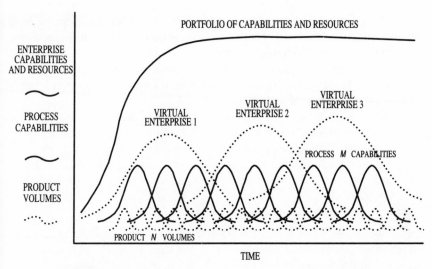

Figure 10-5 Mass-Customized Virtual Enterprises

of consumers, to creating new processes that can provide their own dynamic flow of goods and services.

Many companies are using self-directed and task-focused teams internally to shorten cycles times and to be responsive to changing demands. Some are starting to include vendors, suppliers, partners, and even customers on these teams. But no one has yet created the process capability to quickly bring together (spatially or electronically) the right people to focus on a task no matter where in the internal and external communities they may reside and for whom they may be working.

It may not be doable today, but it will be in the future. In November 1991, the Iacocca Institute at Lehigh University began a national initiative to create "agile manufacturing enterprises": essentially, manufacturers that can mass-customize products, processes, and enterprises. The institute believes that it is crucial to achieve this level of agility if America is to maintain its national competitiveness:

The very developments that today are driving the transformation of the mass production system of manufacturing can serve as a springboard for the U.S. to return to a leadership role in manufacturing by the year 2006. . . .

Where the mass production system achieved low unit costs by producing large quantities of uniform products, the new system achieves agility. It is capable of low unit costs while producing far smaller quantities of high quality, highly customized, products. In an agile enterprise, manufacturing machinery can be reprogrammed quickly to produce new products, in many variations. Products with a high information content, and related commercial services, are being created that will increasingly come to define the competitiveness of a nation's industrial apparatus.

In the mass production system, even with the enhancements of just-in-time and lean production, corporations attempted to do everything themselves. Competition favored large scale, comprehensive, operations. The agile manufacturing system favors smaller scale, modular production facilities, and cooperation between enterprises, each of which contributes a part to a new capability.[18]

One of the most powerful competitive weapons of the agile manufacturing enterprise will be, in the institute's view, "the ability to form virtual companies routinely."[19] To that end, it proposes

a national industrial network, a Factory America Net (FAN). FAN combines a comprehensive industrial data base with services that allow groups of companies to create and operate proprietary virtual entities. Its operation assumes the removal of legal barriers to multi-enterprise collaborations and the creation of standard consortium formation models that make forming a virtual company as straightforward as making a will or forming a corporation.[20]

Of course, this degree of agility will be every bit as useful to service firms, and government departments for that matter, as it is to manufacturing firms. And it appears that it will begin to occur long before 2006. In November 1991, with involvement of the Iacocca Institute and several other industry organizations, the Microelectronics and Computer Technology Corporation (MCC), a consortium of information technology companies, announced the Enterprise Integration Network (EINet) to enable the sharing of business information and services among companies across the United States, and eventually the world.

In the vision of Factory America Net, and potentially in the reality of EINet, companies should be able to initiate, create, and operate virtual enterprises on-line. They should be able to search the network (by themselves or through an infopreneuring broker) for the right knowledge, skills, experiences, and technologies they need to apply to a project, validate potential partners in a number of ways (including face-to-face videoconferencing), create and sign agreements with selected partners, file the necessary documents for the creation of a virtual enterprise, and then exchange all of the information for the running of that enterprise (including market opportunity documents, engineering drawings, prototype specifications, manufacturing or service process standards, customer databases, and so on). Personal meetings and telephone or videophone conversations will of course still be desirable if not necessary for the effective running of a virtual enterprise, but the network will provide the primary mechanism for integrating its value chain.

In all likelihood, the mass customization of virtual enterprises will one day be at the forefront of business competition. It is still far enough into the future that exactly how it will be accomplished is unclear. In the product-process change matrix introduced in Figure 9-2, the virtual enterprise fits into the Invention quadrant of dynamic change in both processes and products. Out of that quadrant will come a constant stream of virtual enterprises, and out of those enterprises will come a dynamic flow—a "mass invention"—of processes and of products that individually may cover the spectrum. As shown in Figure 10-6, virtual enterprises may even be able to develop the occasional breakthrough product that can still be mass-produced for stable markets.

One company that at least comes close to fitting this picture today is Gruppo Financiario Tessile (GFT), headquartered in Turin, Italy. GFT began as a small craft producer of men's clothing but introduced mass-production techniques to the Italian clothing industry after World War II. It grew on the strength of its production capabilities until market turbulence hit the industry in the 1970s, when GFT found that it could not adequately respond to rapid changes in its markets.[21] So, the company set out to reinvent itself, almost single-handedly creating the Italian designer movement in men's suits in the 1980s. It forged agreements with top Italian designers and greatly increased the flexibility of its production processes to produce up to five hundred different styles. It also moved into high-fashion women's wear, for which a typical production run was only ten to twenty units. And after growth slowed in its designer markets, GFT created "diffusion" lines that lowered the price of designer fashions.

To do all of this, GFT created three distinct production processes: its old mass-production process for its continued ready-to-wear lines; a craft-production process for high-fashion women's wear; and

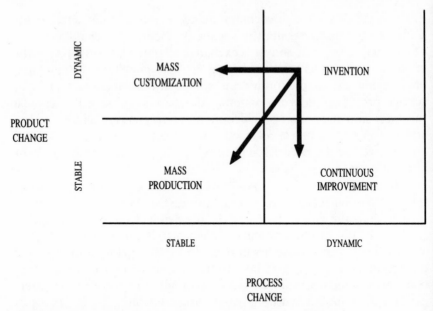

Figure 10-6   Process-Product Change Matrix: Virtual
Enterprise Flow

a mass-customization process for its designer and diffusion lines. The
development and marketing for each type of fashion also took different routes. All came together in the marketing and manufacturing
organizations spread across Europe and the United States that produced and sold GFT's global apparel lines.

As it hit the billion-dollar mark in the late 1980s, however, GFT
found that continued growth required that it localize its apparel for
each country. It decided to reinvent itself yet again, decentralizing
its organization and allowing new product and process ideas and innovations to flow from individual countries back to Turin—the opposite
of what made it successful. As Gene de Nicolais, director of corporate
communications at Gruppo GFT North America, relates, GFT's latest transformation

has led to the group's industrial and marketing flexibility in an industry
primarily set on satisfying the changing tastes and lifestyles of world popula-
tions. GFT's talent for customizing a standardized product has not only
allowed it an insider role in most of the world's principal markets from an
industrial perspective, but has also provided the merchandising and marketing expertise necessary to make the group's product "communicate" in the
language of the market of destination.[22]

GFT has moved from being production-driven to designer-driven to customer-driven. Having reinvented itself several times, it now finds that to continue its growth this must become a constant process. To reach new and changing market opportunities, the group has created many new market-focused companies that in turn constantly forge new alliances with designers, with retailers, and with each other. GFT has planted itself in the Invention quadrant of Figure 10-6, where new product and process innovations flow quickly and are spread throughout the company, landing in the quadrant most appropriate to the particular market opportunity it is going after.

In the old system of Mass Production, significant resources are spent in trying to achieve a sustainable competitive advantage. As this discussion on the future of Mass Customization and the particular case of GFT demonstrates, in the new frontier, with all its accompanying turbulence, there may be no such thing as a sustainable advantage, and it is almost certainly dangerous to believe that there is. Companies must constantly stretch their capabilities, searching out new areas to create advantages first in the dynamic flow of individually customized product and services they produce, eventually in the dynamic flow of processes that allow constant innovation in those products and services, and finally in the dynamic flow of virtual enterprises that will become key to going after and conquering new market opportunities. The progression of advantage in the new frontier of business competition seems clear.

- Mass-customized products and services allow companies to gain advantage in their current markets through fulfilling the wants and needs of individual customers.
- Mass-customized processes would allow companies to enlarge that advantage through constant innovation in new products and services.
- Mass-customized enterprises will one day allow companies to create new advantages through the application of its portfolio of capabilities and resources in concert with the capabilities and resources of any and all firms that together can create and attack new market opportunities.

What is beyond that? The next logical progression from Figure 10-5 would be the ability to mass-customize the development of the capabilities and resources that allow virtual enterprises to be formed. Perhaps this could be accomplished through things like just-in-time education, synergistic cross-discipline skill development, expert system technology, and collaborative computing environments. However, the competitive landscape is still far too unknown for anyone to speculate much on how this advance might come about. At the rate that competition is evolving today, it may not be too long before such speculations are not only conceivable, but doable. For now, let us leave that to the future. For companies in industries struck by market turbulence, the immediate task is ensure a place in that future by shifting from the old ways of Mass Production to Mass Customization, the new frontier in business competition.

Crossing into the New Frontier

In the early 1800s, American pioneers spread west, radiating from New England and the other original colonies, past the Ohio Valley and the Mississippi River, and entered a new frontier, securing a future for the American people. A few decades later, in the mid-1800s, American trailblazers again entered a new frontier that radiated from New England. This frontier became known as the American System of Manufactures, and as it spread and evolved into the system of Mass Production, its practitioners also secured a future for American business and the American people.

That future is now threatened by a changing business environment and new forms of competition more suited to it. In industries struck by increased market turbulence, the system of Mass Production that made America great has become outmoded and is no longer effective. Worse, it is detrimental to the companies that practice it, to their workers, and to America.

But a new frontier in business competition, the paradigm of Mass Customization, is at hand, and yet another group of American pioneers are leading the way, but they are not alone. Competition is no longer domestic but global. Many companies in many other countries have discovered this frontier and are already ferreting out the intricacies of the principle of variety and customization through flexibility and quick responsiveness. It is time for the pioneers to be joined by all other companies whose markets are being hit by the storms of turbulence. The time has come to shift to Mass Customization, the new frontier in business competition. For those who make this shift, the turbulence will not end, but they will once again have their hands at the controls.

Appendix
Research on Market Turbulence

CHAPTER 4 presented the Market Turbulence Map and Variety and Customization Profile as tools that can indicate whether a company should shift to Mass Customization. These tools were validated through a survey of more than 250 people in 164 companies. First this Appendix provides the survey questionnaire, which has been modified slightly for ease of use in analyzing companies today; for example, references to 1991 and 1980 have been replaced by references to "today" and "a decade ago." Following the questionnaire are more detailed results than provided in Chapter 4 to validate the research. Finally, the analysis of five industry segments provides further validation as well as insights into what has been happening across a spectrum of industries, some moving to Mass Customization and some not.

Survey Questionnaire

Part One: Demographic Information

Instructions: Please provide the demographic information requested below on you and your company.

Name: _____

Company: _____

Title: _____

What is the primary business of your company?

This survey will ask you questions about the "business unit" with which you are most familiar. This may be your entire company, a division, or some other business unit. Please give the name of the business unit for which you will be responding and its primary business:

Please indicate the size of your company (with a "C") and your business unit (with a "B") in both annual revenue and number of employees in the appropriate spaces below:

Revenue: __ < $5m __ $5–$49m __ $50–$499m __ ≥ $500m
Employees: __ < 50   __ 50–499   __ 500–4999   __ ≥ 5000

How long have you been with this business unit (years)? ____

With the company? ____ In the same or similar industry? ____

You may find as you complete this survey that you have two or more marketplaces that would yield different results. If so, please respond for your primary or most familiar marketplace, and indicate here which marketplace you used:

Part Two: Market Environment Perceptions

Instructions: Here are seventeen questions about your business unit's market environment. Each question asks for *your perception* of where your business unit stands *today* on a scale between two defined endpoints. Please take a moment or two to think about the question and then place an X at the point on the given line that matches your initial perception. The scale is divided into 100 percentage points with markers at every 5 and 10 points, but please use the level of precision that is meaningful to you.

1. To what extent are the demand levels of your business unit's products unstable and unpredictable?

   To No Extent   To a Great Extent

2. Do your products fill very basic needs, or are they complete luxuries in the minds of your customers, or are they somewhere in between?

   Very Basic Necessities   Complete Luxuries

3. Are your customers' needs and wants easily defined and understood, or are they uncertain and difficult to ascertain, or are they somewhere in between?

   Very Easily Defined   Totally Uncertain

   (scale line)

4. Do all of your customers desire basically the same products (completely homogeneous), or do they demand something unique (completely heterogeneous), or do they lie somewhere in between?

   Completely Homogeneous   Completely Heterogeneous

5. At what rate are the needs and wants of your customers changing?

Very Slowly   Very Quickly

6. To what extent do the prices of your products influence your customers in their decisions to buy your business unit's products?

To No Extent   To a Great Extent

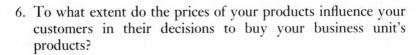

7. To what extent does the quality of your products influence your customers in their decisions to buy?

To No Extent   To a Great Extent

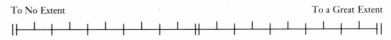

8. To what extent do fashion and style influence your customers in their decisions to buy?

To No Extent   To a Great Extent

9. To what extent does the level of pre- and postsale service influence your customers in their decisions to buy?

To No Extent   To a Great Extent

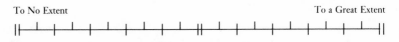

10. To what extent can your customers dictate the prices, conditions, and features of your business unit's products?

To No Extent   To a Great Extent

11. To what extent are your business unit's sales affected by economic cycles (recession, recovery, and expansion)?

To No Extent   To a Great Extent

12. To what extent do you and your competitors battle for market share in your business unit's markets?

To No Extent   To a Great Extent

13. Is competition in your industry based totally on product differentiation, totally on price competition, or is it somewhere in between?

Total Price Competition   Total Product Differentiation

14. Are your business unit's markets completely unsaturated (all sales are to entirely new customers), completely saturated (all possibilities of sales are replacements of or additions to existing products), or somewhere in between?

Completely Unsaturated   Completely Saturated

15. To what extent are your existing products vulnerable to being replaced by substitute products that are of a different nature but perform similar functions?

To No Extent   To a Great Extent

16. Are the product life cycles (first shipment to replacement or withdrawal) of products in your business unit's industry very long and predictable, very short and unpredictable, or somewhere in between?

Very Long, Predictable   Very Short, Unpredictable

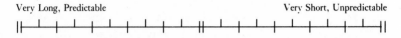

17. To what extent is the rate of product technology changing in your business unit's industry?

To No Extent   To a Great Extent

Thank you for your perceptions of your business unit's current market environment!

Instructions: The questions you have just answered are about *today's* market environment. It is important to understand how much each of these factors has changed over time. Therefore, please think back across the past decade or so and the changes, if any, that have happened to your business unit's market environment during this time.

Then, please take another couple of minutes to go back to the seventeen questions above and quickly indicate your perceptions of your business unit's marketplace a decade ago. (Please use an "O" to mark each line to differentiate between your previous "X"s.) It is all right if you are not as familiar with the environment back then (you may not even have been around); what is important are *your perceptions* of the marketplace environment at that time.

Instructions: The open-ended questions below request more detail about your business unit's market environment. Please write your answers in the space provided, or attach another sheet if you so desire.

1. What do you think have been the most profound changes in your business unit's market environment during the past decade?

2. What do you think are the causes behind these changes?

3. Do you believe your business unit's customers are demanding more variety or customization today than they did a decade ago? Why or why not? If so, how far do you think this trend will go?

Part Three: Product Perceptions

Instructions: The following sixteen questions are about your business unit's products or services. (If your business unit is in a service industry, please interpret the word "product" as "service" whenever it is used below.) Again, each question asks you to indicate *your perception* of where your business unit stands today on a scale between two defined endpoints. Please take a moment or two to think about each question and then place an X at the point on the given line that matches your initial perception. (Note that you will not be asked to go over this section twice; many of the questions refer directly to the changes that have occurred during the past decade.)

1. How does the amount of variety in your business unit's products today compare with that of a decade ago?

   Much Less Variety   About the Same   Much More Variety

2. Does your business unit plan on providing more or less variety in the future?

   Much Less Variety   About the Same   Much More Variety

3. Are your product life cycles (first shipment to withdrawal or replacement) longer or shorter than they were a decade ago?

   Much Longer   About the Same   Much Shorter

   If possible, please indicate the approximate average life cycle length (in years and/or months) of your products now and a decade ago:

   Today: _____ Decade Ago: _____

4. How does the quality of your products today compare with the quality of your products a decade ago?

   Much Lower   About the Same   Much Higher

5. How do the manufacturing/production costs of your products today compare with the costs of your products a decade ago?

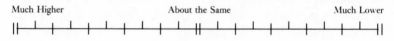

Much Higher   About the Same   Much Lower

6. How do today's products compare with those of a decade ago in meeting your customers' complete needs and wants?

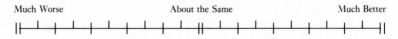

Much Worse   About the Same   Much Better

7. Today, is it more or less important to respond quickly to customer demand for changes with new or modified products?

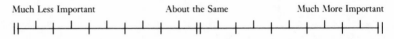

Much Less Important   About the Same   Much More Important

8. How important are product innovations (e.g., new features, new technologies, new products) to the success of your business unit?

Not at All   Absolutely Essential

9. How important are *incremental* product innovations (e.g., new features, modified products) versus *breakthrough* innovations (e.g., new products, new technologies) to the success of your business unit?

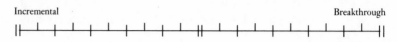

Incremental   Breakthrough

10. To what extent are your products *customized* to individual customers?

Not at All   100% Customized

11. To what extent are your products *customizable* by individual customers (or others outside of your business unit who assist your end customers)?

Not at All   100% Customizable

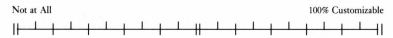

Instructions: If your responses to questions 10 and 11 were *both* "Not at All," please skip questions 12 through 16 and proceed directly to the open-ended questions following them.

12. How does the level of customization (regardless of who does it) in your products today compare with that of a decade ago?

Much Less Customization   About the Same   Much More Customization

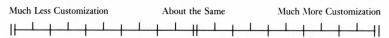

13. Does your business unit plan on providing more or less customization in the future?

Much Less Customization   About the Same   Much More Customization

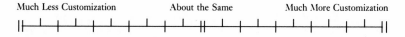

14. Completely "closed customization" means your business unit has to perform all product customization; completely "open customization" means your customers (or others) can perform any and all customizations that can be performed. To what extent are your products closed or open?

Totally Closed   Totally Open

15. "Continuous customization" means that, within some range, your products can be infinitely customized; "discontinuous customization" means there are discrete steps in the level of customization. Where do your products fall on this scale?

Totally Discontinuous   Totally Continuous

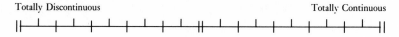

16. "Same-use customization" means that your products perform exactly the same function after customization; "modified-use customization" means that they can perform different but related functions; and "different-use customization" means that your products can perform completely different functions. Where do your products lie on this scale?

Same-Use   Modified-Use   Different-Use

Thank you for your perceptions of your business unit's products!

Instructions: The open-ended questions below request more detail about your business unit's products. Please write your answers in the space provided, or attach another sheet if you so desire.

1. If you are providing more product variety and customization today than a decade ago, why? If not, why not? (If the latter, skip to the next page.)

2. How far do you think the trend toward more variety and customization will go? What are the product limits to customization for your business unit, or is it foreseeable that products could be economically customized for individual customers?

Part Four: Process and Organization Perceptions

Instructions: The six questions below are about your business unit's processes and organization. Again, each question asks you to indicate *your perception* of where your business unit stands today on a scale between two defined endpoints. Please take a moment or two to think about each question and then place an X at the point on the given line that matches your initial perception.

1. Where does your business unit's production process lie on the scale between one-of-a-kind production (where each final product is different from the next) and fully standardized mass production?

One-of-a-Kind   Full Mass Production

2. How does this compare with a decade ago? Today's process is:

More One-of-a-Kind   About the Same   More Mass Production

3. What do you think your business unit will do in the future?

More One-of-a-Kind   About the Same   More Mass Production

4. How much more production flexibility (meaning the ability to change quickly between products) exists in your production process today than a decade ago? Today's process has:

Much Less Flexibility   About the Same   Much More Flexibility

5. Is your product development process (project initiation to product shipment) longer or shorter than a decade ago?

Much Longer   About the Same   Much Shorter

If possible, please indicate the approximate development process length (in years and/or months) of your products now and a decade ago:

Today: _____ Decade Ago: _____

6. To what extent has the structure of your organization and your processes changed in the past decade?

To No Extent   To a Great Extent

Instructions: The open-ended questions below request more detail about your business unit's processes and organization. Please write your answers in the space provided, or attach another sheet if you so desire.

1. If your business unit is providing more product variety and customization today than a decade ago, how is it being done? How have your processes changed?

2. If you are providing more variety and customization, how has your business unit's organization (including employee and supplier relations) changed to provide this variety?

This completes the survey. ***Thank you very much for your participation!***

Research Results and Validation

During the early months of 1991, 1,027 questionnaires were mailed to executives, managers, and a few professionals across an array of companies and industries. About 90 percent of these were graduates of the Sloan School of Management at MIT. Despite the survey's length, the participation rate was quite high: 255 responses were returned, a rate of almost 25 percent.

Survey Participants

These respondents represented 227 business units within 164 companies. Table A-1 gives the distribution of the size of the companies in terms of both revenue and number of employees. Table A-2 provides the same information for the business units. The survey was heavily weighted toward large companies, but was somewhat more evenly weighted across business units.

Table A-3 gives the number of business units from each industry division, as defined by their Standard Industrial Classification codes. Each division, except Agriculture, Forestry, and Fishing, was repre-

Table A-1   Distribution of Business Unit Size

Size in Revenue	# Business Units		Size in Employees	# Business Units	
<$5 million	39	15%	<50	39	15%
$5m–$49m	30	12%	50–499	46	18%
$50m–$499m	68	27%	500–4,999	76	30%
>$500 million	116	46%	>5,000	92	36%
Not given	2	<1%	Not given	2	<1%

Table A-2   Distribution of Company Size

Size in Revenue	# Companies		Size in Employees	# Companies	
<$5 million	28	11%	<50	30	12%
$5m–$49m	18	7%	50–499	26	10%
$50m–$499m	42	17%	500–4,999	42	17%
>$500 million	164	64%	>5,000	154	60%
Not given	3	1%	Not given	3	1%

Table A-3   Distribution of Business Units by Industry Division

Industry Division	# Business Units	
1 Agriculture, Forestry, and Fishing	0	0%
2 Mining	9	4%
3 Construction	2	<1%
4 Manufacturing	140	55%
5 Transportation, Communications, Electric, Gas, and Sanitary Services	32	13%
6 Wholesale Trade	5	2%
7 Retail Trade	2	<1%
8 Finance, Insurance, and Real Estate	15	6%
9 (Other) Services	35	14%
10 Public Administration	11	4%
11 Nonclassifiable (or unknown)	4	2%

sented in the survey. A majority, 55 percent, of the participants represented manufacturing business units, 35 percent were from all of the service industries (Divisions 5–9), 4 percent were from various branches of the government (mostly from the armed services because of their participation in the Sloan School programs), and another 4 percent were from mining and construction.

One interesting piece of demographic information was obtained from asking the participants to place their business units on a scale between one-of-a-kind production and fully standardized mass production. Figure A-1 indicates a breadth of responses. The histogram is weighted toward the full mass production end, with a mean response of 60.

In Chapter 2, Figure 2-1 showed the same histogram for manufacturing and service companies. There, the full breadth of responses was given for *both* types of business units. The responses for services were quite flat across the entire spectrum. Their mean response (49) was lower than that for manufacturing (63), but respondents in service industries clearly did not hesitate to state that their business unit's "production" process was fully a *mass* production process. The possibility for operating within the paradigm of Mass Production clearly exists for service companies.

Figure 2-2 provided the same information for the different business unit sizes. Mass production processes not only exist but predominate within business units of every size. The larger the firm, of

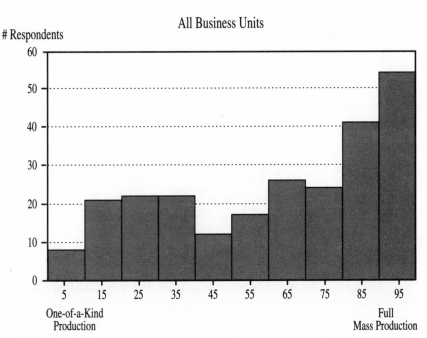

Figure A-1 One-of-a-Kind Production vs. Full Mass Production: All Business Units

course, the more likely it resides on the mass production end of the spectrum. The mean responses for the four sizes were:

- 52 for business units of fewer than 50 employees,
- 56 for those between 50 and 499 employees,
- 63.0 for those between 500 and 4,999 employees, and
- 63.2 for those of 5,000 or more employees.

Results and Validation

Figure A-2 provides a histogram of the average change in the 183 business units whose respondents answered all seventeen market environment questions for both 1980 and 1991. A small majority of business units clustered between zero and a 10-point increase, with a second major cluster between 10 and 20 points.

Table A-4 ranks the market environment factors by how much they changed, on average, since 1980. While fifteen of the factors increased in turbulence, two in fact decreased in market turbulence

Respondents

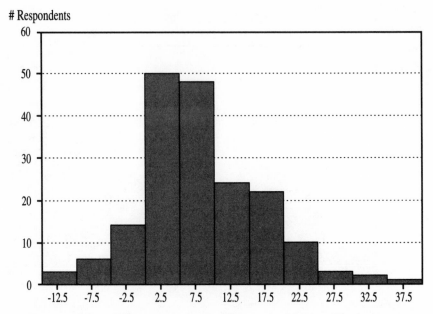

Figure A-2   Histogram of the Change in Market Turbulence

Table A-4   Mean Survey Results: Market Environment Factors
Ranked by Increased Turbulence

Market Environment Factors	1980	1991	Change
Competitive Intensity	56	74	18
Rate of Need/Want Change	40	55	15
Quality Consciousness	62	76	14
Buyer Power	41	54	13
Price Consciousness	51	63	12
Rate of Technology Change	52	64	12
Service Levels	53	64	11
Saturation Levels	53	63	10
Substitutes	41	51	10
Heterogeneity of Wants	46	55	9
Product Life Cycles	28	36	8
Demand Levels	38	45	7
Economic Cycles	54	60	6
Fashion/Style Consciousness	22	25	3
Certainty of Needs	36	39	3
Necessities/Luxuries	30	27	− 3
Price vs. Product Competition	54	50	− 4

since 1980: there were small changes of products moving farther away from the luxury end of the scale toward increasingly becoming necessities (30 to 27), and from the basis of competition being product differentiation toward price competition (54 to 50). However, this does not mean that these factors do not correlate positively with the amount of variety or level of customization. Even though the average of these factors decreased in turbulence over the decade or so under study, those companies which moved toward luxuries and product differentiation did indicate, on average, a greater increase in variety and customization than those which moved in the opposite direction.

As discussed in Chapter 4, the fact that both market turbulence and variety/customization, on average, increased does not demonstrate that the increases are correlated. This was accomplished through least-squares regression to find the best linear fit of the measures of market turbulence given in the Market Turbulence Map—the overall market turbulence in 1991 and its change since 1980 (see Figure 4-4)—with the six measures given in the Variety and Customization Profile (see Figure 4-5). These six were (1) the amount of variety relative to 1980, (2) the amount of future variety, (3) the level of customization relative to 1980, (4) the level of customization in the future, (5) the extent to which products are customized today, and (6) the extent to which they are customizable today.

In addition to these six indicators of the shift to Mass Customization, two new indicators were included in the analysis. The measure *Maximum of Variety, Customization* takes the maximum of each respondent's answers to the questions on the relative levels of variety and customization. Similarly, the measure *Maximum of Future Variety, Customization* takes the maximum of each respondent's answers to the questions on the levels of future variety and customization. The intent of these two indicators is twofold: (1) to capture the fact that the paradigm shift can manifest itself in increased variety *or* customization (as well as both), and (2) eventually to use these two variables as proxies for all of the variety and customization questions, to boil down the amount of information provided into a more manageable whole.

Table A-5 provides the statistical correlations from each of these regression analyses, which indicate how strongly correlated the variables are.[1] Every measure of variety and customization is positively correlated with market turbulence in 1991 and with the change in market turbulence between 1980 and 1991. All but one correlation is statistically significant at the 95 percent level, all but one other at the

Table A-5 Correlations of Measures of Market Turbulence to
Indicators of the Paradigm Shift

Indicators of the Paradigm Shift	Measures of Market Turbulence	
	Market Turbulence in 1991	Change in Market Turbulence
Amount of Variety	.237**	.304***
Future Variety	.295***	.402***
Level of Customization	.189**	.340***
Future Customization	.220**	.408***
Extent Customized	.324***	.061
Extent Customizable	.287***	.154*
Maximum of Variety, Customization	.313***	.350***
Maximum of Future Variety, Customization	.342***	.436***

*Statistically significant at the 95% confidence level
**Statistically significant at the 99% confidence level
***Statistically significant at the 99.99% confidence level

99 percent level, and eleven of the sixteen correlations are statistically significant at the 99.99 percent level.

Still, while the correlation between increased market turbulence and increased variety/customization is extremely strong, correlations cannot prove causality. Detailed analysis of additional statistics (beyond the scope of this discussion)[2] support the following scenario:

- Higher levels of market turbulence *in the 1970s* caused firms to add customization to their products. This manifested itself more in customized than in customizable products. The customization done in this time frame was probably postproduction, added in a somewhat ad hoc manner to standardized products to increase their sales, which would conform to the model of Mass Customization presented in Chapter 3. This focus on customization was continued in the 1980s.
- Continued and increased turbulence in the 1980s through 1991 caused even more customization. However, it seems that the turbulence in the 1980s resulted in even more increased variety. If the firms with higher turbulence in the 1970s began customizing in the 1970s using postproduction processes and then turned their attention to increasing variety within production, their relative levels of customization in 1991 could indeed be less than those

firms whose turbulence started in the 1980s and began customizing in the 1980s.

- Firms also appear to be extrapolating their past experience into the future. While the increased levels of customization and then variety in the 1970s and 1980s may originally have been the result of incremental decisions, many of the firms undergoing an increasingly turbulent market environment now understand that it does not appear to be going away and acknowledge that it is increasing; they therefore recognize that the future will bring even more variety and customization. These are the firms that are making the shift to Mass Customization.

There may be other possible scenarios about what all of the detailed results indicate, but it does seem that increased market turbulence has led to increased variety and customization in the companies surveyed.

It appears from the survey results that change in market turbulence is the more effective predictor of increased variety and customization, as most all of the correlations given in Table A-5 for this measure are higher than those for the level of turbulence in 1991. This can be further seen in Figures A-3 and A-4, which group all of

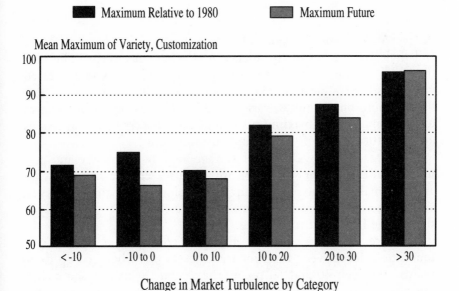

Figure A-3   Mean Results of Maximum Variety, Customization Indicators by Category of Change in Market Turbulence

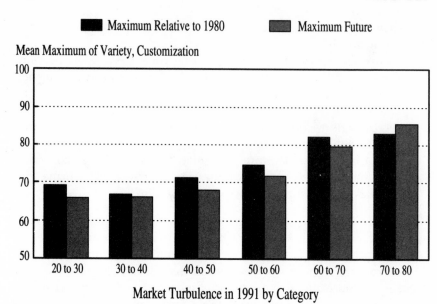

Figure A-4   Mean Results of Maximum Variety, Customization Indicators by Category of Market Turbulence Levels in 1991

the respondents into categories by their change in market turbulence and their static level of turbulence in 1991, respectively. The bars then indicate the mean of the two primary indicators of increased variety and customization: (1) the maximum value of the answers to the questions on amount of variety and level of customization relative to 1980, and (2) the maximum value of the answers to the questions on the future levels of variety and customization.

Figure A-3 shows that the average amount of variety and customization differs very little for any negative change in turbulence and for small positive changes up to 10 points. After that, however, variety and customization increase dramatically and proportionally to the change in market turbulence.

Figure A-4 shows that the average amount of variety and customization differs very little for static levels of turbulence up to 40 points. Between 40 and 60 points the amount increases somewhat, but after 60 points variety and customization increase significantly. However, this increase is not as dramatic as that seen in Figure A-3.

Therefore, managers should weigh the amount of their change in market turbulence more heavily than the current static level in trying to determine whether their industry is undergoing the shift to Mass Customization. Figure 4-6 provided guidelines for this determination.

Differences Across Industries

Five specific industry groups were heavily represented in the survey demographics, enough so that separate analyses could be done to determine whether the shift has occurred in each industry group or whether its extent differs across them. This analysis is quite illuminating. The industry groups are:

1. Automotive companies (including automobile manufacturers and their suppliers), which had 22 (9 percent) of the responses;

2. Information technology companies (including computer and semiconductor manufacturers, software providers, and internal information system business units), which had 35 (14 percent) of the responses;

3. Telecommunications companies (including AT&T, the Regional Bell Operating Companies, and others), which had 31 (12 percent) of the responses;

4. The defense industry (including the armed services and defense contractors), which had 35 (14 percent) of the responses; and

5. Commodity companies (including oil and gas production, petroleum products, mining, and utilities), which had 21 (8 percent) of the responses.

Table A-6 gives the average market turbulence measures for each industry group, and Table A-7 provides the primary indicators of variety and customization. These tables, which are ordered from most to least change in market turbulence, indicate that industries with high and increasing turbulence have seen proportionate increases in their variety and customization. In almost every case, the order of the data in Table A-7 follows the order in Table A-6. A most interesting picture emerges from examining these industry groups in more detail, one that conforms to what is known about these industry groups and the possibility of the paradigm shift in each.

Table A-6 Average Market Turbulence Measures for Five
Industry Groups

Industry Group	1980	1991	Change
Telecommunications	36	54	18
Information Technology	48	60	12
Automotive	53	61	8
Other Business Units	44	51	7
Defense	50	54	4
Commodity	35	39	4
All Business Units	44	53	9

Table A-7 Average Indicators of Variety and Customization for
Five Industry Groups

Industry Group	Amount of Variety	Future Variety	Level of Customization	Future Customization
Telecommunications	81	82	74	78
Information Technology	80	73	74	69
Automotive	76	72	66	66
Other Business Units	72	68	67	65
Defense	53	51	58	58
Commodity	51	53	59	58
All Business Units	70	67	67	66

Automotive Industry Group

The highest turbulence in 1980 (53) was in the automotive group,
whose turbulence then increased by 8 points in 1991. Automobile
manufacturing was one of the first industries to be hit by market
turbulence in the 1970s. The most turbulent factors in 1980 (see
Figure A-5) were dependence on economic cycles, reflecting the oil
shocks of the 1970s; price consciousness, always a big factor in the
industry; saturation levels; and then quality consciousness, competitive intensity, and service levels—all reflecting the tremendous success of the Japanese imports in the 1970s.

By 1980, Japanese automobile manufacturers were well on their
way to making the shift, increasing the number of models produced
each year while decreasing the product life of each model. This in-

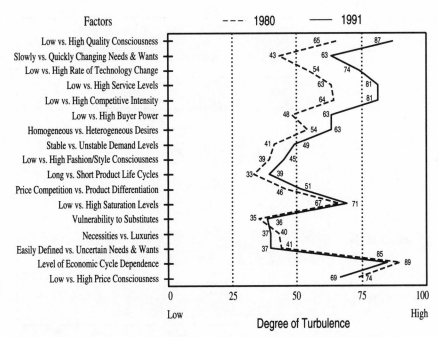

Figure A-5 Market Turbulence Map for Automotive Business Units

creased the turbulence for the American manufacturers even further. Between 1980 and 1991, competitive intensity, quality consciousness, and expected service levels also increased in turbulence. In addition, consumer wants became more heterogeneous, and both the rate of change in their desires and the rate of product technology change increased dramatically. This was probably caused by the tremendous variety that became available to them in the 1980s not only from Japanese but from American producers as well. As Figure A-6 shows, American manufacturers also greatly increased their variety and, to a lesser extent, their levels of customization in the 1970s and 1980s. The respondents expect this trend to continue into the future.

It appears that the increased variety and customization in this industry is no longer just the sum of incremental decisions but may reflect the beginnings of a true shift from Mass Production to Mass Customization. As an executive at one of the American automobile manufacturers stated in response to one of the open-ended questions:

[Customers] are demanding more variety to meet their new needs/circumstances. The manufacturers have demonstrated that they can customize

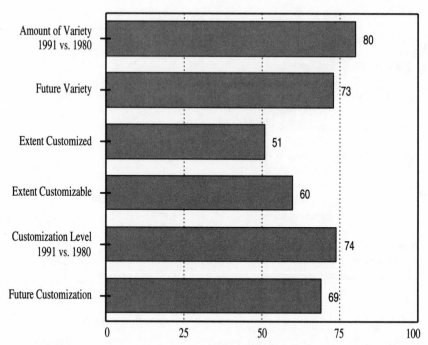

Figure A-6 Variety and Customization Profile for Automotive Business Units

products to meet these new expectations and I believe the trend will be endless as automakers find more ways to economically justify smaller production runs, while providing more variety/choice to the customer. . . . Obstacles to economical justification will surface from time to time but will be overcome.

Another respondent, an executive with one of the big three auto manufacturers, said: "I think the capability to get to a lot size of one is critical—if nothing else than to get your 'mind right!'"

Unfortunately, the roots of Mass Production run very deep in Detroit. Its reaction to the recession of 1990–1991 was limited by its history of traditional responses: lengthen development cycles, lay off employees, squeeze suppliers, and ask for more protectionist measures. But, over the long haul, the industry has begun taking many of the steps necessary to shake off the old mentality. It is only a matter of time before they make the shift—or lose out almost completely to the Japanese manufacturers, who are fast becoming grounded in the new paradigm.

Information Technology Industry Group

The information technology group had the second highest turbulence in 1991 (60), just one point behind the automotive group, but the movement was greater: 12 points since 1980. Figures A-7 and A-8 provide the detailed information for this industry. As the Market Turbulence Map shows, four factors became less turbulent in the 1980s (demand levels, necessities/luxuries, certainty of needs, and price competition versus product differentiation), while every other factor moved largely in the direction of greater turbulence. Leading the way were saturation levels, competitive intensity, vulnerability to substitutes, and quality consciousness.

As the Variety and Customization Profile demonstrates, during the 1980s the amount of variety and customization increased dramatically—in an industry already renowned for high degrees of both. This industry is the only one of those analyzed whose products are more customizable than they are customized. Many of the business units surveyed appear to be moving in the direction of Mass Customization, as a sample of responses indicates.

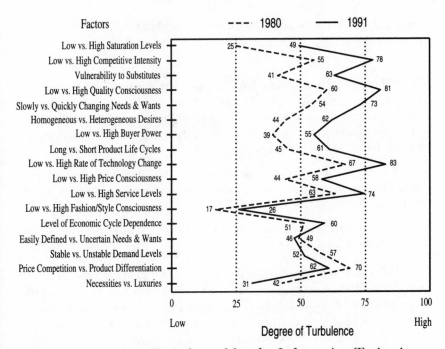

Figure A-7 Market Turbulence Map for Information Technology Business Units

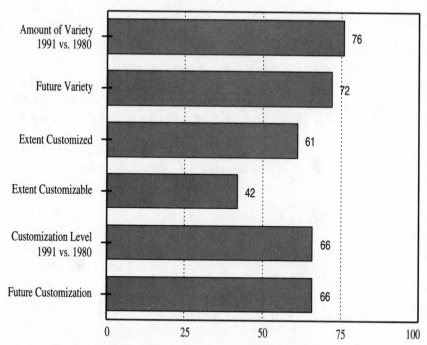

Figure A-8 Variety and Customization Profile for Information Technology Business Units

[The trend toward more variety and customization] will continue at [an] accelerated pace. Ultimately [the] overwhelming majority of systems will be tailored & customized. Only commodity items will not. . . . The product[s] will have "no" limits to customization. Software can do that. The limiting factor will be skilled people.

The trend toward customization will continue into the foreseeable future. There is the potential that products will be customized for individual customers. It occurs today in some cases.

Our software now requires a method for self-customization or it won't sell. In 1980, a fixed application was OK.

But the computer industry is coming under increasing pressure from its customers to standardize both hardware and software, so that they will not be locked in to one manufacturer but can easily switch vendors. A respondent from a computer manufacturer that uses the industry-standard UNIX operating system stated that [customers] want less variety/customization and more standards. The economics of standard hardware and software products are compelling. The trend will move as far and as fast as we (vendors) can push it because it is a competitive weapon.

However, as seen earlier in this chapter during the discussion of buyer power, standards do not remove the need for variety and customization but change its locus from operating systems, for example, to hardware and application software. The numbers of minicomputer manufacturers going after particular market segments would not be so great if they could not pick the UNIX operating system from off the shelf to reduce their development costs, and they would make few sales if their products didn't operate (thanks to standards) in computer networks with equipment from other manufacturers. Similarly, the proliferation of hundreds of personal computer models would be impossible without the standard DOS operating system.

To view the powerful trend toward industry standards as customers demanding less variety and customization, as the respondent above appears to have done, is missing the point. This same respondent revealed that his business unit was providing a great deal more variety (90 on the 100-point scale) and customization (60) than in 1980, and would provide even more in the future (70 on both). Yet his understanding of the industry was so wrapped up in standards that he would say customers wanted less variety and customization. Just as automobile buyers want to be able to switch from model to model without having to learn how to drive each new one, computer customers want to be able to switch from system to system without having to learn how to operate each new one—provided that the system can be customized to solve their unique business problems.

Telecommunications Industry Group

The telecommunications industry underwent by far the greatest increase in market turbulence, from 36 to 54. The reason, of course, is the breakup of the old Bell system in 1984. In 1980, the average turbulence in telecommunications was essentially the same as that of commodity business units (36 and 35, respectively), because, with the regulation of AT&T, telephone service *was* essentially a commodity. The breakup, however, unleashed new market forces on that giant company and on the Regional Bell Operating Companies that changed the nature of telecommunications in the United States.

As the Market Turbulence Map shown in Figure A-9 demonstrates, every market environment factor became more turbulent except for price competition versus product differentiation, which remained at the same level. The competitive intensity in the industry skyrocketed (from 35 to 73), as did the vulnerability to substitutes (29 to 60). Other factors that increased by 20 or more points were the rate of change in both product technology and customer wants; buyer power; shorter product life cycles; and price consciousness. All of these can be directly attributed to the Bell system breakup.

The results of the dramatically increased turbulence can be seen in Figure A-10. The amount of variety and level of customization relative to 1980 is almost identical to that of the information technology industry group, but owing to the rate of change in its market environment, the telecommunications industry is forecasting more variety and customization—more than in the information technology industry, and much more than in its own recent past.

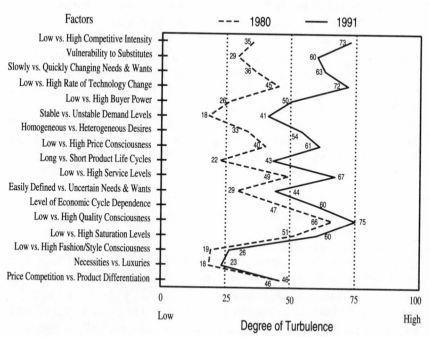

Figure A-9 Market Turbulence Map for Telecommunications Business Units

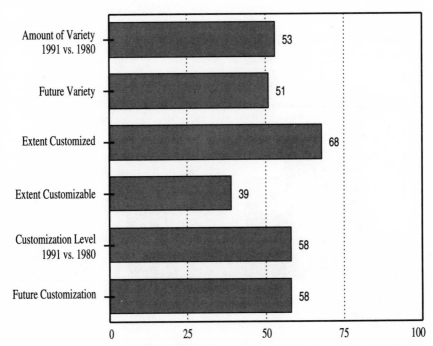

Figure A-10 Variety and Customization Profile for Telecommunications Business Units

As Figure A-11 demonstrates, despite the fact that it consists of mostly service companies, the telecommunications industry is very much an industry of mass-production processes. If the responses to the open-ended questions are any indication, this industry understands better than any other that mass-produced products and services can and will be individually customized. Many respondents acknowledged the power of individual customization. These three are typical.

Microlevel need can eventually be met on a custom basis at the same unit cost as today's mass production.

Price is still the dominant selection factor [but] the postindustrial shift toward customization is likely to accelerate in this industry. . . . [There is] no technological limit—individual customization will be available if the market wants it.

[Regarding variety and customization, there will be] far more! This is because [customers] have seen what can be done and imagined the extensions that should be available. This will ultimately lead to "mass customization"

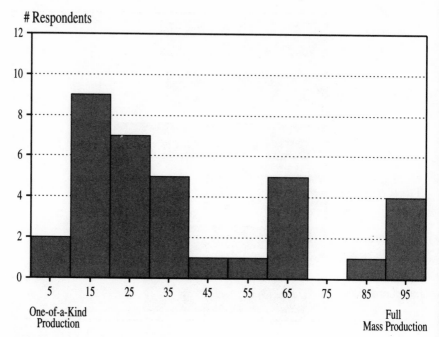

Figure A-11   One-of-a-Kind vs. Full Mass Production: Telecommunications Business Units

where customers will "create" their own versions of products to their own specifications.

Both the information technology and telecommunications industry have the software and hardware technology to provide full customization at virtually the same price as standardized goods. It appears that the telecommunications industry is striving hardest to reach that point.

Defense Industry Group

The defense industry group (including the armed services, whose respondents were mostly from research laboratories or product development groups), which had the second highest turbulence in 1980 (50), didn't change all that much by 1991, increasing its turbulence by "only" 4 points. As a glance at its Market Turbulence Map (Figure A-12) shows, none of the factors changed as dramatically as the other industries. The biggest change (17 points) was in price consciousness,

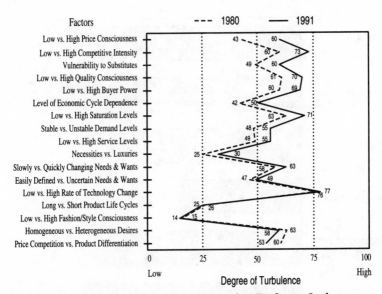

Figure A-12 Market Turbulence Map for Defense Industry Business Units

no surprise given the budget arguments of the 1980s. Competitive intensity, quality consciousness, and vulnerability to substitutes were the only other factors to increase by 10 or more points. The only factor to reach the 75-point mark (which it did in both time frames) was the rate of product technology change, which has always been significant in the defense industry.

Directly corresponding to the small increase in market turbulence was the small increase in variety and customization, as seen in Figure A-13. However, a market environment in the 50- to 54-point range is still quite turbulent, and the base amount of variety and particularly customization in the defense industry remains high—far higher than that of any other industry group. As one defense contractor stated: "What they want and pay for they will get."

It would be difficult to say, however, that the defense industry has made the shift to Mass Customization, for most contractors have never really been mass producers or "mass" anything. Defense products are generally of much smaller lot sizes than general industry and are customized to the specifications of the Pentagon and its branches. Low costs and volume production have never been hallmarks of this

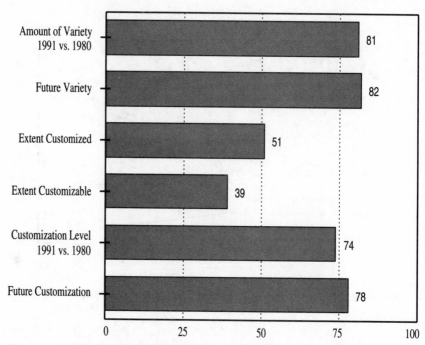

Figure A-13 Variety and Customization Profile for Defense
Industry Business Units

industry. As Figure A-14 shows, the defense sample in this survey
was indeed weighted toward one-of-a-kind production.

Commodity Industry Group

Businesses that provide commodity products (e.g., oil and gas, petroleum products, mining, and utilities) had low turbulence in both 1980
and 1991. As Figure A-15 shows, there were no large changes in any
of the factors. The Variety and Customization Profile given in Figure
A-16 is exactly what one would expect: only small increases in variety
and customization relative to 1980 and in the future, with little customization of today's products. Obviously, no paradigm shift is occurring in the commodity businesses surveyed. In reply to the open-
ended question on whether customers are demanding more variety or
customization, one respondent simply indicated "not applicable."

However, over time the potential is there. Saturation levels, competitive intensity, and price consciousness are all highly turbulent.

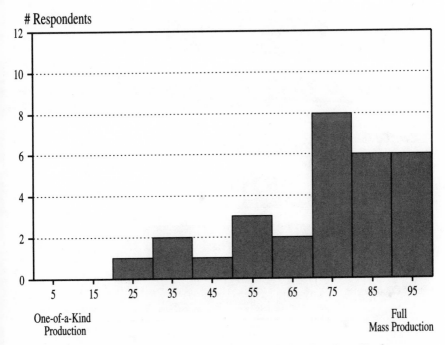

Figure A-14   One-of-a-Kind vs. Full Mass Production: Defense
Industry Business Units

Demand levels have become a little less stable and predictable; the
rate of change in customers' needs and wants has increased slightly;
quality consciousness has moved over into the turbulent half of the
scale; and buyers are gaining more power. While it is unlikely that
something as cataclysmic as the breakup of the Bell system will occur
to move these other commodities into a highly turbulent market environment almost overnight, something like utility deregulation, a prolonged oil glut, or the innovation of cheap, efficient alternative fuels
could move segments to explore significantly higher levels of variety
and customization.

   The past ten or twenty years have, for example, produced multiple varieties of gasoline available at the pump. Several respondents
from electric utilities noted that, while they can't provide much variety, customers do want customized rate structures. A provider of
petroleum lubricants said that many customers are demanding more
variety and customization, demand that is going not to the large pro-

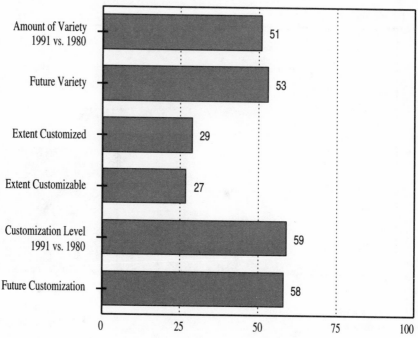

Figure A-16 Variety and Customization Profile for Commodity
Business Units

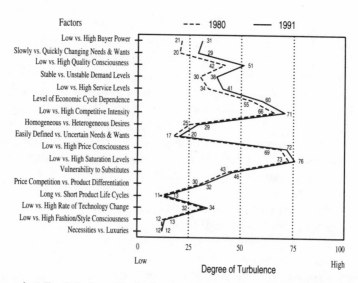

Figure A-15 Market Turbulence Map for Commodity Business
Units

ducers but to "specialty houses." And as noted in Chapter 3, many personal care items—shampoo, soap, toothbrushes, diapers—were once commodities but are now characterized by high levels of variety and innovation. It can happen. Managers in commodity companies should track their market turbulence and understand that the situation may change.

The analysis of these five industry groups reveals that all differ in the degrees of change in market turbulence and variety/customization, and that these differences conform to what is known about each industry group. Through the use of the Market Turbulence Map and the Variety and Customization Profile, we were able to discern to what extent the shift from Mass Production to Mass Customization is occurring. The greater the increase in market turbulence within each industry group, the greater the increase in variety and customization.

Notes

Chapter 1

1. This parable was originally suggested by Jim Utterback of MIT and the late William Abernathy of Harvard.

2. The key points in this story can be found in the introduction and the 1854–1855 reports from English observers in America provided in Nathan Rosenberg, ed., *The American System of Manufactures: The Report of the Committee on the Machinery of the United States 1855 and the Special Reports of George Wallis and Joseph Whitworth 1854* (Edinburgh: Edinburgh University Press, 1969). A partial listing of specific references includes:

- Focus on the low end of product categories: pp. 281–282.
- Imitators of products, not inventors: pp. 65–66.
- Fear of overwhelming England with imports: p. 193.
- Advice to emulate the American System: pp. 128–129.
- Manufacturing system based on workers, machinery, and flow of materials: p. 193.
- High skills of workers and their productivity: pp. 15, 27–29, 121–122, 283.
- Worker cooperation to constantly improve quality of products: p. 14.
- High attendance and cleanliness of workers: p. 194.
- High education level of workers and praise for education system: pp. 28, 283.
- Rapid diffusion of innovation to somewhat cooperating competitors: pp. 59–60, 65.
- Reliance on subcontractors: pp. 116–117.
- Homogeneous culture: pp. 7, 282.

3. W. W. Rostow, *The World Economy: History and Prospect* (Austin: University of Texas Press, 1978), pp. 52–53, cited in Alfred D. Chandler, Jr., *Scale and Scope: The Dynamics of Industrial Capitalism* (Cambridge, Mass.: The Belknap Press of Harvard University Press, 1990), p. 4.

4. Throughout, management systems and paradigms such as the American System and Mass Production are capitalized because of their influence across countries and industries, differentiating them from the activities and outputs of individual firms, for example, "mass-producing" particular products or services.

5. Michael L. Dertouzos, Richard K. Lester, Robert M. Solow, and the MIT Commission on Industrial Productivity, *Made in America: Regaining the Productive Edge* (Cambridge, Mass.: MIT Press, 1990), p. 166.

6. The term "mass customization" was coined by Stanley M. Davis in *Future Perfect* (Reading, Mass.: Addison-Wesley, 1987).

Chapter 2

1. Michael J. Piore and Charles F. Sabel, *The Second Industrial Divide: Possibilities for Prosperity* (New York: Basic Books, 1984), p. 19.

2. Ibid.

3. For a full discussion of the American System and the rise of Mass Production, see Nathan Rosenberg, ed., *The American System of Manufactures: The Report of the Committee on the Machinery of the United States 1855 and the Special Reports of George Wallis and Joseph Whitworth 1854* (Edinburgh: Edinburgh University Press, 1969); and David A. Hounshell, *From the American System to Mass Production 1800–1932: The Development of Manufacturing Technology in the United States* (Baltimore: Johns Hopkins University Press, 1984).

4. Michael H. Best, *The New Competition: Institutions of Industrial Restructuring* (Cambridge, Mass.: Harvard University Press, 1990), p. 29.

5. Nathan Rosenberg, *Technology and American Economic Growth* (Armonk, N.Y.: M. E. Sharpe, 1972), pp. 25–27.

6. Ibid., pp. 90–92. Rosenberg notes that "at one point in the Napoleonic Wars (1811) the British government had in its possession some 200,000 musket barrels which were useless because of the absence of a sufficient supply of skilled armorers to make or repair the locks" (p. 92).

7. Rosenberg, *The American System of Manufactures*, pp. 59–60.

8. See Rosenberg, *Technology and American Economic Growth*, pp. 97–107.

9. Nathan Rosenberg, *Perspectives on Technology* (Cambridge, England: Cambridge University Press, 1976), p. 162.

10. William J. Abernathy, Kim B. Clark, and Alan M. Kantrow, *Industrial Renaissance: Producing a Competitive Future for America* (New York: Basic Books, 1983), pp. 32–33. See also Hounshell, *From the American System to Mass Production 1800–1932*, for descriptions of how the entrepreneurs of the period focused on the production process involved in the American System.

11. "Report from the Select Committee on Scientific Instruction," Parliamentary Papers, 15 (1867–8) Question 6722, quoted in Rosenberg, *The American System of Manufactures*, p. 15. This is not an isolated quote; the reports published in this volume frequently praise American workers, especially in relation to those in England.

12. See Piore and Sabel, *The Second Industrial Divide*, p. 46.

13. Abernathy, Clark, and Kantrow, *Industrial Renaissance*, pp. 33–34.

14. Rosenberg, *Technology and American Economic Growth*, p. 102.

15. Quoted in Alexis de Tocqueville, *Journeys to England and Ireland* (1958), J. P. Mayer, ed., p. 111, cited in H. J. Habakkuk, *American and British Technology in the Nineteenth Century: The Search for Labour-saving Inventions* (Cambridge, England: Cambridge University Press, 1962), p. 57.

16. No real distinction is made here between mass production processes as used in the automobile industry, continuous process methods as used in the aluminum industry, machine-tending processes as used in the textile industry, or, for that matter, the assembly-line-like techniques used in many service industries. Each shares most of the common traits of the system of Mass Production discussed in this chapter.

17. These examples can be found in Alfred D. Chandler, Jr., *The Visible Hand: The Managerial Revolution in American Business* (Cambridge, Mass.: The Belknap Press of Harvard University Press, 1977), pp. 249–258; and Hounshell, *From the American System to Mass Production 1800–1932*, pp. 10–11. See also Rosenberg, *Technology and American Growth*, pp. 107–116; and for a more detailed history of the development of the assembly line, Siegfried Giedion,

Mechanization Takes Command: a contribution of anonymous history (New York: Oxford University Press, 1948), pp. 77–127.

18. Hounshell, *From the American System to Mass Production 1800–1932*, p. 237.

19. Chandler, *The Visible Hand*, p. 280.

20. See Best, *The New Competition*, pp. 36–37; and Hounshell, *From the American System to Mass Production 1800–1932*, p. 9. Interestingly, the only sector of the American System that seemed to focus on low costs were government-sponsored armament manufacturers.

21. Best, *The New Competition*, pp. 47–55; and Piore and Sabel, *The Second Industrial Divide*, pp. 190–191. This cycle, the heart of Mass Production, is fully explored later in this chapter.

22. Hounshell, *From the American System to Mass Production 1800–1932*, pp. 223–224, 274.

23. Ibid., pp. 247–248.

24. Chandler, *The Visible Hand*, p. 491.

25. Frederick W. Taylor, *The Principles of Scientific Management* (New York: W. W. Norton, 1967; originally published in 1911), p. 36.

26. See Chapter 4 for a description of this research.

27. Thomas S. Kuhn, *The Structure of Scientific Revolutions*, 2d ed., enlarged (New York: New American Library, 1986), p. 19.

28. In examining scientific communities and the structure of revolutions in the ideas, thoughts, and theories of those communities, Kuhn, ibid., broadened what was then an obscure word meaning an "example or pattern," and in particular an especially clear or typical example, an "archetype," into something more. In a postscript to the second edition of *The Structure of Scientific Revolutions* (p. 144), he relates that

in much of the book the term "paradigm" is used in two different senses. On the one hand, it stands for the entire constellation of beliefs, values, techniques, and so on shared by the members of a given community. On the other, it denotes one sort of element in that constellation, the concrete puzzle-solutions which, employed as models or examples, can replace explicit rules as a basis for the solution of the remaining puzzles of normal science.

In both these senses, as seen in this chapter and in Chapter 5, the word *paradigm* applies to the system of Mass Production in America.

29. Joel Arthur Barker, *Discovering the Future: The Business of Paradigms* (St. Paul: ILI Press, 1988), p. 14; emphasis deleted.

30. Piore and Sabel, *The Second Industrial Divide*, pp. 190–191. While the following presentation is original, I am heavily indebted for the view given here of Mass Production as a reinforcing feedback loop with inherent limits to Michael Piore and Charles Sabel of MIT. Another example of this type of view (without limits, however) may be found in Robert Ayres and Ehud Zuscovitch, "Technology and Information: Chain Reactions and Sustainable Economic Growth," *Technovation* 10:3 (1990), pp. 163–183.

31. We normally view things like the producer/consumer relationship as a linear chain of cause and effect rather than as a system with reinforcing feedback loops. This latter view is promoted by the System Dynamics Group at MIT. For an understanding of this view of the world and more information on how to create and read diagrams like Figure 2-3, see Peter M. Senge, *The Fifth Discipline: The Art and Practice of the Learning Organization* (New York: Doubleday Currency, 1990).

32. Ibid., p. 83.

33. See Robert H. Hayes and William J. Abernathy, "Managing Our Way to Economic Decline," *Harvard Business Review* (July–August 1980), pp. 67–77.

Chapter 3

1. Michael H. Best, *The New Competition: Institutions of Industrial Restructuring* (Cambridge, Mass.: Harvard University Press, 1990), pp. 137–138.

304

2. Joel Arthur Barker, *Discovering the Future: The Business of Pardigms* (St. Paul: ILI Press, 1988), p. 15.

3. William J. Abernathy, Kim B. Clark, and Alan M. Kantrow, *Industrial Renaissance: Producing a Competitive Future for America* (New York: Basic Books, 1983), pp. 15–16.

4. Ibid., pp. 15–29 in particular.

5. Data for Western automobile firms are from Antony M. Sheriff and Kentaro Nobeoka of MIT, with the detail included for 1980–1987 in Sheriff, "Product Development in the Automobile Industry: Corporate Strategies and Project Performance," master's thesis, MIT, June 1990.

6. Joel D. Goldhar and Theodore W. Schlie, "Computer Technology and International Competition: Part 2: Managing the 'Factory of the Future' to Achieve Competitive Advantage," *Integrated Manufacturing Systems*, vol. 2, no. 2, p. 27.

7. Gary Hamel and C. K. Prahalad, "Corporate Imagination and Expeditionary Marketing," *Harvard Business Review* (July–August 1991), pp. 81–92. Data are from the table on p. 88.

8. Kathleen Deveny, "Toothbrush Makers Hope to Clean Up with Array of 'New, Improved' Products," *The Wall Street Journal*, October 22, 1991, pp. B1, B10.

9. Greg Prince, "Their Mug Runneth Over," *Beverage World* (September 1991), p. 20.

10. Data are from John C. Maxwell, Jr., of Wheat First Securities.

11. James Scarpa, "McDonald's Menu Mission," *Restaurant Business*, July 1, 1991, p. 117.

12. Ibid., p. 115.

13. Quoted in Lois Therrien, "McRisky," *Business Week*, October 21, 1991, p. 117.

14. Scarpa, "McDonald's Menu Mission," p. 110.

15. Ronald V. Dolan, "Focus on Products and Perspectives: Ronald V. Dolan, President, First Colony Life Insurance Company," *Broker World* (January 1988), p. 42.

16. Robert A. Shafto, "Looking Toward the 21st Century," *LIMRA's Marketfacts* (July/August 1990), p. 35.

17. See David C. Jones, "The New England Starts $50M Tech. Project," *National Underwriter*, September 10, 1990, p. 8, and Christopher Lindquist, "The New England's World Class Life," *Computerworld*, July 8, 1991, pp. 57, 60.

18. Stephen P. White, "Old Truisms Won't Get You Far in the '90s," *American Banker*, July 17, 1991, p. 4.

19. Quoted in Barry I. Deutsch, "A Conversation with Philip Kotler," *Bank Marketing* (December 1990), p. 19.

20. The Mass Customization feedback loop could be presented in a number of ways, but is shown as the reversal of the Mass Production feedback loop for simplicity and ease of comparison.

21. For the view that the American economy is in fact going back to Craft Production as the primary paradigm of management, see Glenn Bassett, *Management Strategies for Today's Project Shop Economy* (New York: Quorum Books, 1991).

22. For an excellent discussion of advanced manufacturing technologies, see Hamid Noori, *Managing the Dynamics of New Technology: Issues in Manufacturing Management* (Englewood Cliffs, N.J.: Prentice-Hall, 1990).

23. Ibid., pp. 140–145.

24. These themes are treated in more depth in Chapter 6, "The New Competition."

25. Stanley M. Davis, *Future Perfect* (Reading, Mass.: Addison-Wesley, 1987), p. 157.

26. Obviously, there are limits and perils to the paradigm of Mass Customization, just as there are to that of Mass Production. These are discussed in Chapter 10.

Chapter 4

1. See Thomas S. Kuhn, *The Structure of Scientific Revolutions*, 2d ed., enlarged (New York: New American Library, 1986), pp. 64–75; and Joel Arthur Barker, *Discovering the Future: The Business of Paradigms* (St. Paul: ILI Press, 1988), pp. 40–45.

2. This follows the definition of turbulence as "more events per unit of time" provided in Rashi Glazer, "Marketing in an Information-Intensive Environment: Strategic Implications of Knowledge as an Asset," *Journal of Marketing* (October 1991), pp. 1–19.

3. William J. Abernathy and James M. Utterback, "Patterns of Industrial Innovation," *Technology Review* (June–July 1978), pp. 40–47.

4. See Jacob M. Schlesinger, "Japanese Get First Crack at New Gadgets as Firms Use Local Stores to Test Demand," *The Wall Street Journal*, December 3, 1990, pp. B1, B7.

5. William J. Abernathy, Kim B. Clark, and Alan M. Kantrow, *Industrial Renaissance: Producing a Competitive Future for America* (New York: Basic Books, 1983), pp. 15–29 in particular. For a discussion by Utterback of how the Japanese have been successful at entering an industry after a dominant design has emerged (which was previously unheard of) through continual product innovation, see James M. Utterback and Freddy F. Suárez, "Innovation, Competition, and Industry Structure," Working Paper #29–90, International Center for Research on the Management of Technology, MIT, December 1990, pp. 29–35 in particular.

6. See Jeremy Main, "The Winning Organization," *Fortune*, September 26, 1988, pp. 27–28; and George Stalk, Jr., and Thomas M. Hout, *Competing Against Time* (New York: Free Press, 1990), p. 109.

7. Before I conducted the research discussed later in this chapter, it was fairly clear that increased price consciousness would yield greater turbulence, but uncertain whether it would lead to greater variety and customization. However, the research did find that the correlation existed (see Table 4-3 and the Appendix).

8. As an example, for a description of how segment retreat in the face of Japanese competition caused the British motorcycle industry to continue believing it was profitable and viable until it was finally overwhelmed, see The Boston Consulting Group Limited, *Strategy Alternatives for the British Motorcycle Industry: A Report Prepared for the Secretary of State for Industry* (London: Her Majesty's Stationery Office, 1975).

9. Many of the structural factors are directly related to the concept of industry structure and dynamics given in Michael E. Porter, *Competitive Strategy: Techniques for Analyzing Industries and Competitors* (New York: Free Press, 1980).

10. Michael S. Piore and Charles F. Sabel, *The Second Industrial Divide: Possibilities for Prosperity* (New York: Basic Books, 1984), pp. 165–183.

11. Ibid., p. 184.

12. Decreasing product reliability to decrease time to replacement ("planned obsolescence") is another alternative that has little merit in today's quality-oriented world.

13. Jennifer Pellet, "A Surge in New Candy Products," *Discount Merchandiser* (September 1990), pp. 56–59.

14. In particular, I am not using the term "product life cycle" in the sense of the cycle that entire classes of products go through: introduction, growth, maturity, and decline.

15. Alvin Toffler, *Future Shock* (New York: Bantam Books, 1970), pp. 19–35 in particular.

16. See Glazer, "Marketing in an Information-Intensive Environment: Strategic Implications of Knowledge as an Asset," pp. 1–19, and Tjerk Huppes, *The Western Edge: Work and Management in the Information Age* (Boston: Kluwer Academic Publishers, 1987) for excellent expositions of this subject.

17. The information in this map was provided by the corporation's director of Market Analysis as part of the survey described later in this chapter.

18. For a complete description of this research and all its findings, see Buddie Joseph Pine II, "Paradigm Shift: From Mass Production to Mass Customization," master's thesis, MIT, June 1991.

19. While the survey uses words like "product" and "production" throughout, respondents from service companies are specifically asked to translate "product" into "service," and so on. Only a handful of respondents, most of whom were either consultants or in the defense industry, indicated that the wording was inappropriate for them.

20. Least-squares regression determines the line that best fits the data by minimizing the squares of the distances of all of the data points to that line. If the resulting line indicates that an increase in one measure corresponds to an increase in another, then the two measures are

said to be correlated. To say that a correlation is "statistically significant at the 95 percent confidence level" means that there is only a 5 percent chance that the result could happen by chance and a 95 percent chance that the two measures are indeed correlated.

21. While the correlation between the extent to which products are customized and the change in market turbulence is positive, it is not statistically significant.

22. More empirical evidence that supports this finding can be found in Sunder Kekre and Kannan Srinivasan, "Broader Product Line: A Necessity to Achieve Success?" *Management Science* (October 1990), pp. 1216–1231. These authors studied the self-reported information from more than 1,400 business units contained in the Profit Impact of Marketing Strategies database and found that firms with broader product lines achieved higher market share, greater profits, *and* lower costs. The authors had hypothesized that higher costs would be associated with broader product lines.

23. See Pine, "Paradigm Shift," Appendix B, for a description of how these rankings were conducted. Two results should be noted. First, saturation levels come up dead last, probably because high levels of saturation may be the most important reason that some companies decided to retreat from turbulent market segments rather than stay and fight by increasing variety and customization. While this factor cannot predict what individual companies will do, it is still useful for predicting where the industry itself is headed. Second, even though Figure 4-4 shows two market environment factors decreasing in turbulence (necessities versus luxuries and price competition versus product differentiation), an increase in turbulence in these two factors still correlated with increases in variety and customization, as Table 4-3 shows.

Chapter 5

1. See, for example, Michael H. Best, *The New Competition: Institutions of Industrial Restructuring* (Cambridge, Mass.: Harvard University Press, 1990); William J. Abernathy, Kim B. Clark, and Alan M. Kantrow, *Industrial Renaissance: Producing a Competitive Future for America* (New York: Basic Books, 1983); and Philip Kotler, Liam Fahey, and Somkid Jatusripitak, *The New Competition* (Englewood Cliffs, N.J.: Prentice-Hall, 1985).

2. Siegfried Giedion, *Mechanization Takes Command: a contribution of anonymous history* (New York: Oxford University Press, 1948), p. 93.

3. Seymour Melman, "The Rise of Administrative Overhead in the Manufacturing Industries of the United States, 1899–1947," *Oxford Economic Papers* 3 (1951), p. 66; cited in William Lazonick, *Competitive Advantage on the Shop Floor* (Cambridge, Mass.: Harvard University Press, 1990), pp. 229–230.

4. Alfred D. Chandler, Jr., *The Visible Hand: The Managerial Revolution in American Business* (Cambridge, Mass.: The Belknap Press of Harvard University Press, 1977), p. 236.

5. Ibid., p. 8. It should be pointed out that Chandler's tone in describing the permanence, power, and growth of organizational hierarchies is not the negative one presented here.

6. Rosabeth Moss Kanter, *The Change Masters: Innovation and Entrepreneurship in the American Corporation* (New York: Simon & Schuster, 1983), p. 18.

7. See Lazonick, *Competitive Advantage on the Shop Floor*, pp. 222–228.

8. John Anderson, *General Statement of the Past and Present Condition of the Several Manufacturing Branches of the War Department* (London: H.M.S.O., 1857), p. 31, cited in Nathan Rosenberg, *The American System of Manufactures: The Report of the Committee on the Machinery of the United States 1855 and the Special Reports of George Wallis and Joseph Whitworth 1854* (Edinburgh: Edinburgh University Press, 1969), p. 66.

9. Richard Florida and Martin Kenney, *The Breakthrough Illusion: Corporate America's Failure to Move from Innovation to Mass Production* (New York: Basic Books, 1990), p. 19.

10. Michael L. Dertouzos, Richard K. Lester, Robert M. Solow, and the MIT Commission on Industrial Productivity, *Made in America: Regaining the Productive Edge* (Cambridge, Mass.: MIT Press, 1990), p. 67.

11. Florida and Kenney, *The Breakthrough Illusion*, p. 21.

12. Ibid., p. 28.

13. See, for example, Frederick E. Webster, Jr., "Rediscovery of the Marketing Concept," *Business Horizons* (May–June 1988), pp. 29–39.

14. Philip Kotler, *Marketing Management: Analysis, Planning, Implementation, and Control*, 7th ed. (Englewood Cliffs, N.J.: Prentice-Hall, 1991), p. 13. Kotler, professor of international marketing at the Kellogg Graduate School of Management, Northwestern University, is one of the world's leading experts on marketing. The discussion here on the focus of the marketing function in Mass Production companies is more or less an amalgamation of three concepts Kotler gives as "the production concept," "the product concept," and "the selling concept." All are inferior, under most circumstances, to "the marketing concept," which Kotler defines as "determining the needs and wants of target markets and delivering the desired satisfactions more effectively and efficiently than competitors" (p. 16).

15. American automakers have had to rework cars for export to Japan to meet government regulations. Since this is work performed after manufacturing rather than changes designed into cars, it has been quite expensive. In 1982, rework cost Ford $400 to $500 per car exported to Japan (Kotler, Fahey, and Jatusripitak, *The New Competition*, p. 56).

16. Harold Poling, quoted in Alex Taylor III, "Ford to the Feds: Help Detroit," *Fortune*, September 9, 1991, p. 132. In response to criticism on this specific issue, Ford, GM, and Chrysler announced, in October 1991, that they would produce a right-hand drive model for Japan—sometime in the mid-1990s. Meanwhile, Honda produces right-wheel drive in its Marysville, Ohio, plant and in 1991 surpassed GM in exporting the most cars from America to Japan.

17. This includes trying to sell the government on protectionism, as Mr. Poling was doing.

18. Edward N. Cole, quoted in "GM Takes the High Ground in the Battle of Detroit," *Fortune*, May 1, 1969, p. 71, cited in Kotler, Fahey, and Jatusripitak, *The New Competition*, p. 47.

19. Richard Gerstenberg, quoted in "The Small Car Blues at General Motors," *Business Week*, March 16, 1974, p. 79, cited in ibid., p. 57.

20. Kotler, *Marketing Management*, p. 15.

21. Anonymous, quoted in James P. Womack, Daniel T. Jones, and Daniel Roos, *The Machine That Changed the World* (New York: Rawson Associates, 1990), p. 174.

22. Peter Drucker, *Management: Tasks, Responsibilities, Practices* (New York: Harper & Row, 1973), pp. 64–65.

23. For an excellent description of this entire process for Japanese producers, see Kotler, Fahey, and Jatusripitak, *The New Competition*. For details on the television set example, see also Liam Fahey and Michael Radnor, "The Product-Market Strategies of U.S. and Japanese Firms in the U.S. Consumer Electronics Marketplace," in Sang M. Lee and Gary Schwendiman, *Management by Japanese Systems* (New York: Praeger, 1982), pp. 334–346.

24. D. J. Collis, R. Phelps, and N. Donohue, "General Electric—Consumer Electronics Group," Case #389-048. Boston: Harvard Business School, 1989.

25. Stanley W. Angrist, "Inspired Management," *The Wall Street Journal*, June 28, 1991, p. A11, citing Ira C. Magaziner and Mark Patinkin, *The Silent War: Inside the Global Business Battles Shaping America's Future* (New York: Random House, 1989).

26. The latter two effects were significant factors in the television industry takeover. The Japanese did use inflated prices in their home market to subsidize their exports to the United States, and their long-term home market need for smaller TV sets for the smaller homes and apartments in Japan left them ideally positioned for the movement by U.S. consumers to purchase smaller TVs as second sets. See Fahey and Radnor, "The Product-Market Strategies of U.S. and Japanese Firms in the U.S. Consumer Electronics Marketplace."

27. H. Thomas Johnson and Robert S. Kaplan, *Relevance Lost: The Rise and Fall of Management Accounting* (Boston: Harvard Business School Press, 1987), pp. 6–7.

28. Ibid., Chapters 2 and 3.

29. Ibid., pp. 125–126.

30. Robert H. Hayes and William J. Abernathy, "Managing Our Way to Economic Decline," *Harvard Business Review* (July–August 1980), p. 70. See also Michael T. Jacobs, *Short-Term America: The Causes and Cures of Our Business Myopia* (Boston: Harvard Business School Press, 1991).

31. Johnson and Kaplan, *Relevance Lost*, p. 197.

32. For the automobile industry as an example, see Susan Helper, "How Much Has Really Changed between U.S. Automakers and Their Suppliers?" *Sloan Management Review* (Summer 1991), pp. 15–28.

33. Johnson and Kaplan, *Relevance Lost*, Chapter 7.

34. Ibid., pp. 185–186.

35. See ibid., Chapter 8, and H. Thomas Johnson, "Managing Costs: An Outmoded Philosophy," *Manufacturing Engineering* (May 1989), pp. 42–46.

36. Federal Trade Commission, *Statistical Report on Mergers and Acquisitions*, 1977, p. 106, Table 19, cited in Richard A. Brealey and Stewart C. Myers, *Principles of Corporate Finance*, 3d ed. (New York: McGraw-Hill, 1988), p. 796.

37. Richard S. Teitelbaum, "LBOs Really Didn't Pay, Say the Chiefs," *Fortune*, August 26, 1991, p. 73.

Chapter 6

1. Proponents of the cultural view include Ezra F. Vogel in *Japan as Number One* (Cambridge, Mass.: Harvard University Press, 1979); and William Ouchi in *Theory Z* (Reading, Mass.: Addison-Wesley, 1982).

2. Proponents of the conspiracy view include Marvin Wolf in *The Japanese Conspiracy* (New York: Empire Books, 1983); Pat Choate, *Agents of Influence* (New York: Alfred A. Knopf, 1990); and William J. Holstein, *The Japanese Power Game: What It Means for America* (New York: Plume, 1991).

3. Proponents of the management view include James C. Abegglen and George Stalk, Jr., *Kaisha, the Japanese Corporation* (New York: Basic Books, 1985); and Philip Kotler, Liam Fahey, and Somkid Jatusripitak, *The New Competition* (Englewood Cliffs, N.J.: Prentice-Hall, 1985).

4. In fact, according to Haruo Shimada, "The Perceptions and Reality of Japanese Industrial Relations," in Lester C. Thurow, ed., *The Management Challenge: Japanese Views* (Cambridge, Mass.: MIT Press, 1985), pp. 42–66, the labor market in Japan is much more flexible and mobile than management books on Japan have tended to portray. Lifetime employment in the large corporations is limited by compulsory retirement at ages fifty-five to sixty, when most people move on to a secondary job until they really retire in their late sixties. During recessions, workers above this age are among the first to be dismissed. Further, "10 to 20 percent of all employees leave their firm every year. . . . Roughly half of newly hired people have had an occupational experience somewhere else. Recent graduates account for only a quarter to a third of total recruits" (pp. 47–49).

5. See, for example, Michael H. Best, *The New Competition: Institutions of Industrial Restructuring* (Cambridge, Mass.: Harvard University Press, 1990), pp. 167–202.

6. See Koniyasu Sakai, "The Feudal World of Japanese Manufacturing," *Harvard Business Review* (November–December 1990), pp. 38–49.

7. Abegglen and Stalk, *Kaisha*, Chapter 4, pp. 67–90. The "Asian Tigers" or "Gangs" of Four and Five mentioned earlier are rapidly going through the same phases.

8. Ibid., p. 72.

9. A 1980 survey of more than 200 U.S. and almost 300 Japanese CEOs from the top 1,000 corporations in each country found (among many things) that the firms from the two countries differed little in the percentages that used mass production, continuous process, or job shop (small batch) production technologies. However, a much higher percentage of American firms used large batch technology (35 to 25 percent), while a much higher percentage of Japanese firms used "custom" technology (20 to 13 percent). See Tadao Kagono et al., "Mechanistic vs. Organic Management Systems: A Comparative Study of Adaptive Patterns of American and Japanese Firms," in Kazuo Sato and Yasuo Hoshino, eds., *The Anatomy of Japanese Business* (Armonk, N.Y.: M. E. Sharpe, 1984), pp. 27–61 and p. 38 in particular.

Today, the percentage of Japanese corporations signifying custom production technology would probably be much higher. The percentage is also probably understated as many Japanese companies that have become flexible in production and small-lot oriented still refer to their systems as "mass production." For example, the president of Seiko Instruments Inc., Reinosuke Hara, in "Current and Future Manufacturing Industry," *Management Japan* (Spring 1990), pp. 11–16, states that Japan has progressed from "standardised product with simplified function" in the 1960s to "product with multiple function" in the 1970s to "system product for individual taste" in the 1980s (p. 14). But at the same time, he states that Japan is focused on "standardised, mass volume" and the United States on "custom-made oriented" products (p. 13), reflecting a defense industry orientation. The Japanese have yet to discover the phrase "mass customization," but they know its meaning well.

10. Abegglen and Stalk, *Kaisha*, p. 90. A similar prediction from the mid-1980s was made by Kenneth J. McGuire in *Impressions from Our Most Worthy Competitor: An Examination of Japanese Approaches to Managing Manufacturing Resources* (Falls Church, Va.: American Production and Inventory Control Society, 1984), p. 29:

There is also the misconception that the Japanese are only effective where there is a high volume in narrow product lines in a mass production environment, and that they are quite inflexible in custom-made products produced in low volumes. Although that belief may be reassuring to many American manufacturers, it is not true. . . . Making large volumes in very small lots, then intermixing those small lots with expanding variety has enabled many [Japanese] manufacturers to enter the marketplace for custom, one-of-a-kind products with equivalent competitive advantages. The export market has not been a prime target for custom products as yet, although some machine tools and similar equipment are already entering the North American markets. Other custom products will follow when the efficiencies of manufacture offset the logistics of supply factors. That discomforting fact will become more evident in the future.

11. Michael J. Piore and Charles F. Sabel, *The Second Industrial Divide: Possibilities for Prosperity* (New York: Basic Books, 1984), p. 17.

12. Best, *The New Competition*, p. 204. For an excellent discussion of Italy's resurgence and how it is based on the flexible specialization model of organization, see Giorgio Inzerilli, "The Italian Alternative: Flexible Organization and Social Management," *International Studies of Management & Organization*, vol. 20, no. 4, pp. 6–21.

13. Charles F. Sabel, "Flexible Specialization and the Re-emergence of Regional Economies," in Paul Hirst and Jonathan Zeitlin, eds., *Reversing Industrial Decline? Industrial Structure and Policy in Britain and Her Competitors* (Oxford: Berg Publishers, 1989), p. 22. The first two Italys are "the impoverished South and the old industrial triangle of Genoa, Turin, and Milan" (p. 22), the latter of which was more traditionally focused on Mass Production.

14. For a thorough explanation of these associations in the Third Italy, see Best, *The New Competition*, Chapter 7.

15. Sabel, "Flexible Specialization and the Re-emergence of Regional Economies," p. 22. Additional information on these industrial communities can be found in primary sources referenced in this article. The list could go on to include similar districts in France, Spain, and elsewhere.

16. Piore and Sabel, *The Second Industrial Divide*, pp. 219–220. They make the interesting point that "looked at from this perspective, the Japanese have stood the Fordist paradigm on its head: instead of using general-purpose equipment to produce special-purpose machines, they are doing the reverse—using special-purpose equipment to produce general-purpose machines to fill the craft needs of the rest of the metalworking industry" (p. 219).

17. See Zoltan J. Acs, "Innovation and Technical Change in the U.S. Steel Industry," *Technovation*, 7 (1988), pp. 181–195; Terence P. Paré, "The Big Threat to Big Steel's Future," *Fortune*, July 15, 1991, pp. 106–108; and Michael L. Dertouzos, Richard K. Lester, Robert M. Solow, and the MIT Commission on Industrial Productivity, *Made in America: Regaining the Productive Edge* (Cambridge, Mass.: MIT Press, 1990), pp. 285–287. The cooperative nature of minimills is enhanced by the practice of "informal information trading," discovered by Stephan Schrader in "Informal Technology Transfer Between Firms: Cooperation Through Information Trading," *Research Policy* (April 1991), pp. 153–170. See Christoph Scherrer, "Mini-Mills: A New Growth Path for the U.S. Steel Industry?" *Journal of Economic Issues* (December 1988), pp. 1179–1200, for an alternative (and minority) view that the success of minimills "has been

based on short-term profit maximization: sub-standard wages and working conditions as well as neglect of R&D and manpower training" (p. 1194).

18. AnnaLee Saxenian, "Regional Networks and the Resurgence of Silicon Valley," draft paper, Department of City and Regional Planning, University of California at Berkeley, January 1989. See also Saxenian, "The Political Economy of Industrial Adaptation in Silicon Valley," Ph.D. diss., MIT, 1988; and Allen Scott and Michael Storper, "High Technology Industry and Regional Development: A Critique and Reconstruction," *International Social Science Review* (May 1987), pp. 215–232.

19. Sabel, "Flexible Specialization and the Re-emergence of Regional Economies," p. 23. See also E. W. Soya and A. J. Scott, "Los Angeles: Capital of the Late Twentieth Century," *Society and Space* (September 1986).

20. Susan Christopherson and Michael Storper, "The Effects of Flexible Specialization on Industrial Politics and the Labor Market: The Motion Picture Industry," *Industrial and Labor Relations Review* (April 1989), p. 334.

21. Best, *The New Competition*, pp. 228–233, provides an interesting account of the reactions to competitive pressures by two regions of small furniture makers—one, in North London, that took individual approaches that resulted in 23 of 25 manufacturers going out of business within fifteen years; the other, in the Third Italy, where developing a sense of community (Best uses the term "collective identity") and reacting with flexible specialization strategies resulted in a fivefold increase in exports in virtually the same time span.

22. Piore and Sabel have been criticized on the one hand for not providing enough concrete examples of flexible specialization to support its theoretical constructs, and on the other for outlining a single model of economic development that attempts to encompass too many different economic organizations. However, additional research since the publication of *The Second Industrial Divide* in 1984 has found many more examples and filled out the underpinnings of the theory, and applications of flexible specialization strategies have been used successfully in a number of public policymaking forums. For a discussion of these points, see Paul Teague, "The Political Economy of the Regulation School and the Flexible Specialisation Scenario," *Journal of Economic Studies*, vol. 17, no. 5, pp. 32–54.

23. The similarity is great enough that most of the companies discussed would fit under Piore and Sabel's definition of flexible specialization provided in *The Second Industrial Divide*. They feel flexible specialization is not limited to small companies, but includes IBM, Boeing, Du Pont, Dow, and other large American corporations, as well as the networked industries of Japan. For "unlike the mass producers, these firms do not produce long runs of standardized products; and their size results from the high capital requirements of their products—not economies of scale, as in mass production" (p. 267). The key factor for Piore and Sabel is whether the enterprise or community revives and uses craft or craftlike forms of production. In the view of Mass Customization presented here—particularly for the dynamic extended enterprise—the new paradigm is really a synthesis of the best parts of both craft and mass modes of production. Economies of scale (and scope) can be realized to provide low costs, even while the end product still has high levels of variety and individual customization obtained through production flexibility generally anchored in the skills and inherent flexibility of production workers.

24. Best, *The New Competition*, pp. 147–148.

25. Abegglen and Stalk, *Kaisha*, pp. 112–115.

26. Ibid., p. 114. Further data on the automobile industry, complete through the 1980s, can be found in James P. Womack, Daniel T. Jones, and Daniel Roos, *The Machine That Changed the World* (New York: Rawson Associates, 1990), Chapter 4 in particular. The best example in the automobile and possibly any other industry is the Toyota production system. Toyota's chief production engineer and founder of the system, Taiichi Ohno, has described the history, practices, and future of this system in *Toyota Production System: Beyond Large-Scale Production* (Cambridge, Mass.: Productivity Press, 1988), and, with Setsuo Mito, *Just-in-Time: For Today and Tomorrow* (Cambridge, Mass.: Productivity Press, 1988).

27. This point is the central theme of two books by Philip R. Thomas with Kenneth R. Martin: *Competitiveness Through Total Cycle Time: An Overview for CEOs* (New York: McGraw-Hill, 1990), and *Getting Competitive: Middle Managers and the Cycle Time Ethic* (New York: McGraw-Hill, 1991).

28. This point is made regarding New United Motors Manufacturing, Inc., the joint venture between Toyota and General Motors in Fremont, California, by Mike Parker and Jane Slaughter, "Management by Stress," *Technology Review* (October 1988), pp. 36–44.

29. Janice A. Klein, "The Human Costs of Manufacturing Reform," *Harvard Business Review* (March–April 1989), pp. 60–66.

30. "Research and Development in Japan: 1989 Update," *JEI Reports*, June 23, 1989, cited in Richard Florida and Martin Kenney, *The Breakthrough Illusion: Corporate America's Failure to Move from Innovation to Mass Production* (New York: Basic Books, 1990), p. 149.

31. Abegglen and Stalk, *Kaisha*, p. 128. They add: "Not all foreign companies fell into the trap. A few toughminded and farsighted firms, like IBM and Texas Instruments, used their technology as bludgeons to beat down the barriers to entry into Japan to build wholly owned operations there. But such companies were few."

32. While the consumer electronic examples are well known, an interesting account of how Japanese automakers during the 1980s went from "low-tech weaklings to high-tech wonders" through imitating and improving old technology of automobile engines can be found in Womack, Jones, and Roos, *The Machine That Changed the World*, pp. 131–132.

33. Dertouzos et al., *Made in America*, pp. 76–77.

34. A host of literature has appeared on this point in the last decade or so. Some of the best and most pertinent are: Larry Hirschhorn, *Beyond Mechanization: Work and Technology in a Postindustrial Age* (Cambridge, Mass.: MIT Press, 1984); Ken C. Kusterer, *Know-How on the Job: The Important Working Knowledge of "Unskilled" Workers* (Boulder, Colo.: Westview Press, 1978); and Roy B. Helfgott, "Moving beyond Taylorism," *International Journal of Technology Management*, vol. 2, nos. 3/4 (1987), pp. 459–471.

35. The New Competition frequently starts out newly hired development personnel on production lines to cement the integration of innovation and production in their minds at the beginning of their careers. See, for example, the case of Japanese automakers in Womack, Jones, and Roos, *The Machine That Changed the World*, pp. 129–130.

36. Broad support for this practice was found by Edwin Mansfield in his study of a random sample of 125 Japanese and American firms in a broad cross section of industries, reported in "Technological Creativity: Japan and the United States," *Business Horizons* (March–April 1989), pp. 48–53. He found that the Japanese introduced products and processes more quickly than the Americans, 18 percent more quickly according to the Japanese and 6 percent more quickly according to the Americans. Further, the costs of commercial introduction were 23 percent lower according to the Japanese and 10 percent lower according to the Americans. While these numbers may not seem large, given all the press on how the Japanese are so much faster and less costly, a 10 to 20 percent advantage compounded over even a few years can yield an absolutely huge difference. Mansfield's data further show that in Japan "firms take about 25 percent less time and spend about 50 percent less money to carry out an innovation based on external technology than one based on internal technology" (p. 50). There were essentially no differences between American and Japanese firms in the costs and time to develop internal technologies.

37. George Stalk, Jr., and Thomas M. Hout, *Competing Against Time* (New York: Free Press, 1990), p. 109.

38. Kim B. Clark and Takahiro Fujimoto, *Product Development Performance: Strategy, Organization, and Management in the World Auto Industry* (Boston: Harvard Business School Press, 1991), p. 137.

39. Kim B. Clark, "Project Scope and Project Performance: The Effect of Parts Strategy and Supplier Involvement on Product Development," *Management Science* (October 1989), pp. 1247–1263.

40. Abegglen and Stalk, *Kaisha*, pp. 146–147.

41. See Florida and Kenney, *The Breakthrough Illusion*, pp. 161–164; Mansfield, "Technological Creativity: Japan and the United States"; and Kagono et al., "Mechanistic vs. Organic Management Systems." In their research, the latter found that Japanese companies allocated twice the expenditures to basic research on new technologies than did American companies (16 to 8 percent) (p. 44).

42. Zoltan Acs and David Audretsch, *Innovation and Small Firms* (Cambridge, Mass.: MIT Press, 1990), pp. 150–154 in particular.

43. Don E. Kash views this capability in foreign countries as the most serious threat to the United States' technological leadership. See *Perpetual Innovation: The New World of Competition* (New York: Basic Books, 1989).

44. Gary Hamel and C. K. Prahalad, "Corporate Imagination and Expeditionary Marketing," *Harvard Business Review* (July–August 1991), p. 90.

45. "The Battle for Market Share," *Tokyo Business Today* (September 1988), p. 14.

46. Kotler, Fahey, and Jatusripitak, *The New Competition*, Chapter 3, which uses the automobile industry as an example. Additional examples are offered throughout the book.

47. Stan Davis and Bill Davidson, *2020 Vision: Transform Your Business Today to Succeed in Tomorrow's Economy* (New York: Simon & Schuster, 1991), pp. 15–16.

48. Tom Peters, "All Markets Are Now Immature," *Industry Week*, July 3, 1989, p. 14.

49. Bennett Daviss, "Laid-back Computers," *Discover* (January 1991), p. 61. The technology in the washing machine, "fuzzy logic," decides the appropriate action based on the vague information available to it and is becoming increasingly popular in home appliances.

50. Best, *The New Competition*, p. 159, says that "perhaps nothing better captures the distinguishing substance of the two paradigms" than that "in America accounting became the language of the elite in business," while in Japan nonfinancial measures, such as statistical quality measures, are the language of everyone, even hourly workers.

51. Toshiro Hiromoto, "Another Hidden Edge—Japanese Management Accounting," *Harvard Business Review* (July–August 1988), p. 22.

52. Ford S. Worthy, "Japan's Smart Secret Weapon," *Fortune*, August 12, 1991, pp. 72–75.

53. For example, the consortium created through Computer Aided Manufacturing–International, Inc. (CAM-I) to improve the state of accounting includes among its members companies like Motorola, Kodak, and General Electric, which are focused on increasing their variety and customization. See *Cost Management for Today's Advanced Manufacturing: The CAM-I Conceptual Design*, edited by Callie Berliner and James A. Brimson (Boston: Harvard Business School Press, 1988).

54. Worthy, "Japan's Smart Secret Weapon," p. 74.

55. Ibid., p. 75. Michiharu Sakurai, "The Influence of Factory Automation on Management Accounting Practices: A Study of Japanese Companies," in *Measures for Manufacturing Excellence*, Robert S. Kaplan, ed. (Boston: Harvard Business School Press, 1990), pp. 39–62, found that in companies like this, the profitability hurdle is often return on sales (ROS) instead of return on investment (ROI): "ROS can clearly reveal the profitability of each product in an environment of high product variety. It is almost impossible for companies producing high-variety, low-volume products to compute ROI for each product. On the other hand, it is easy to compute ROS for each product" (p. 56).

56. Kagono et al., "Mechanistic vs. Organic Management Systems," p. 36.

57. Berliner and Brimson, *Cost Management for Today's Advanced Manufacturing*, p. 227. See also Sakurai, "The Influence of Factory Automation on Management Accounting Practices."

Chapter 7

1. Quoted in Taiichi Ohno, *Toyota Production System: Beyond Large-Scale Production* (Cambridge, Mass.: Productivity Press, 1988), p. 91.

2. Ibid., p. 95.

3. Quoted by Norman Bodek in Publisher's Foreword to ibid., p. ix.

4. For the complete story behind IBM Rochester winning the Malcolm Baldrige National Quality Award, see Roy A. Bauer et al., *The Silverlake Project: Transformation at IBM* (New York: Oxford University Press, 1992).

5. For a description of this process, see B. J. Pine II, "Design, Test, and Validation of the Application System/400 through Early User Involvement," *IBM Systems Journal*, vol. 28, no. 3 (1989), pp. 376–385.

6. The group that designed, developed, and put in place the original early external involvement process was a cross-functional team made up of both development and marketing personnel. It was a fine example of how a flexible work team can accomplish a task requiring flexibility, responsiveness, and varied skills and experiences. There were actually four or five self-directed teams comprised of various combinations of permanent employees, loaners, full- and part-time temporaries, and retirees brought back for part-time work. While the normal IBM employee-to-manager ratio was about ten to one at the time, this activity had only one manager for a department that varied between twenty and seventy people, depending on the monthly and sometimes weekly requirements. For more information, see B. J. Pine II and S. E. Aldrich, "Early External Involvement at IBM Rochester," IBM Technical Report 07.1664, October 1991.

7. Interestingly, it accomplished this by working directly with IBM programmers from Rochester, Minnesota, in one of the activities spawned by the success of IBM's early external involvement program discussed above. For more information on the application, Bally Express Service Timetable (BEST), see LindaMay R. Patterson, "Bally Makes Its BEST Better," *NEWS 3X/400* (November 1990), pp. 8–14.

8. Quoted in William J. Hampton, "What Is Motorola Making at This Factory? History," *Business Week*, December 5, 1988, p. 168H.

9. Quoted in Rita R. Schreiber, "The CIM Caper," *Manufacturing Engineering* (April 1989), p. 85.

10. Quoted in Jagannath Dubashi, "The Bandit Standoff," *Financial World*, September 17, 1991.

11. Schreiber, "The CIM Caper," p. 87.

12. Quoted in Bernard Avishai and William Taylor, "Customers Drive a Technology-Driven Company: An Interview with George Fisher," *Harvard Business Review* (November–December 1989), p. 112.

13. Ibid., p. 113. Fisher believes that Mass Customization plays to American strengths, that American companies are more flexible and adaptive than Japanese companies, and therefore that America is uniquely positioned to take advantage of the shift away from Mass Production.

14. The information in this illustration can be found primarily in Christian Pinson, "Swatch" case study (Fontainebleau, France: INSEAD-CEDEP, 1987). See also Margaret Studer, "SMH Leads a Revival of Swiss Watchmaking Industry," *The Wall Street Journal*, January 21, 1992, p. B4.

15. Pinson, "Swatch," p. 3.

16. Ibid., p. 4.

17. Seiko has also moved away from Mass Production and is now a leader in mass-customizing watches. According to Lewis H. Young, "Product Development in Japan: Evolution vs. Revolution," *Electronic Business*, June 17, 1991, p. 75, Seiko "offers more than 1,000 models of watches. But all are based on only four or five watch movements; their multiplicity derives from various combinations of movements, cases, dials, and hands. Seiko introduces 100 such variations every six months."

18. Rosalind Resnick, "A Top Gun Comes to the Rescue of CPI," *Electronic Business*, September 9, 1991, p. 80.

19. Ibid., p. 82.

20. *Computer Products, Inc. 1990 Annual Report*, pp. 2–3.

21. The Government Electronics business was sold by CPI at the end of 1991 so the company could focus on its industrial customers.

22. Wallys Conhaim, "French Videotex: Reaching Out for New Markets," *Information Today* (January 1991), p. 28.

23. William H. Davidson, "Transforming Operator Services: The Evolution of an Info-business in Telecommunications Services," Mesa Research: IBM Advanced Business Institute paper, December 1991. Much of the information in this illustration can be found here. See also Shlomo Maital, "Why the French Do It Better," *Across the Board* (November 1991), pp. 7–10.

24. "Mad about Minitel," *TE&M*, October 1, 1991, pp. 82–86.

25. Michel Dupagne, "French and US Videotex: Prospects for the Electronic Directory Service," *Telecommunications Policy* (December 1990), p. 492.

26. Stan Davis and Bill Davidson, *2020 Vision: Transform Your Business Today to Succeed in Tomorrow's Economy* (New York: Simon & Schuster, 1991), p. 167.

27. See Mark Mehler and Ronit Addis Rose, "Plug into the Power," *Success* (June 1990), pp. 37–43; and Ann Ryan, "Salvaging a Near Miss," *Minnesota Ventures* (November/December 1991), pp. 74–77.

28. See also Laura O'Connell, "Mixing and Matching Musical Tastes," *Computerworld*, July 23, 1990, p. 16.

29. Ballard is also working on reducing the cost of the system, increasing its reliability, and enhancing its usability so that customers can enter their selections themselves. This is intended to give the Personics system a cost structure equivalent to or better than mass-produced cassette tapes.

30. See David J. Teece, "Profiting from Technological Innovation: Implications for Integration, Collaboration, Licensing and Public Policy," *Research Policy* (December 1986), pp. 285–305.

31. Richard Zoglin, "Inside the World of CNN," *Time*, January 6, 1992, p. 32.

32. Quoted in William A. Henry III, "History as It Happens," *Time*, January 6, 1992, p. 26.

33. Ibid., p. 24.

34. Daniel Pearl, "Turner Broadcasting Is Developing Multimedia Products for Home PCs," *The Wall Street Journal*, February 7, 1992, p. B6. The article indicates that "Ted Turner . . . is intrigued with products that let people pick and choose programs from computers. But he is hedging his bets. 'It might be too complicated to be a mass item,' he said in an interview last week. 'It's like work.'"

35. For one way of doing this, see D. L. Bates and John E. Dillard, "Desired Future Position—A Practical Tool for Planning," *Long Range Planning* (June 1991), pp. 90–99.

36. B. Charles Ames, "Survival Insurance: Market-Driven Management," *Creating Corporate Success: The 1990 International Conference Executive Summary* (Oxford, Ohio: The Planning Forum, 1990), p. 3.

37. For an excellent discussion of strategic flexibility, see Sara L. Beckman, "Manufacturing Flexibility: The Next Source of Competitive Advantage," in Patricia E. Moody, ed., *Strategic Manufacturing: Dynamic New Directions for the 1990s* (Homewood, Ill.: Dow Jones–Irwin, 1990), pp. 107–132. See also John C. Camillus and Deepak K. Datta, "Managing Strategic Issues in a Turbulent Environment," *Long Range Planning* (April 1991), pp. 67–74.

38. See Peter Schwartz, *The Art of the Long View* (New York: Doubleday Currency, 1991), for a description of how scenario planning was developed at Shell and how it can be used today.

39. Christopher Knowlton, "Shell Gets Rich by Beating Risk," *Fortune*, August 26, 1991, pp. 79–82.

Chapter 8

1. Representative of the best references on the use of flexible technologies are: Hamid Noori, *Managing the Dynamics of New Technology: Issues in Manufacturing Management* (Englewood Cliffs, N.J.: Prentice-Hall, 1990); James Brian Quinn and Penny C. Paquette, "Technology in Services: Creating Organizational Revolutions," *Sloan Management Review* (Winter 1990), pp. 67–78; Joel D. Goldhar, Mariann Jelinek, and Theodore W. Schlie, "Competitive Advantage in Manufacturing through Information Technology," *International Journal of Technology Management*, Special Publication on the Role of Technology in Corporate Policy (1991), pp. 162–180; and Brandt R. Allen and Andrew C. Boynton, "Information Architecture: In Search of Efficient Flexibility," *MIS Quarterly* (December 1991), pp. 435–445.

2. See Ramchandran Jaikumar, "Postindustrial Manufacturing," *Harvard Business Review* (November–December 1986), pp. 69–76.

3. It appears that most companies starting down the path of Mass Customization begin with postproduction customization because it is relatively simple and quick to implement. This

is supported by the survey discussed in Chapter 4. See Buddie Joseph Pine II, "Paradigm Shift: From Mass Production to Mass Customization," master's thesis, MIT, June 1991.

4. See Charles J. Bashe et al., *IBM's Early Computers* (Cambridge, Mass.: MIT Press, 1986), p. 583.

5. David Mercer, *The Global IBM: Leadership in Multinational Management* (New York: Dodd, Mead, 1987), pp. 216–217. The "building block" approach described here also provides a good example of using modular components to customize end products.

6. Helen Pike, "Restoring the Personal Touch," *Computerworld*, July 30, 1990, pp. 51, 54.

7. Where it is available, all customers, not only Gold customers, receive this service. Not to be outdone, Marriott is testing mobile computers in its courtesy vans to check guests in on their way from the airport.

8. H. Skip Weitzen with William ("Biff") Genda, *Infopreneurs: Turning Data into Dollars* (New York: John Wiley, 1988), p. 35.

9. Quoted in Subrata N. Chakravarty and Dana Wechsler Linden, "Dow Jones: A Belt, Suspenders and Elastic Waistband," *Forbes*, February 3, 1992, p. 69.

10. See Donald T. Hawkins, "Customized Information: 'No, I Don't Want "All the News That's Fit to Print," ' " *ONLINE* (September 1990), pp. 117–120. INDIVIDUAL has purchased several companies—and/or their subscriber lists—that have failed at customized news services, including Tele/scope Networks, Inc., and Pinpoint Information Corp. The costs of these other services were too high for the market because of labor-intensive manual search techniques.

11. Many companies have created their own customized newspapers to provide their employees with the information they need. See Michael S. Gelinne, "Creating an Internal Customized News Service," *ONLINE* (July 1991), pp. 52–57, for the example of Glaxo Inc.

12. Faith Popcorn, *The Popcorn Report: Faith Popcorn on the Future of Your Company, Your World, Your Life* (New York: Doubleday Currency, 1991), p. 47.

13. Survey of 1,475 ATM users by PULSE/Financial Interchange Inc., cited in Connie Kenjura-Maples, "ATMs: The People's Choice," *Texas Banking* (October 1991), p. 11.

14. "Design Cubed = T-Shirts Plus," *Chain Store Age Executive* (May 1988), pp. 126–132.

15. Note that in each of these examples, the final manufacturing step is actually thought of as a service by the customers. They can be considered customized services performed on standardized products.

16. AT&T is experimenting with Domino's on a new service that combines a seven-digit number, eliminating the 800 area code, with "Store Finder" software that takes seven to eleven seconds to find the closest store location, matching the caller's phone number with the store on computerized maps. See Anthony Ramirez, "The Pizza Version of Dialing '911,' " *New York Times*, September 9, 1991.

17. See Marj Charlier, "Restaurants Mobilize to Pursue Customers," *The Wall Street Journal*, June 10, 1991, pp. B1, B4.

18. Much of the information in this illustration comes from William H. Davidson, "Transforming Claims Processing Services: The Evolution of an Info-Business in Property and Casualty Insurance," Mesa Research: IBM Advanced Business Institute paper, December 1991.

19. See also B. G. Yovovich, "Risky Business," *CIO* (March 1990), pp. 20–28; and Stephen Phillips, "Bad Risks Are This Insurer's Best Friends," *Business Week*, November 12, 1990, p. 122.

20. See also Rick Friedman, "Progressive Targets 24-Hour Claims Settlement," *Insurance & Technology* (October/November 1990), pp. 6–8.

21. Davidson, "Transforming Claims Processing Services," pp. 7–8. See also Julia King, "Re-engineering Puts Progressive on the Spot," *Computerworld*, July 15, 1991, p. 58.

22. In addition to numerous articles by each, see Tom Peters, *Thriving on Chaos* (New York: Alfred A. Knopf, 1987); George Stalk, Jr., and Thomas M. Hout, *Competing Against Time* (New York: Free Press, 1990); and Philip R. Thomas with Kenneth R. Martin, *Competitiveness Through Total Cycle Time: An Overview for CEOs* (New York: McGraw-Hill, 1990), and *Getting Competitive: Middle Managers and the Cycle Time Ethic* (New York: McGraw-Hill, 1991).

23. See J. Meredith, "The Strategic Advantages of the Factory of the Future," *California*

Management Review (Spring 1987), pp. 28–29, cited in Noori, *Managing the Dynamics of New Technology*, p. 82.

24. "Quick Response in the Apparel Industry," Harvard Business School Note #9-690-038, p. 4.

25. Robert M. Frazier, "Quick Response in Soft Lines," *Discount Merchandiser* (January 1986), pp. 42, 44, cited in ibid., p. 1.

26. "Quick Response in the Apparel Industry," ibid., pp. 8–9.

27. Textile industry representative, "Time-Based Competition Conference," December 1988, quoted in Joseph D. Blackburn, "The Quick-Response Movement in the Apparel Industry: A Case Study in Time-Compressing Supply Chains," in Joseph D. Blackburn, ed., *Time-Based Competition: The Next Battleground in American Manufacturing* (Homewood, Ill.: Business One Irwin, 1991), p. 265.

28. Although it has yet to make it all the way out to the customer, Benetton, with its ability to manufacture "gray stock" sweaters, warehouse them, and later dye them to match consumer trends, is moving one step closer to point-of-delivery customization. However, it would be better to move the final dye step to the stores, and it might be even better to forgo point-of-delivery customization and instead shorten the manufacturing cycle to avoid the costs of warehousing. This is especially true of other manufacturers who would be much more at risk of failing to sell the intermediate merchandise than Benetton with its gray stock.

29. Tom Peters, "Time-Obsessed Competition," *Management Review* (September 1990), p. 16.

30. James Aaron Cooke, "How *Quick Response* Works at Haggar," *Traffic Management* (November 1991), pp. 30–32.

31. Lisa Cedrone, "Chalking Up Record Sales," *Bobbin* (April 1991), pp. 44–52.

32. Tom Peters, "Beyond Speed: We're All in the Fad-&-Fashion Business," *Industry Week*, June 3, 1991, p. 22.

33. "How High-Tech Tailors Are Saving a Stitch in Time," *Business Week*, April 14, 1986, p. 92G, cited in Peters, *Thriving on Chaos*, p. 133.

34. This point is indeed important. See Peter Senge, *The Fifth Discipline: The Art and Practice of the Learning Organization* (New York: Doubleday Currency, 1990), pp. 27–54 in particular, for a description of how this whipsaw can occur and how devastating it can be. See also D. R. Towill, "Supply Chain Dynamics," *International Journal of Computer Integrated Manufacturing*, vol. 4, no. 4 (1991), pp. 197–208.

35. Alvin Toffler, *The Third Wave* (New York: Bantam Books, 1980), pp. 265–288.

36. Thomas with Martin, in *Competitiveness Through Total Cycle Time* and *Getting Competitive*, calls this effect "Cycles of Learning," which forms the basis for his work on reducing total cycle time.

37. Alvin P. Lehnerd, "Revitalizing the Manufacture and Design of Mature Global Products," in Bruce R. Guile and Harvey Brooks, eds., *Technology and Global Industry: Companies and Nations in the World Economy* (Washington, D.C.: National Academy Press, 1987), p. 51.

38. Ibid., pp. 61–62.

39. See John Huey, "The New Power in Black & Decker," *Fortune*, January 2, 1989, pp. 89–94.

40. John Pierson, "FORM + FUNCTION: Molding Tool Designs to Cause No Harm," *The Wall Street Journal*, March 11, 1991, p. B1.

41. See Kaoru Takahashi and Hidetsugu Fujii, "New Concept for Batchwise Specialty Chemicals Production Plant," *Instrumentation and Control Engineering* (September/October 1990), pp. 19–22.

42. Processes designed for the mass production of commodity chemicals are still much cheaper—but only if market demand is stable enough to justify inventorying the output of long production runs.

43. See also Paul Gillin, "Custom Tours at Package Prices? No Problem," *Computerworld*, August 6, 1990, pp. 63, 69.

44. Karl T. Ulrich and Karen Tung, *Fundamentals of Product Modularity*, Working Paper #3335-91-MSA, Sloan School of Management, MIT, September 1991. Mix modularity is not included in this paper, which deals with discrete manufacturers and not process operators or

service providers. Also, Ulrich and Tung use the term "fabricate-to-fit" instead of "cut-to-fit" for the same reason.

45. Toshio Suzue and Akira Kohdate describe techniques for redesigning products and production processes to reduce component variety and process complexity while maintaining or increasing end product variety in *Variety Reduction Program: A Production Strategy for Product Diversification* (Cambridge, Mass.: Productivity Press, 1990). See also Gordon V. Shirley, "Models for Managing the Redesign and Manufacture of Product Sets," *Journal of Manufacturing and Operations Management*, vol. 3 (1990), pp. 85–104; and Roy Rothwell and Paul Gardiner, "Robustness and Product Design Families," in Mark Oakley, ed., *Design Management: A Handbook of Issues and Methods* (Cambridge, England: Basil Blackwell, 1990).

46. Brian Dumaine, "How Managers Can Succeed Through Speed," *Fortune*, February 13, 1989, pp. 55–56. See also D. Quinn Mills, *Rebirth of the Corporation* (New York: John Wiley, 1991), pp. 20–21.

47. "Komatsu: Ryoichi Kawai's Leadership," Case #390-037. Boston: Harvard Business School.

48. Susan Moffat, "Japan's New Personalized Production," *Fortune*, October 22, 1990, p. 132.

49. Anonymous manager, quoted in Stanley M. Davis, *Future Perfect* (Reading, Mass.: Addison-Wesley, 1987), p. 160.

50. Ulrich and Tung, *Fundamentals of Product Modularity*, p. 11.

51. Amy Cortese, "Greener Acres Ahead in Publishing," *Computerworld*, September 4, 1989, pp. 55, 59. See also Patricia W. Hamilton, "*Farm Journal* Feels Its Oats," *D&B Reports* (July/August 1988), pp. 22–25.

52. See Jill Roth, "Book Marks," *American Printer* (January 1991), pp. 44–47; and Rick Pastore, "High-Tech Heroes II: Business and Related Services: McGraw-Hill, Inc.," *Computerworld*, July 1, 1991, p. 58.

53. "Manufacturing 21 Report: The Future of Japanese Manufacturing," *AME Research Report* (Wheeling, Ill.: Association for Manufacturing Excellence, 1990), p. 26.

54. See Mary Emrich, "A New Wrinkle in Auto Body Manufacture—And Guess Who's Doing It," *Manufacturing Systems* (August 1991), p. 46. Nissan has already moved to daily production plans and has developed an information system that allows each customer to know within two hours of entering a custom order when the car will arrive. During production, the customer's full name is placed right on the windshield, giving that car priority over dealer inventory cars and allowing personal attention should any delay occur. See "New Information System Gives Customers Firm Delivery Dates," *Business JAPAN* (September 1991), pp. 22–23.

55. "Manufacturing 21 Report," pp. 25–26. For additional discussion of the coming use of modularity in automobile manufacture, see "The Arrival of Haute Carture," *The Economist*, July 29, 1989, pp. 53–54.

56. See, for example, John W. Verity and Evan I. Schwartz, "Software Made Simple," *Business Week*, September 30, 1991, pp. 92–100.

57. See Michael Cusumano, *Japan's Software Factories: A Challenge to U.S. Management* (New York: Oxford University Press, 1991).

58. Quinn and Paquette, "Technology in Services," p. 67.

59. Ibid., p. 69.

60. Steve Barnett, ed., *The Nissan Report: An Inside Look at How a World-Class Japanese Company Makes Products That Make a Difference* (New York: Doubleday Currency, 1992), pp. 67–73. Most of the problems discussed on pp. 71–73 could be solved through proper modularity.

61. See Jan Klatten, "Case Studies from the US Auto Market: The Impact of Product Policy on Manufacturability," master's thesis, MIT, June 1991. In 1992, General Motors announced it would once again increase its component sharing across vehicles, including a reduction of the number of platforms. Unlike the 1970s, however, GM says it will make sure each model retains its distinctiveness.

62. Ulrich and Tung, *Fundamentals of Product Integrity*, p. 8.

63. David K. Murotake and Thomas J. Allen, "Computer Aided Engineering and Project Performance: Managing a Double-Edged Sword," Working Paper #47-91, The International Center for Research on the Management of Technology, MIT, August 1991.

Chapter 9

1. The depiction of the integrated organization as a stacked value chain was suggested by Andrew Boynton of the University of Virginia Darden School of Management.

2. William J. Abernathy and James M. Utterback, "Patterns of Industrial Innovation," *Technology Review* (June–July 1978), pp. 40–47.

3. Of course, a basic tenet of Mass Customization is to focus on the individual wants and needs of every customer and provide customized products and services to fulfill those desires. Individual customers take on more importance than in the days of the "anonymous, homogeneous market," but it is customers and their requirements that become of utmost importance to a firm, not the particular products or services that are sold. This is a complete reversal from Mass Production.

4. See Hamid Noori, "The Decoupling of Product and Process Life Cycles," *International Journal of Production Research*, vol. 29, no. 9 (1991), pp. 1853–1865.

5. Andrew C. Boynton and Bart Victor, "Beyond Flexibility: Building and Managing the Dynamically Stable Organization," *California Management Review* (Fall 1991), p. 54. The terms used in the product-process change matrix presented here are significantly different than those originally published by Boynton and Victor because of the results of ongoing research they are conducting in concert with the author and the IBM Advanced Business Institute.

6. Ibid., pp. 60–61. Similar conclusions were reached by Noori, "The Decoupling of Product and Process Life Cycles," and by Paul S. Adler, "Managing Flexible Automation," *California Management Review* (Spring 1988), pp. 34–55.

7. Boynton and Victor, "Beyond Flexibility," p. 59. For further information on Corning, see Andrew C. Boynton, *Corning Telecommunications Division: The Flexible Manufacturing System*, case series, case numbers UVA-IT-005, -006, and -007, Darden Graduate School of Business, University of Virginia.

8. Boynton and Victor, "Beyond Flexibility," p. 58.

9. In addition to Boynton and Victor, a number of authors have emphasized this changing definition of the firm. These include David J. Teece, "Economies of Scope and the Scope of the Enterprise," *Journal of Economic Behavior and Organization*, 1 (1980), pp. 223–247; C. K. Prahalad and Gary Hamel, "The Core Competence of the Corporation," *Harvard Business Review* (May–June 1990), pp. 79–91; and James Brian Quinn and Penny C. Paquette, "Technology in Services: Creating Organizational Revolutions," *Sloan Management Review* (Winter 1990), pp. 67–78.

10. The idea that an inherent part of the system of Mass Production is the need for specialized machinery that cannot itself be produced by mass production methods is known as "industrial dualism," and can be found in Michael J. Piore, "Dualism as a Response to Flux and Uncertainty," and "The Technological Foundations of Dualism and Discontinuity," in Suzanne Berger and Michael J. Piore, eds., *Dualism and Discontinuity in Industrial Societies* (Cambridge, England: Cambridge University Press, 1980), pp. 13–81.

11. This finding by Boynton and Victor is consistent with the survey results reported in Chapter 4 and with the discussion of strategy given in Chapter 7.

12. This creates a "new dualism" between the Mass Customization and Continuous Improvement quadrants, analogous to the industrial dualism of the Mass Production axis. Another reason this may be occurring is that as companies move to modularity as a method of mass customization and flexible manufacturing systems as a tool, they will require standardized parts and general-purpose machinery that, in today's environment, can best be produced by firms in the Continuous Improvement quadrant.

13. Two of the best resources on this are B. Charles Ames and James D. Hlavacek, *Market Driven Management: Prescriptions for Survival in a Turbulent World* (Homewood, Ill.: Dow Jones–Irwin, 1989); and George S. Day, *Market Driven Strategy: Processes for Creating Value* (New York: Free Press, 1990).

14. The best resource in this area is Richard C. Whitely, *The Customer Driven Company: Moving from Talk to Action* (Reading, Mass.: Addison-Wesley, 1991). See pages 39–64 in particular.

15. See, for example, ibid., pp. 42–44; and Richard J. Schonberger, *Building a Chain of Customers: Linking Business Functions to Create the World Class Company* (New York: Free Press, 1990).

16. For descriptions of the use of internal customers by a number of companies, see Tim R. V. Davis, "Satisfying Internal Customers: The Link to External Customer Satisfaction," *Planning Review* (January–February 1992), pp. 34–37; and Jason Magidson and Andrew E. Polcha, "Creating Market Economies Within Organizations: A Conference on 'Internal Markets,'" *Planning Review* (January/February 1992), pp. 37–40.

17. Among the best references on process redesign are George D. Robson, *Continuous Process Improvement: Simplifying Work Flow Systems* (New York: Free Press, 1991); Thomas H. Davenport and James E. Short, "The New Industrial Engineering: Information Technology and Business Process Redesign," *Sloan Management Review* (Summer 1990), pp. 11–27; Michael Hammer, "Reengineering Work: Don't Automate, Obliterate," *Harvard Business Review* (July–August 1990), pp. 104–112; and H. James Harrington, *Business Process Improvement: The Breakthrough Strategy for Total Quality, Productivity, and Competitiveness* (New York: McGraw-Hill, 1991).

18. For a good discussion on how to do this, see Roy L. Harmon and Leroy D. Peterson, *Reinventing the Factory: Productivity Breakthroughs in Manufacturing Today* (New York: Free Press, 1990), pp. 179–202. For a detailed discussion and case studies on the Japanese practice of "single-minute exchange of dies," see Shigeo Shingo, *A Revolution in Manufacturing: The SMED System* (Cambridge, Mass.: Productivity Press, 1985).

19. Quoted in Thomas Teal, "Service Comes First: An Interview with USAA's Robert F. McDermott," *Harvard Business Review* (September–October 1991), p. 126.

20. Gary Hamel and C. K. Prahalad, "Corporate Imagination and Expeditionary Marketing," *Harvard Business Review* (July–August 1991), pp. 81–92. Expeditionary marketing is also discussed in Chapter 6.

21. Eric von Hippel, *The Sources of Innovation* (New York: Oxford University Press, 1988).

22. U.S. Congress, Office of Technology Assessment, *Technology and the American Economic Transition: Choices for the Future* (Washington, D.C.: U.S. Government Printing Office, 1988). Interestingly, only low-wage manufacturing and some services networks became less interdependent during the analysis period of 1972 and 1984. Apparel manufacture makes up the predominant portion of low-wage manufacturing, so the Quick Response program begun in 1985 would have made the apparel network much more interdependent than reflected in this study.

23. Tom Peters, "Part One: Get Innovative or Get Dead," *California Management Review* (Fall 1990), p. 23.

24. This distinction was suggested by Michael Piore of MIT. See also Ikujiro Nonaka, "The Knowledge-Creating Company," *Harvard Business Review* (November–December 1991), pp. 96–104.

25. V. R. Basili, "Software Development: A Paradigm for the Future," *Proceedings of the 13th Annual International Computer Software & Applications Conference*, Orlando, Florida, September 20–22, 1989.

26. Since any component of knowledge, processes, tools, techniques, and products can be brought to bear at the appropriate time, this mass customization is accomplished through sectional modularity.

27. D. Quinn Mills, *Rebirth of the Corporation* (New York: John Wiley, 1991), pp. 29–30.

28. Others who foresee the movement to value chain disaggregation, although they may use different terminology, include Peter F. Drucker, "The Coming of the New Organization," *Harvard Business Review* (January–February 1988), pp. 45–53; Peters, "Part One: Get Innovative or Get Dead"; Stan Davis and Bill Davidson, *2020 Vision: Transform Your Business Today to Succeed in Tomorrow's Economy* (New York: Simon & Schuster, 1991), pp. 15–16; James Brian Quinn, Thomas L. Doorley, and Penny C. Paquette, "Beyond Products: Services-Based Strategy," *Harvard Business Review* (March–April 1990), pp. 58–68; Ravi S. Achol, "Evolution of the Marketing Organization: New Forms for Turbulent Environments," *Journal of Marketing* (October 1991), pp. 77–93; Raymond E. Miles and Charles C. Snow, "Fit, Failure and the Hall of

Fame," *California Management Review* (Spring 1984), pp. 10–28; and Michael J. Piore and Charles F. Sabel, *The Second Industrial Divide: Possibilities for Prosperity* (New York: Basic Books, 1984).

29. For example, for a discussion of how power transformers are customized, see E. Agerman, "On the Design Process for Customized Products and Demands upon a Technical Information System," *Annals of the CIRP*, vol. 40, no. 1 (1991), pp. 161–164. The author was in charge of the design department for ABB's power transformers, a group firmly planted in the Invention quadrant of the product-process change matrix during the 1960s. Interestingly, as the shift to lowering costs through design modularity began about 1965, Agerman says ABB described the process as "design systematics," very similar to the term "systematic customization" used by Håkan West for Valmet Paper Machinery's shift from Invention to what is called here Mass Customization.

30. Quoted in William Taylor, "The Logic of Global Business: An Interview with ABB's Percy Barnevik," *Harvard Business Review* (March–April 1991), p. 99.

31. Ibid.

32. Gary S. Vasilash, "Hitting Homers Even in the Off-Season," *Production* (November 1989), p. 112. See also Koniyasu Sakai, "The Feudal World of Japanese Manufacturing," *Harvard Business Review* (November–December 1990), pp. 38–49.

33. Russell Johnston and Paul R. Lawrence, "Beyond Vertical Integration—the Rise of the Value-Adding Partnership," *Harvard Business Review* (July–August 1988), p. 97.

34. Don Schreiber, "Redefining IBM—A Spectrum of Businesses," *Think*, no. 1 (1992), p. 28.

35. Quoted in ibid., p. 29. See also Jon Iwata, "A Close-up View of a Turbulent Year," *Think*, no. 1 (1992), pp. 14–18.

36. Quoted in " 'Affiliates' Make Businesses More Competitive," *Think*, no. 1 (1992), p. 33.

37. Nell Margolis, "ISSC Could Be Role Model for Parent IBM," *Computerworld*, December 2, 1991, p. 99.

38. " 'Affiliates' Make Businesses More Competitive," p. 33.

39. See F. J. Aquilar and A. Bhambri, "Johnson & Johnson (A)" and "Johnson & Johnson (B)," Cases 384-053 and 384-054. Boston: Harvard Business School, 1983.

40. Wayne Eckerson, "Johnson & Johnson Develops CIM Guide," *Network World*, December 24, 1990, pp. 13–14.

41. This is the thesis of Amy Glasmeier, "Technological Discontinuities and Flexible Production Networks: The Case of Switzerland and the World Watch Industry," *Research Policy* (October 1991), pp. 469–485.

42. Ibid., p. 482.

Chapter 10

1. The topic of product and process shocks, or discontinuities, is handled thoroughly with many (primarily mass production) examples in James M. Utterback and Linsu Kim, "Invasion of a Stable Business by Radical Innovation," in Paul R. Kleindorfer, ed., *The Management of Productivity and Technology in Manufacturing* (New York: Plenum Press, 1986), pp. 113–151.

2. See ibid.

3. Michael W. Miller, "As Phone Technology Swiftly Advances, Fears Grow They'll Have Your Number," *The Wall Street Journal*, December 13, 1991.

4. See, for example, Michael W. Miller, "Citicorp Creates Controversy with Plan to Sell Data on Credit-Card Purchases," *The Wall Street Journal*, August 21, 1991, pp. B1, B7. The controversy surrounding both credit card and telephone companies' use of sales data is raised to a higher level by merchants who object to *their* transactions with *their* customers being used for gain by a third party.

5. Thomas J. Meyer, "Home Brew: Orgy of Caf," *The Wall Street Journal*, January 27, 1992, p. A10.

6. See, for example, Thomas Sowell, "George Eastman, We Need You," *Forbes*, September 16, 1991; and Bruce Nussbaum and Robert Neff, " 'I Can't Work This Thing!' " *Business Week*, April 29, 1991, pp. 58–66.

7. The best resource for designing products that do not induce information overload is Donald A. Norman, *The Design of Everyday Things* (New York: Doubleday Currency, 1988).

8. The Magic Mirror and Elizabeth Arden examples are from Stanley M. Davis, *Future Perfect* (Reading, Mass.: Addison-Wesley, 1987), pp. 176–177.

9. John Pierson, "FORM + FUNCTION: Molding Tool Designs to Cause No Harm," *The Wall Street Journal*, March 11, 1991, p. B1.

10. In 1990, IBM researchers used a scanning tunneling microscope to move individual atoms; according to one expert, similar devices should soon "make it possible to deliver single atoms or small molecular building blocks to a binding point on a molecule and thus custom-build molecules atom by atom and building block by building block" (Jon Roland, "Custom-Building Molecules," *The Futurist* [March–April 1991], pp. 34–35). For information on how virtual reality is already being implemented, see Howard Rheingold, *Virtual Reality* (New York: Summit Books, 1991). This is a fast-moving technology. For example, MCA Inc., a subsidiary of Matsushita, is investigating mass-customizing movies by allowing patrons to individualize the experience in specially built virtual reality theaters.

11. Figure 10-1 could have production cycle times as a balancing loop attached to mass customization processes, just as development cycle limits are attached to short product development cycles. However, since the two become so intertwined as they move closer to zero and are treated together here, this level of complexity was not added to the figure.

12. Christoph-Friedrich von Braun, "The Acceleration Trap," *Sloan Management Review* (Fall 1990), pp. 49–58, and "The Acceleration Trap in the Real World," *Sloan Management Review* (Summer 1991), pp. 43–52.

13. The imagery of the New Competition as "net advantage creators" and the Old Competition as "net advantage imitators," as well as the notion of a firm as a "portfolio of capabilities and resources" used later in this section, are from the work of Gary Hamel of the London Business School.

14. In one well-documented occurrence, it took the Ford Motor Company nine months or more of very little production to change over to the Model A from the Model T in 1927–1928. While certainly not typical, it is indicative of the system of Mass Production. See David A. Hounshell, *From the American System to Mass Production 1800–1932: The Development of Manufacturing Technology in the United States* (Baltimore: Johns Hopkins University Press, 1984), pp. 279–292.

15. Tom Peters, in "Part One: Get Innovative or Get Dead," *California Management Review* (Fall 1990), p. 10, advocates that companies "license [their] most advanced technology" to all comers to "turn up the heat" and ensure that constant innovation occurs in both products and processes.

16. The term "virtual enterprise" appears to have first been used by Jan Hopland and Charles Savage, "Virtual Teams and Flexible Enterprises," *Digital Technical Management Education Program News* 3 (July 1989), cited in Charles M. Savage, *Fifth Generation Management: Integrating Enterprises through Human Networking* (Bedford, Mass.: Digital Press, 1990), p. 236, note 19. Savage defines "virtual" from its computer science origin as "being such in force or effect, though not actually or expressly such" (p. 181).

17. This is bus modularity, in which the structure of a generic enterprise makes up the bus, and people with the right knowledge, skills, and experiences as well as technology with the right characteristics from different companies are the components that "plug" into the enterprise structure.

18. *21st Century Manufacturing Enterprise Strategy: An Industry-Led View*, vol. 1 (Bethlehem, Pa.: Iacocca Institute, Lehigh University, 1991), p. 2. See also *21st Century Manufacturing Enterprise Strategy: Infrastructure*, vol. 2 (Bethlehem, Pa.: Iacocca Institute, Lehigh University, 1991).

19. Ibid., vol. 1, p. 9.

20. Ibid.

21. See Richard M. Locke and Cristiano Antonelli, "International Competitiveness,

Technological Change and Organizational Innovation: Strategy and Structure of the Italian Apparel Industry in the 1980's," in Donald Lessard and Cristiano Antonelli, eds., *Managing the Globalization of Business* (Napoli, Italy: Editoriale Scientifica, 1990), pp. 151–172. For further details on this illustration, see Robert Howard, "The Designer Organization: Italy's GFT Goes Global," *Harvard Business Review* (September–October 1991), pp. 28–44.

   22.   Gene de Nicolais, "Innovation Sweeps the Fashion Industry," *Europe* (June 1989), p. 20.

Appendix

   1. Correlation figures lie between −1 and 1, with negative values indicating negative correlations. The farther the number is from zero, the stronger the correlation. Correlations tend to go up and down with the slope of the least-squares regression line.

   2. See Buddie Joseph Pine II, "Paradigm Shift: From Mass Production to Mass Customization," master's thesis, MIT, June 1991, Chapter 6, for this complete analysis.

Index

323

ety at lower, 113; growth in real, 81; high, and long cycle times, 87; high, of variety, 82; inventory carrying, 82; low, and high profits, 124; low, and short cycle times, 115; low average, 81; low inventory carrying, 112; low total, 112–113
Crafted with Pride in the U.S.A. Council, 191
Craft Production, 9, 13, 19, 48, 50, 113; and flexible specialization, 104–105, 106
Craftsmen, 9, 12, 13
Create-A-Book, 202–203, 251
Custom Cut Technologies (CCT), 193, 203, 204
Customer(s): ability to respond quickly to desires of, 119–120; consolidation shocks, 244–246; disgruntled and disloyal, 91–92, focus, loss of, 88; focus on individual, 222–223; servicing intermediate and internal, 223–225. See also Needs/wants, customer
Custom Vêtement Associates, 193
Cusumano, Michael, 209–210
Cut-to-fit modularity, 203–204
Cycle times: high costs and long, 87; low costs and short, 115
Cypress Semiconductor, 106

Dairy Queen, 186
Dartmouth College, 210
DataFAX Communications Corp., 178
Davis, Stan, Future Perfect, 50
deBarros, Len, 147
Decisions, sound long- and short-term, 123
Decoupling, of product and process life cycles, 255–256
Deluxe Corporation, 158, 160
Deluxe Forms Centers, 158
Demand: factors, market turbulence and, 55–61; homogeneous vs. heterogeneous, 57–59; levels, stability and predictability of, 31, 55–56, 89
"De-maturity," 35, 57
d'Estaing, Valéry Giscard, 156
Development cycle limits, 249–253, 321n11
Dialog Information Services, Inc., 178, 183

Digital audio tape (DAT), 246
Digital Equipment Corporation, 36
Disaggregation, of value chain, 232–239, 319n28
Diversification, diverted attention of management to, 99
Dodge, 56
Doing, thinking and: integration of, 112; separation of, 82, 230
Domino's, 41, 186, 188, 315n16
DOS operating system, 62
Dow, 310n23
Dow Jones & Co., 177
Dow Jones News/Retrieval, 177, 209
Drucker, Peter, 92
Du Pont, 28, 191, 310n23
Dynamic extended enterprise, 109–110
Dynamic stability, 215–221, 255–256

Eastman Kodak Co., 28–29, 206–207, 312n53
Economic cycles, degree of influence of, 62–63
Economic order quantity (EOQ), 50
Economies: of integration, 49; of scale, 16, 48, 49; of scope, 48, 49
Efficiency: operational, 20, 80–84, 85, 110; through stability and control, 28, 32, 44; total process, 110–113
Elizabeth Arden, Inc., 248–249
Emery, Mark, 38, 252–253
Employment Solutions Corp., 236
Empowerment, of people and teams, 229–230
Englert, Inc., 185–186, 203
Enterprise(s): dynamic extended, 109–110; mass customization of, 258; virtual, 258, 260–261, 321n16
Enterprise Integration Network (EINet), 260
Enterprise Leasing, 61
Environment, creating demanding and stressful, for management and workers, 113
Espresso bars, 247
ETA S.A., 150
Execution, and journey to Mass Customization, 169–170
Exports: high sales domestically and through, 120; lack of, 93

About the Author

Joe Pine is a program manager with IBM's client executive education center, the Advanced Business Institute. He is responsible for research into leading-edge management and strategy issues that is incorporated into executive education and IBM management consulting practices. Mr. Pine conducts both original research and supports university research through grants, joint projects, and ongoing discussions and debates with leading business school professors throughout the world.

Prior to joining the Advanced Business Institute, Mr. Pine held a number of technical and managerial positions within IBM. He has received numerous awards for his achievements, including IBM's Outstanding Innovation Award and an invitation from the chairman to attend the company's Corporate Technical Recognition Event. He graduated from the University of Wisconsin-Stout with a Bachelor of Science degree in applied mathematics in 1980, and from the MIT Sloan School of Management with a Masters of Science degree in the management of technology in 1991. He is a member of The Planning Forum (The International Society for Strategic Management and Planning), its Research and Education Foundation, and the Strategic Management Society.